LANDSCAPE, MEMORY A

Anthropology, Culture and Society

Series Editors:
Professor Thomas Hylland Eriksen, University of Oslo
Dr Katy Gardner, University of Sussex
Dr Jon P. Mitchell, University of Sussex

RECENT TITLES

Land, Law and Environment:
Mythical Land, Legal Boundaries
Edited by ALLEN ABRAMSON AND
DIMITRIOS THEODOSSOPOULOS

The Trouble with Community:
Anthropological Reflections on
Movement, Identity and Collectivity
VARED AMIT AND NIGEL RAPPORT

Anthropology and the Will to Meaning:
A Postcolonial Critique
VASSOS ARGYROU

The War of Dreams:
Exercises in Ethno-Fiction
MARC AUGÉ

Orange Parades:
The Politics of Ritual, Tradition and Control
DOMINIC BRYAN

Identity and Affect:
Experiences of Identity in a Globalising World
Edited by
JOHN R. CAMPBELL AND ALAN REW

Risk Revisited
Edited by PAT CAPLAN

Macedonia:
The Politics of Identity and Difference
Edited by JANE K. COWAN

Ethnicity and Nationalism:
Anthropological Perspectives
THOMAS HYLLAND ERIKSEN

A History of Anthropology
THOMAS HYLLAND ERIKSEN AND
FINN SIVERT NIELSON

Small Places, Large Issues:
An Introduction to Social
and Cultural Anthropology
THOMAS HYLLAND ERIKSEN

Life on the Outside:
The Tamil Diaspora and
Long-Distance Nationalism
ØIVIND FUGLERUD

Anthropology, Development and
the Post-modern Challenge
KATY GARDNER AND DAVID LEWIS

Power and its Disguises:
Anthropological Perspectives on Power
JOHN GLEDHILL

Youth and the State in Hungary:
Capitalism, Communism and Class
LÁSZLÓ KÜRTI

Locating Cultural Creativity
Edited by JOHN LIEP

Cord of Blood:
Possession and the Making of Voodoo
NADIA LOVELL

Ethnography and Prostitution in Peru
LORRAINE NENCEL

Witchcraft, Power and Politics:
Exploring the Occult in
the South African Lowveld
ISAK A. NIEHAUS with ELIAZAAR MOHLALA
AND KALLY SHOKANE

Power, Community and the State:
The Political Anthropology
of Organisation in Mexico
MONIQUE NUIJTEN

Social Mobility in Kerala:
Modernity and Identity in Conflict
FILIPPO OSELLA AND CAROLINE OSELLA

Negotiating Local Knowledge:
Power and Identity in Development
Edited by
JOHAN POTTIER, ALAN BICKER
AND PAUL SILLITOE

Class, Nation and Identity:
The Anthropology of Political Movements
JEFF PRATT

Bearing Witness
FIONA C. ROSS

Race, Nation and Culture:
An Anthropological Perspective
PETER WADE

LANDSCAPE, MEMORY AND HISTORY

Anthropological Perspectives

EDITED BY
PAMELA J. STEWART AND ANDREW STRATHERN

Pluto Press
LONDON • STERLING, VIRGINIA

First published 2003
by PLUTO PRESS
345 Archway Road, London N6 5AA
and 22883 Quicksilver Drive,
Sterling, VA 20166–2012, USA

www.plutobooks.com

British Library Cataloguing in Publication Data
A catalogue record for this book is available from
the British Library

ISBN 0 7453 1967 X hardback
ISBN 0 7453 1966 1 paperback

Library of Congress Cataloging in Publication Data applied for

10   9   8   7   6   5   4   3   2   1

Designed and produced for Pluto Press by
Chase Publishing Services, Fortescue, Sidmouth EX10 9QG, England
Typeset from disk by Stanford DTP Services, Towcester, England
Printed and bound in the European Union by
Antony Rowe, Chippenham and Eastbourne, England

CONTENTS

1. Introduction   1
   Pamela J. Stewart and Andrew Strathern
2. Iconic Images: Landscape and History in the Local Poetry of
   the Scottish Borders   16
   John Gray
3. Céide Fields: Natural Histories of a Buried Landscape   47
   Stuart McLean
4. Landscape Representation: Place and Identity in
   Nineteenth-century Ordnance Survey Maps of Ireland   71
   Angèle Smith
5. Memories of Ancestry in the Forests of Madagascar   89
   Janice Harper
6. Moon Shadows: Aboriginal and European Heroes in an
   Australian Landscape   108
   Veronica Strang
7. History, Mobility and Land Use Interests of Aborigines and
   Farmers in the East Kimberly in North-West Australia   136
   Ruth Lane
8. Co-present Landscapes: Routes and Rootedness as Sources
   of Identity in Highlands New Guinea   166
   Michael O'Hanlon and Linda Frankland
9. 'Island Builders': Landscape and Historicity Among the
   Langalanga, Solomon Islands   189
   Pei-yi Guo
10. Biography, Ecology, Political Economy: Seascape and
    Conflict in Jamaica   210
    James G. Carrier
Epilogue   229
Andrew Strathern and Pamela J. Stewart

Notes on Contributors   237
Index   240

LIST OF FIGURES

6.1a Distant view of Jimmy Inkerman's memorial at
      Trubanamen   109
6.1b Close-up view of memorial   109
6.2   The Australian Stockman's Hall of Fame in Longreach,
      North Queensland   121
7.1   Ord River Valley looking north from Kununurra   137
7.2   Proposed Ord Stage 2 Project Area showing
      Conservation Area and Aboriginal land claims   138
7.3   The East Kimberley Region   141
7.4   John Mack, horticulturalist   154
7.5   Bush meeting of Miriuwung women convened by the
      Northern Land Council to discuss the Ord Stage 2
      proposal   157
8.1   Standing atop the *bolyim* house, men of Komblo Kulka clan
      consume pork fat at the climax to their Pig Festival   171
8.2   Walking home with a netbag of sweet potato, a Wahgi
      woman passes by the roadside the decaying hulk of a
      truck, parked at its owner's settlement, adjacent to a grave 184

1 INTRODUCTION

Pamela J. Stewart and Andrew Strathern

The topic of landscape has recently come more to the fore in anthropological interests. Ethnographers have realised from their field experiences how perceptions of and values attached to landscape encode values and fix memories to places that become sites of historical identity. Such perceptions shift, either gradually or dramatically, over time, so that landscape becomes a form of codification of history itself, seen from the viewpoints of personal expression and experience. This notion has proved particularly fruitful as a focus for work in parts of the world where social and cultural anthropology have had to make their way alongside history, sociology and politics. At the same time the concept of landscape has proved strategic for interpreting materials from many parts of the world.

In this collection of papers we highlight the significance of this topic for studies of identity. Thus, the materials here look at particular individuals, emplaced within a physical environment, who interact with others within their social environment through their remembered and imaginary experiences. These expressions of identity are not reified or locked in time but are historically positioned in the dynamics of temporal space. The generalised applicability of this approach is evident from the range of geographical locations included in this volume: Scotland, Ireland, Madagascar, Papua New Guinea, Australia, the Solomon Islands and Jamaica. One of the common tropes of ethnographic enquiry has always been that of 'setting'. The beginning chapters of most ethnographic treatises lay out the place in which the research was conducted and the temporal location of the study. But one of the criticisms of some ethnographic studies has been a lack of historicity in representation and of details on the intersubjectivity of the peoples being discussed. The authors here use history and memory to explore the economic, political and social events that impact perceived visions of landscape and the perceived placement of people within these settings.

In terms of identity, our view is that two crucial elements are at work: notions of *memory* and notions of *place*. Together these occupy a conceptual space analogous to that which *community* once held in the social anthropology of some societies. Memory and place, via landscape (including seascape), can be seen as crucial transducers whereby the local, national and global are brought into mutual alignment; or as providing sites where conflicts between these influences are played out. Such a theoretical scheme can also be seen as providing an alternative way of studying identity to the concentration on nationalism and national senses of identity as phenomena *per se*. It can help to re-establish a sphere of studies for social anthropology that would integrate aspects of earlier community-based approaches with approaches that emphasise political change, citizenship, national identity, historical influences, and similar broad factors.

Landscapes are also dramatically changed from time to time not only by urban planning, roads and factories but also by the wide-scale epidemics that affect farming, such as the spread of foot and mouth disease in the UK and elsewhere. These epidemiological disasters pose a challenge to understanding the experience of farmers and others who value the countryside in different ways (e.g. tourists who often come to rural farming areas in places like Scotland simply to see the farming landscape with its varied hues, odours, livestock and topography). The project that we pursue here should help to bring out a better understanding of the intertwining aspects of landscape, memory and history in ethnographic presentation and make readers in general aware of its significance.

The materials presented here explore the topic of landscape, memory and history in greater depth and in a broader geographical range than has previously been done. A strong emphasis on changing perceptions of history as expressed in ideas about landscape is central to this project, taking landscape in the broad senses laid out in the volumes edited by Hirsch and O'Hanlon (1995), Bender (1993), and Bender and Winer (2001). This involves the examination of landscape as seen initially by the viewer and 'a second landscape which is produced through local practice and which we come to recognise and understand through fieldwork and through ethnographic description and interpretation' (Hirsch 1995: 2).

The word 'landscape' was introduced into English as a technical term of painters (cf. *Oxford English Dictionary*). Thus, taken as a term to describe the artistic presentation of a scene, it can well be applied to the creative and imaginative ways in which people place themselves within their environments. No two people will paint the same landscape since no two people will mentally see the same images or be able to technically reproduce the seen images at the same level of expertise. Cultural knowledge gained from living within a social landscape determines the pictures that people construct. Ethnographers struggle to interpret the information given to them in terms of these verbal pictures.

One of the main ideas here is to incorporate history into these trends, and so to endow them with temporal depth and subjectivity. This project of incorporating history into our discussion gives strength to our perspective, in part differentiating it from previous work done on the topic. We see history as involved continuously in the making and remaking of ideas about place, realigning or differentiating place in relation to notions of community. Essentially, we argue that landscape provides a wider context in which notions about place and community can be situated. This context crucially includes historically defined power relations and how these are both imposed and resisted at local levels (see Head 2000 for examples from Australia).

The sense of place and embeddedness within local, mythical, and ritual landscapes is important. These senses of place serve as pegs on which people hang memories, construct meanings from events, and establish ritual and religious arenas of action. Veronica Strang has described 'cosmological landscapes' in her prior writing on Australian Aboriginal peoples and Australian White farmers in Northern Queensland (1997). Simon Schama (1995) has explored what we might call an 'environmental landscape' that connects human and spirit dwelling places, including forests, mountains, rivers and streams. He looked at the topic of landscape and memory as expressed in artistic representations in paintings from certain parts of Western Europe and North America, focusing on what these images might tell us about the societies in which these individual artists were working. This is one way in which material culture can be used to represent meanings of landscape.

Two regions in which we ourselves have been interested to explore this topic are in the Highlands of Papua New Guinea (Stewart and Strathern 2000, 2002a) and in the Lowlands of Scotland (Strathern and Stewart 2001). In both of these regions we have shown the ways in which people manifest their local, and in some instances their national, senses of self-recognition and social identity. Folktales, myths, oral histories, ballads, ritual incantations and ordinary stories of daily life all invoke in real or imagined detail the spatial positionings of a community of people. Our research in Ayrshire, Scotland, has shown, among other things, how places with historical significance can be appropriated through their perceived cultural heritage status so as to strengthen political identities. Likewise, our work among the Duna people of Papua

New Guinea has demonstrated how *malu* (genealogical narratives) identify groups of people with specific parts of the local area and that this knowledge of emplacement can be a strong tool in battles over compensation claims when outside companies come into the region to extract natural resources (e.g. oil).

While we see the concepts of place, community and landscape as intersecting or overlapping, we do not regard them as synonyms. The idea of landscape gives us a meaningful context into which we can set notions of place and community, but we need to give these concepts definitions that at least partially separate them. In our view landscape refers to the perceived settings that frame people's senses of place and community. A place is a socially meaningful and identifiable space to which a historical dimension is attributed. Community refers to sets of people who may identify themselves with a place or places in terms of notions of commonality, shared values or solidarity in particular contexts. Landscape is thus a contextual horizon of perceptions, providing both a foreground and a background in which people feel themselves to be living in their world. While we may tend to think of this in rural terms or as an aspect of 'nature' it may apply equally to urban and rural sites because they are all equally moulded by human actions and/or by human perceptions. It is such acts of moulding that give to landscape its character of being a *process* that Hirsch refers to (Hirsch 1995: 5). It is a process because its shape at any given time reflects change and is a part of change. Nevertheless it often serves as a crucial marker of continuity with the past as well as a reassurance of identity in the present and a promise for the future. Ideas about landscape often turn time into space or express time through space, as happens for example in New Guinea origin stories that describe pathways of migration taken by group ancestors to their historical locations (Stewart and Strathern 2001a).

The idea of landscape, then, both modifies ideas about place and community and may be called on to support or enrich them. It also grants a flexibility to concepts of identity and belonging as forged through individual historical experience. This point may help to reconcile two seemingly contradictory approaches or emphases in the study of place seen as 'home'. In one approach home and place are considered to be fixed points, while in the other the stress is on movement through points, in which travel itself provides the feeling of being 'at home' (see Rapport and Dawson 1998). While we can accept that either notion could form the basis of a sense of belonging, since belonging is essentially an idea and ideas are plastic, we can also suggest that persons travel with their own inner landscapes. They remember particular places through images of how they looked and what it felt like to be there; or they develop such images through photographs, films, or narratives from others. What they are remembering or creating here are landscapes, to which they have a connection; and such landscapes can travel with people, giving them a sense of 'home' when they are not 'at home'. The person who stays in one place may not see that place as 'home'. The person who travels may carry 'home' around as a tangible point in fluidity. Home may also be multiple: it need not be just one place, but numbers of places that show correspondences of association, landscapes that have relationships attached to them. While there may literally be some people for whom travel itself provides a sense of continuity, for other people the experience of travel coexists with senses of identity that are in counterpoint with it, and our argument here is that those senses of identity are often most forcibly tied up with senses of landscape, of how a place appears as an ordered form of environment *within which* place and community are perceived.

The sense of community that is established through emplacement encompasses both the living and the dead as well as the spirit world. For example, among the Duna people of the Aluni Valley in the Southern Highlands Province of Papua New Guinea the non-corporeal part of a human body (the 'soul', *tini*) is thought to reside in limestone shelters in the forested areas around the settlements after a person dies. The non-skeletal substance of the human body is said to be reabsorbed by the local ground (*rindi*) and is thought to replenish the fertility of the place in general. In the past the bones of the deceased were bundled and placed into limestone ossuaries, providing a 'home' for the person's *tini*.[1] The *tini* is encouraged to depart to these ossuaries at funerals and afterwards at grave sites by mourning songs that women specialise in singing. These laments invoke local place names and describe familiar landscape features that serve to place the dead firmly within the environmental and community framework of the group while serving the equally strong function of embedding the singer within her social nexus. We refer to this as the 'embodiment of landscape'. This concept is one that is vital in understanding the phenomenology of emplacement. In these Duna songs the *tini* is often evocatively animated through a parallelism with birds.

> My daughter, like a ribbon-tail bird,
> Wearing your little apron . . .
> Go up . . . up there,
> Where the rocks stand out.
> (Sung by a Duna women whose daughter had died, 1998)

As demonstrated by Duna mourning songs, an important aspect of how landscapes gain their meanings has to do with naming. The names of locations within areas record the forms of human experience that have occurred within them. Such names may also provide a kind of archaeology of meanings, recording aspects of history that may otherwise be forgotten, or environmental features that are no longer there. From our experience in Papua New Guinea, this is one of the strikingly abundant ways in which people see and negotiate their relationship with the environment itself, and their perception goes well beyond the boundaries of their own small place or community, while within such a place their knowledge is likely to be more detailed. For example, in the Hagen area, in the Western Highlands Province, a given clan area is exhaustively divided into small locality names identified with garden spots, pathways, past battle sites and other locales where events make up a maze of local history. Those who know these names best are most able to handle disputes regarding access to land. They also know how the names appear in songs that commemorate emotive aspects of history (see Stewart and Strathern 2002b). Ongka, of the Kawelka group in Hagen, had such a knowledge of songs relating to pre-colonial times of fighting between groups, including songs reportedly sung by leaders among the enemies of his group, or songs made against such leaders by his own people, which gave an emotive and epic dimension to the politics of conflict. One song by Ongka's mother's people, the Kawelka Kundmbo, describes how an enemy, Tape of the place Komapana, went to hide in the hills of Mokla, and they came to muster at a lookout point called Ekit Kuk 'with big black plumes in a bamboo tube', ready to pursue him if necessary (Strathern and Stewart 1999: 122). The plumes in the song are of the *mek* bird, the *Astrapia stephaniae*, Princess Stephanie's Bird of Paradise (Beehler et al. 1986: 228), used both as a striking part of ceremonial headdresses and to adorn the tops of war shields. When not immediately in use these plumes might be carefully stored in long bamboo tubes. The clansmen in the song picture themselves as holding their plumes in latent readiness for wear as they contemplate the territory, including Komapana and Mokla, into which their enemy had for the time being fled. This enemy would also be lying in wait to make his return. The name Ekit Kuk means 'the place of flowers where one emerges'. It is a striking high point in a clearing from which the land dips sharply to the south, clad in forest beech trees, down to a valley and then rises again in another set of hills on which grasslands and gardens intermix with forest, framed further away by the massive flanks of the Mount Hagen mountain range (a similar view appears on the back cover of our book *Arrow Talk: Transaction, Transition, and Contradiction in New*

Guinea Highlands History, Strathern and Stewart 2000a). Ekit Kuk is just at the intersection between Kawelka territory and the land of the Minembi, a more populous and powerful group whose members have in the past been largely traditional enemies of the Kawelka. A colonially constructed road runs through it and down to Minembi territory.[2] In the mid-1980s, many years after the time of the Kawelka song about Komapana Tape, a Christian cross was set up at Ekit Kuk marking a truce between the Kawelka and the Minembi following renewed fighting between them, this time with guns (Strathern 1992, 1993; Strathern and Stewart 2000a). Mention of the name Ekit Kuk can trigger powerful memories in people. Its position in the landscape lends intensity to the meaning of the song. Fifty such named places appear in the index of Ongka's life narrative, representing just a selection of the names he probably knew and held in his mind's eye as a part of his life (see Strathern and Stewart 1999).

For the Duna people of the Aluni Valley in the Southern Highlands Province, far west of Hagen, we have observed a similar panoply of names stretched across the vistas of forest, clearings, settlements and mountain tops, investing every spot with particular meaning, often tied in with sacred sites of origin, or points on ritual trackways where ancestral figures stopped to sleep; but equally with remembered garden sites, or rock shelters in which people have slept and acquired through dreams powers against witchcraft; or sites where marsupials are plentiful, where mushrooms abound, or where there are groves of fruit pandanus trees (see Strathern and Stewart 2000b). Historical memories of former ritual sites remained powerful sources of knowledge and emotion for Duna leaders in the 1990s, and were beginning to acquire a new use in the marshalling of narratives about the landscape to be used in negotiations with companies and exploring for oil, as we have noted (Stewart and Strathern 2000, 2002a). The knowledge enshrined in *malu* is also matched and replicated in Duna songs and in ballads (*pikono*) (Strathern and Stewart 1997, 2000c; Stewart and Strathern n.d.). The same men who are holders of *malu* knowledge are often expert in these genres; just as a leader like Ongka in Hagen had a store of artistic as well as political knowledge, all encapsulated in an aesthetic of landscape. This we refer to as the 'inner landscape of the mind'. This knowledge is transportable and can be objectified through sharing, or it can remain private. In either case, it remains a source of identity.

A familiar context in which such knowledge and the emotions linked to it, appears, is in the context of recollection and commemoration, perhaps tied to senses of nostalgia. We have previously pointed to the power of this motif in the Scottish poetry of diaspora, as shown poignantly in the poems of Violet Jacob (Strathern and Stewart 2001: 89–93). Jacob herself, after being brought up in the House of Dun, north of Montrose in Scotland, spent the early part of her married life in India where she was enamoured of the place, its people, and its ambience. Her diary of the time in India was illustrated by her watercolour representations of the place and its people (Jacob 1990). She was the daughter of the 18th Laird of Dun, and her natal family had been in possession of its lands there for 400 years or more by the time of her birth in 1863. In 1931 she wrote an account of the Lairds of Dun, described in the *Mainstream Companion to Scottish Literature* as 'a loving social history of her family's heritage and also a hymn of praise to the countryside of her birth' (Royle 1993: 158). In her poems she often takes up the position of, or addresses, some other category of person through whom she sets up an identification with herself or a difference from herself. In one poem she takes the role of a speaker addressing visitors to her own home area in Scotland, saying what they will see, all the sights familiar to the speaker. They will see the place the speaker knows well, but will not see it in the same way. The speaker will never forget the Sidlaw Hills, Craig Oule, 'the stars of Scotland' above Strathmore estate at Glamis. The visitors (tourists) may see these places in all directions from the windows of their lodgings, but:

> Fegs! Ye may see them wi' yer een,
> I see them wi' my he'rt!
> (quoted in Strathern and Stewart 2001: 91)

The poem marks a contrast, as well as an identification, between inner and outer landscapes. In the poem, the outer landscape is described as the tourists may see it. But they see it with their eyes only. The speaker sees it from experience (with the heart), even though living far away and unable to gaze immediately on it. This inner landscape merges the perceived experience of the place with the imagined symbolic meaning of the place to the individual. Landscape in a meaningful sense thus encompasses environment plus relationship to it and the cross-cutting ties of relationships that emerge from or exist in a place. When persons of Scottish descent seek their places of origin back in Scotland they make this cathexis of environment plus relationship based on whatever knowledge and personal or inherited memories they have, and it is this that recreates in them a sense of identity as Paul Basu (2001) in Bender and Winer's edited volume points out (cf. also Dawson and Johnson 2001 in the chapter immediately before Basu's). In the same volume Aidan O'Sullivan writes of crannogs in Ireland, small fortified dwellings constructed in lakes from the early medieval period onward (O'Sullivan

2001: 96). They were craft and trading centres that were rebuilt over time and used as the residences of aristocrats and as stores for weapons and wealth goods right through to the sixteenth century. During the Tudor invasion of Ireland they came to be seen by the invaders as sites of resistance to English power, and marks of 'the wildness and peculiarity of the Irish' (2001: 97). What is of particular interest here is that the Irish themselves must have seen these crannogs in a very different way, incorporating the idea of resistance but also endowing them with greater or longer-term memories: a side of the topic that could further be explored, as well as the question of how people today see these dwelling places. The Ordnance Survey maps of Ireland mark these crannogs as sites of historic interest along with standing stones and other markers of 'prehistory'. But such elements have always the potential to be reborn as 'heritage' and tied in with national sentiments. Everything depends on how 'the heart' sees them as 'inner landscape'. The 'contestation of landscape', to which the contributors to Bender and Winer's volume allude (see also Bender 1998), depends on inner landscapes being seen differently in this way. Thus, these images are based on memories and associations that feed into ideology but are based primarily in subjectivity and experience.

The subjectivity of emplacement is an undeniable part of the human psyche. Examples abound from writers who have become well known through their detailed evocation of place as a space for humanity, such as Henry Thoreau's *Walden*: 'A lake is the landscape's most beautiful and expressive feature. It is earth's eye; looking into which the beholder measures the depth of his own nature' (Bode 1975: 435) or Emily Dickinson's poetry and prose: 'How luscious is the dripping of February eaves! It makes our thinking Pink –' (Shurr 1993: 50). Works such as A.A. Milne's *The House at Pooh Corner* and Lewis Carroll's *Alice's Adventures in Wonderland* are excellent examples of the importance of placement in the stories of individual actions and events as seen in the mind's eye. A fine example of how poetry is used in this way is Matsuo Bashō's elegant poem:

> Look at the moon!
> the embarrassment
> of being awakened.
> (Shirane, trans. 1998: 95)

Landscape is an important concept in applying historical perspectives to archaeological work where it is used in planning 'heritage management' and in interpreting the emotional significance and political impact of human settlements. Also, through an employment of the tropes

– landscape, memory and history – it becomes possible to examine more closely ethnographic diversities as they are contextualised spatially and temporally. Thus, we can avoid the use of overgeneralised clumpings of people into categories such as 'Europeans', 'Melanesians' and the like.

The 11 September 2001 terror attacks in New York city have shown how important objects of the urban landscape (e.g. buildings) can be in the formation of identities (in this instance symbols of 'America'). Memories of this landscape have been reflected in the narratives of New Yorkers since the event and will be referred to in historical accounts for years to come. Through the pictorial and written images of Afghanistan that were frequently published in US newspapers after the terror attacks, Americans also became more aware of a place and a people that seemed to some to be impossibly remote – the mountainous passes, arid zones, and mud walls were presented as one-dimensional images for the mind's eye to use in emplacing events in that country.

Our edited collection contributes new insights into the theorising of landscape, memory and history. The chapters cover a wide range of cases from around the world, including Scotland, Ireland, Madagascar, Australia, Papua New Guinea, the Solomon Islands and Jamaica. While people look at landscape as an expression of enduring values, they also contest and negotiate about it in terms of conflicting notions of these values. Landscape can thus become a vehicle for many themes: attachments to land, conflicts over land, the use of images of the past in the social construction of identities, and variant views of history, development and change. The chapters in this book explore the rich complexity of these themes, tying them to actual historical processes and to people's changing interpretations of these. Landscape proves to be a vital concept for bringing together 'materialist' and 'symbolist' perspectives in anthropology: that is to say, ones that stress politics and economics and ones that stress cultural meanings. In landscape analysis these factors are brought together and shown to be interrelated, providing a way to re-cast earlier forms of debate. The intersection of memories and history with how people see themselves in relation to their environment is vital to the understanding of people's placements and movements through social contexts.

Our main objective here is to bring together a set of focused studies that advance our appreciation of the place of ideas about landscape in anthropological analysis, by stressing the themes of history and memory. The present chapter (1) introduces the topics explored in this volume. Chapter 2 (Gray) discusses the work of past and present poets who have celebrated the Borders area of the Scottish Lowlands, highlighting the connections in this area between farming, the landscape, poetry and images of the nation. Drawing on the work of a contemporary farmer and poet, Tim Douglas, Gray shows how the multiple historical ironies of a divided landscape are brought out by Douglas by adopting a balladic style and personifying the issues that have characterised the relationship of the Scots to the English in terms of a *dramatis personae* of Borders figures and politicians. He also enters into the paradox of weather – surely a strong influence on the perception of landscape – and wittily suggests that for all the drear quality of the persistent rain in Scotland, this very aspect is itself an enduring part of senses of identity.

Chapter 3 (McLean) considers the Irish bog as colonial topography, as a repository of prehistory, and as a site of environmentalist debates and discussions on development and change. McLean's chapter brings out well the different ways in which landscapes are imbued with meaning, in terms of whether they are used in the context of ideas about 'heritage' or ideas about 'development'. This is a recurring theme in discussions in the United Kingdom, with its high population density and extensive industrialisation. 'Heritage' tends to come into play, as we ourselves have noted in our work in Ireland and Scotland, when 'development' has played itself out. In relation to Ireland, another point can be made: the cutting of peat-turf, seen by some conservationists as a threat to the bog environment, is seen by the cutters themselves and other commentators as a part of an Irish identity.

Chapter 4 (Smith) examines the colonial process involved in the making of the British Ordnance Survey map of Ireland from 1824 onward. Maps represent multiple ways of seeing the landscape and its meanings, informed by social memories, politics and the power to produce representations. Changing maps of Ireland illustrate the struggle there between colonialism and nationalism. This theme is well illustrated by the interpretations placed on crannogs, artificial island forts built on lakes as refuges and strongholds. The crannog now stands for resistance to outsiders, an honourable notion. To the British who mapped the topography and its dwellings, crannogs simply represented a relic from the past. For visitors and tourists today the original colonial purpose of the Ordnance Survey maps is not immediately relevant. Instead the maps are an invaluable resource for getting around and marking in places of interest, including crannogs (which, incidentally, are also found in Scotland).

Chapter 5 (Harper) shows how concepts of the forest in Madagascar refer to contested terrains, understood differently by forest residents and conservationists. The establishment of a national park and the interventions of international conservationists have created a field of contests between local peoples and outsiders relating to the landscape. This is a classic theme of a clash of interests and philosophies. Conservationists in this regard act like 'development experts' even though their overt aims are different. They seek to control the landscape by constraining the activities of local people, which are often seen as wasteful or ignorant. Local knowledge, based on practice, is displaced in favour of an outside philosophical or ideological scheme of imposed goals. We see here also a familiar contrast between embodied experience and external programmes, each giving the landscape a different kind of value. The chapters by Gray, McLean and Smith all explore conflicts that revolve around this contrast and its historical transformations.

Chapter 6 (Strang) displays two very different perceptions of landscape connected with a conflict in Cape York, Australia in the early 1900s. An Aboriginal Australian speared an Australian settler, and both men have memorial sites dedicated to them which express the identities and values of their historically opposed groups. Chapter 7 (Lane) examines changes in ideas of landscape associated with the contested processes of pastoralism in the Kimberley mountains, north-west Australia. The study sets these processes into a wider picture of agriculture, tourism and Aboriginal land use over time, marked by Committees of Investigation and court hearings.

Chapters 6 and 7 explore the effects of power on the landscape, as shown in the unequal contest between settlers and indigenes. In Strang's account it is interesting to see that the memorial site for the settler has become overgrown and neglected as his reputation waned after his death and historical trends changed. Interesting in Lane's account is the replacement of pastoralism with crop-farming as a focus of values for settlers. This is linked with changes in relationships with Aborigines, the recognition of indigenous land rights, and the continuing problems of sharing the use of the landscape by peoples with different needs and orientations. Here again, the 'heritage' versus 'development' schema is in place.

Chapter 8 (O'Hanlon and Frankland) explores how the Australian colonial administration in Highlands New Guinea laid great stress on road-making, and how local peoples came to see such roads as the marks of progress. At a later time these roads have come to be seen as corridors of threat and danger. This ambivalent historical perception of the introduced roads is matched by an indigenous ambivalent perception of the 'roads' of marriage between clan groups in the Wahgi area. Chapter 9 (Guo) examines indigenous ideas in the Solomon Islands about the historical appropriation of the landscape and its modern-day transformation in the context of tourism and nation-making. Landscape is one of the means of conceptualising history and identity for the Langalanga people, who have shifted from the artificial islands they once built in the coastal sea to living on the mainland. Langalanga memories define local identity in terms of these islands, and the link with them is also made in tourist brochures for visitors. The islands thus become symbols for Langalanga identity.

A marked empirical contrast between the situations in the Wahgi (in Chapter 8) and in Langalanga (in Chapter 9) is that in the former case we find a much greater emphasis on conflict and ambivalence, stemming from the contradictions brought by change. Vehicular roads, originally constructed by local labour in the Wahgi area and throughout the Highlands of Papua New Guinea, were at first seen as hallmarks of modernity and progress, opening up hinterlands to economic opportunities. Now many of these roads are seen as the vectors of danger and violence from criminals and hostile clans. This perception runs in parallel with ideas about 'roads of marriage'. Perhaps in part because of modern changes, these too are seen as sources of danger; although in pre-colonial times also this must have been the case. For the Langalanga people, the contradiction between their current residence and their artificial islands of the past (seemingly built for similar reasons to the Irish crannogs) is resolved by turning the islands into a tourist icon enshrining 'heritage'. Heritage is thus brought into alignment with development.

Chapter 10 (Carrier) neatly encapsulates many of the dominant themes found in the earlier chapters of the book. It delineates the conflict between conservationists and local fishers in contemporary Jamaica. Conservationists see the sea waters in universalistic terms connected with the preservation of 'the environment'. Fishers see these waters as tied in with their livelihood and their daily experience. Both sets of people have further been impacted by external agencies and by tourism. In Carrier's words, 'the result of these processes is that the waters . . . are a disputed landscape, burdened with history'. We take up the themes of heritage versus development and the overall relationships of landscape to conflict further in our Epilogue to this volume.

NOTES

1. Nowadays bodies are buried in holes dug in the ground but within the burial chamber a platform-like structure is built similar to the wooden platforms that were used in the past when bodies were exposed to the elements and allowed to decay in the air prior to the collection of the bones of the deceased for secondary burial in the high forest limestone crannies. The 'modern' coffin has an opening positioned so as to allow the body fluids to drain away from the bones, dripping onto and soaking into the earth. Some people still recover the bones of their kin from these burials so as to place the remains in the high forest where it is thought that a category of powerful female spirit (*Payame Ima*) looks after the *tini* of the deceased (Stewart and Strathern 1999b, 2001b).

These same female spirits are said to be the overseers of various ecological resources, controlling their abundance and quality (Stewart and Strathern 2002a).

2. Like many of the road systems in the Highlands of Papua New Guinea, this one has seriously deteriorated in its condition over the years. In 1997, when we drove to Ekit Kuk, the driver (Pamela J. Stewart) of the four-wheel drive truck found the road to be treacherous with mud slides and fallen boulders along the way. For further narratives of 'roadscapes' in Papua New Guinea see Stewart and Strathern (1999a) and O'Hanlon and Frankland (this volume).

REFERENCES

Basu, Paul (2001)'Hunting Down Home: Reflections on Homeland and the Search for Identity in the Scottish Diaspora', in B. Bender and M. Winer (eds) *Contested Landscapes: Movement, Exile and Place*. Oxford: Berg, pp. 332–48.

Beehler, B., T. Pratt and D. Zimmerman (1986) *Birds of New Guinea*. Princeton, NJ: Princeton University Press.

Bender, B. (ed.) (1993) *Landscape: Politics and Perspectives*. Oxford: Berg.

—— (1998) *Stonehenge: Making Space*. Oxford: Berg.

Bender, B. and M. Winer (eds) (2001) *Contested Landscapes: Movement, Exile and Place*. Oxford: Berg.

Bode, C. (ed.) (1975) *The Portable Thoreau*. New York: Penguin Books.

Dawson, A. and M. Johnson (2001) 'Migration, Exile and Landscapes of the Imagination', in B. Bender and M. Winer (eds) *Contested Landscapes: Movement, Exile and Place*. Oxford: Berg, pp. 319–32.

Head, L. (2000) *Second Nature: The History and Implications of Australia as Aboriginal Landscape*. New York: Syracuse University Press.

Hirsch, E. (1995) 'Introduction', in E. Hirsch and M. O'Hanlon (eds) *The Anthropology of Landscape: Perspectives on Place and Space*. Oxford: Clarendon, pp. 1–30.

Hirsch, E. and M. O'Hanlon (eds) (1995) *The Anthropology of Landscape: Perspectives on Place and Space*. Oxford: Clarendon.

Jacob, V. (1990) *Diaries and Letters from India 1895–1900*. Edinburgh: Canongate.

O'Sullivan, A. (2001) 'Crannogs: Places of Resistance in the Contested Landscapes of Early Modern Ireland', in B. Bender and M. Winer (eds) *Contested Landscapes: Movement, Exile and Place*. Oxford: Berg, pp. 87–102.

Rapport, N. and A. Dawson (eds) (1998) *Migrants of Identity: Perceptions of Home in a World of Movement*. Oxford: Berg.

Royle, T. (1993) *The Mainstream Companion to Scottish Literature*. Edinburgh: Mainstream Publishing.

Schama, S. (1995) *Landscape and Memory*. London: HarperCollins.

Shirane, H. (1998) *Traces of Dreams: Landscape, Cultural Memory, and the Poetry of Bashō*. Stanford, CA: Stanford University Press.

Shurr, W. (ed.) (1993) *New Poems of Emily Dickinson*. Chapel Hill: University of North Carolina Press.

Stewart, P.J. and A. Strathern (1999a) 'Death on the Move: Landscape and Violence on the Highlands Highway, Papua New Guinea', *Anthropology and Humanism* 24(1): 20–31.

—— (1999b) 'Female Spirit Cults as a Window on Gender Relations in the Highlands of Papua New Guinea', *Journal of the Royal Anthropological Institute* 5(3): 345–60.

—— (2000) 'Naming Places: Duna Evocations of Landscape in Papua New Guinea', *People and Culture in Oceania* 16: 87–107.

—— (2001a) 'Origins versus Creative Powers: The Interplay of Movement and Fixity', in A. Rumsey and J. Weiner (eds) *Emplaced Myth: Space, Narrative, and Knowledge in*

Aboriginal Australia and Papua New Guinea Societies. Honolulu: University of Hawai'i Press, pp. 79–98.

—— (2001b) *Humors and Substances: Ideas of the Body in New Guinea*. Westport, CT and London: Bergin and Garvey.

—— (2002a) *Remaking the World: Myth, Mining and Ritual Change among the Duna of Papua New Guinea*. Washington, DC: Smithsonian Institution Press.

—— (2002b) *Gender, Song, and Sensibility: Folktales and Folksongs in the Highlands of New Guinea*. Westport, CT and London: Praeger Publishers.

Stewart, P.J. and A. Strathern (eds) n.d. *Worlds of Song: Expressive Genres and Historical Change*. (manuscript in preparation).

Strang, V. (1997) *Uncommon Ground: Cultural Landscapes and Environmental Values*. Oxford: Berg.

Strathern, A. (1992) 'Let the Bow Go Down', in R.B. Ferguson and N. Whitehead (eds) *War in the Tribal Zone*. Santa Fe: School of American Research Press, pp. 229–50.

—— (1993) *Voices of Conflict*, Ethnology Monograph Series no. 14. Pittsburgh: Dept of Anthropology, University of Pittsburgh.

Strathern, A. and P.J. Stewart (1997) 'Ballads as Popular Performance Art in Papua New Guinea and Scotland', JCU, Centre for Pacific Studies Discussion Papers Series, School of Anthropology and Archaeology, James Cook University of North Queensland, No. 2, pp. 1–17.

—— (1999) *Collaborations and Conflicts: A Leader Through Time*. Fort Worth, TX: Harcourt Brace College Publishers.

—— (2000a) *Arrow Talk: Transaction, Transition, and Contradiction in New Guinea Highlands History*. Kent, OH and London: Kent State University Press.

—— (2000b) *The Python's Back: Pathways of Comparison between Indonesia and Melanesia*. Westport, CT and London: Bergin and Garvey, Greenwood Publishing Group.

—— (2000c) 'Melpa Ballads as Popular Performance Art', in D. Niles and D. Crowdy (eds) *Ivilikou: Papua New Guinea Music Conference and Festival*. Boroko, PNG: Institute of PNG Studies, pp. 76–84.

—— (2001) *Minorities and Memories: Survivals and Extinctions in Scotland and Western Europe*. Durham, NC: Carolina Academic Press.

2 ICONIC IMAGES: LANDSCAPE AND HISTORY IN THE LOCAL POETRY OF THE SCOTTISH BORDERS

John Gray

Grab the land. Deface the soil.
Snatch the industry and oil.
Tell us what we may or may not do.
We don't know what we're waiting for
But Wolfe is waiting by the door,
And he may have the final laugh on you.

It's often said, 'If England sneezes
Scotland catches cold and freezes.'
What could keep us from this source of fear?
Would independent Wolfe's direction
Help protect us from infection
Or would our germ-resistance disappear.

Nothing sure and nothing certain:
Glorious dawn or final curtain?
Harold Wilsons, Heaths or Wolfes or Thorpes?
Who will leap down from his fence

Restoring truth and confidence
Before this vibrant nation is a corpse?
(From 'Cross Roads' [1974] in Douglas n.d. b: 10)

The epigraph is part of a longer poem, 'Cross Roads', composed by Tim Douglas, a hill sheep farmer and well-known local poet of the Scottish Borders. It was written in response to the UK General Elections held on 28 February 1974 in which the Scottish National Party (SNP) polled 22 per cent of the vote in Scotland but won only 7 of the 71 Scottish seats. In notes accompanying the poem he wrote that 16 seats would have been 'a fair share'. The Scotland-wide electoral recognition of the SNP and resurgence of 'The Scottish Question', that is, of Scotland's place in the British state, continued the momentum of the earlier and surprising by-election of 1967 in which SNP took the seat of Hamilton in Lanarkshire – one of the Labour Party's safest – with 46 percent of the vote (see Devine 2000: 574). The poem and several others, written between 1970 and 1986, are persuasions and reflections upon the contemporary ambiguities of the identity of Scotland as a separate but subordinate nation and whether its destiny lay in the United Kingdom but within its own devolved Parliament in Edinburgh or in Home Rule and self-government as a separate state (Strathern and Stewart 2001: 99–129). As Caton suggests in his study of poetry in Yemen, a debate over national identity and status, such as that occurring in Scotland throughout the latter decades of the twentieth century, is a context of social reconstruction in which art can play an active part in the 'emergence [rather than just the reproduction] of culture in social action' (1990: 260–1).

My aim in this chapter is to analyse a subset of Douglas's poems, those composed about Scotland and its identity – an identity that in his poems consists of two dimensions: a 'cultural' dimension based upon and reflected by a distinctive history, landscape, weather, language, sporting teams, economics and a taste for whisky; and a political dimension based upon relations between the Scottish nation and United Kingdom state. I treat these poems as both artistic and social practice in that they entail 'both the creation of art and the production of social and political reality in the same act of composition' (Caton 1990: 21). The social and political reality they bring into being is characterised by multi-faceted, multi-level ironies: the situational irony of the incongruous political circumstances of Scotland as a separate nation with a distinct cultural identity and at the same time as dependent and subordinate within the British state;[1] the historical irony of Scottish resistance to its subjugation and unequal status with little lasting effect; the self-irony of mocking the hubris of nations within the United Kingdom that take themselves and their identity too seriously; and the poetic irony of leaving the reader/listener uncertain as to the poet's intent in evoking these ironies.

Even though the theme of the poems is about the whole of Scotland, the poet and the poetry are local. Douglas uses two closely related themes/images – themselves filled with irony – about the Borders region to localise his poetic persuasions about Scotland as separate nation/dependent state. The first is a distinctive episode and a distinctive set of agents in the history of the Anglo-Scottish Borders. From the fourteenth to the sixteenth century, the border region was the scene of the sporadic and drawn-out Wars of Independence between Scotland and England. During this period there was incessant cross-border raiding by 'reivers' – bands of riders mobilised by local lairds – who have come to represent to the people of the Scottish Borders the spirit of resistance to domination by England and now to the United Kingdom epitomised by the Westminster Parliament. The other theme-image is the unique landscape, including the inclement weather, of the Borders hills which to outsiders appears bleak and foreboding but which to the people of the Borders is beautiful ('bonny') and provides their most important sense of identity and belonging to a place.

> For home, where the landscapes are bonny,
> 'Though the wind of the winter blows cold
> Whether misty, or snowy, or sunny,
> To a love that is richer than gold.
> For home, where our hearts keep returning
> Wherever our footsteps are led.
> We are filled with a desperate yearning
> To be back by the banks of the Jed.[2]
> (from 'Jedwater' [*c.* 1980] in Douglas n.d. b: 139)

Historically, the reivers and the landscape of their exploits were the frontline of the violent struggle to resist domination by England. Poetically, the same reivers and their landscape become synecdoches for Scotland as a whole in Douglas's reflections upon the nation's contemporary identity and the controversy of 'The Scottish Question'.

WHY POETRY?

Each period and each social group has had and has its own repertoire of speech forms for ideological communication. (Volosinov [1929] 1986 in Caton 1990: 262)

Poetry, as verse or ballad, has been – and if Douglas is any indication – continues to be the genre of choice for people of the Scottish Borders when interpreting and constructing their own local culture and history. In the late eighteenth century, Sir Walter Scott travelled throughout the Scottish Borders collecting poems, ballads and stories, often directly from those who recited, sung or told them, 'as a vital record ... of the way of life of a definable region' (Reed 1991: 7). He published his collection as *The Minstrelsy of the Scottish Borders* whose aim was to 'contribute something to the history of my native country; the peculiar features of whose manners and character are daily melting and dissolving into those of her sister and ally' (Scott 1931: 70). He organised the poems into 'historical' and 'romantic' categories, and added a category of those that are 'imitations of the ancient ballad'. Many of the historical poems are romanticised accounts of the exploits of the Borders Reivers.[3] His collection is a testament to the widespread use of the poetic genre by 'ordinary people' of the Borders to celebrate their history and culture. Some of these local poets were, like Douglas himself, shepherds. Two of the most well-known shepherd-poets of the Borders are James Hogg, the Ettrick Shepherd, and Henry Scott Riddell of Teviotdale. Hogg wrote both poetical works, some of which are included in Scott's collection, and prose. His writing in both genres often portrayed local Borders culture and traditions.[4] Riddell is probably best known for his tribute to Scotland, 'Scotland Yet' (1871: 1), in which images of landscape – howes and knowes (low ground and hill tops), dales and vales – express Scotland's distinctiveness and its inherent right to freedom as a separate nation:

> The heath waves wild upon her hills,
>   And, foaming frae the fells,
> Her fountains sing o' freedom still,
>   As they dance down the dells;
> And weel I loe the land, my lads,
>   That's girded by the sea;
> Then Scotland's vales and Scotland's dales,
>   And Scotland's hills for me;
> We'll drink a cup to Scotland yet,
>   Wi' a' the honours three.
> (Riddell 1871: 1)

David Cameron details a similar pattern of local poetry composed by ordinary people in rural locales in the eighteenth century. His study of farmtouns throughout Scotland, *The Ballad and the Plough*, describes the ever-present composition and use of poetry by farmtoun people to express their grievances, to praise their Clydesdales, and just to 'pass the time' (1987: 38–43).

There are indications in his poetry that Douglas self-consciously sees himself continuing in this Borders cultural tradition of using the poetic genre to interpret local history and society. The opening lines of his poem 'Souden Kirk', 'It fell about the Lammas tide', is the same as the opening of one of the most well-known verses from Scott's *Minstrelsy*, 'The Battle of Otterbourne', which gives an account of how in 1388 the Earl of

Douglas was killed in defeating the English armies and capturing Henry Hotspur, Lord Percy. The ironic heroism of the tale is that despite being killed, Douglas 'led' his troops into the battle.[5] Further, like Scott's poem, Douglas's is about the Battle of Otterbourne as an image of the relations between Scotland and England; Scott celebrates Douglas's historical resistance to subjugation by England and Douglas (the poet), perhaps, a contemporary acceptance of Scotland's place in the United Kingdom:

> It fell aboot the Lammas tide
> Six centuries lang syne
> That beacons lit the Border side
> Frae Otterburn tae Tyne.
> No more shall Border beacons blaze
> The desperate days are done,
> In peaceful pastures sheep may graze
> The battle has been won.
> (From 'Souden Kirk' [1986] in Douglas n.d. b: 293)

TIM DOUGLAS – SHEPHERD AND POET

Tim Douglas was born in 1943 into a family that had been farming a large Borders farm for over 300 years (Douglas n.d. a).[6] He started writing poetry in 1969 (Douglas 1983: ii). The earliest poems I have in the collection (Douglas n.d. b) are from 1970 and the latest one was composed in October 1986. During the periods of my fieldwork in the Scottish Borders between 1981 and the mid-1990s, he was the tenant of a farm near the small hamlet of Bonchester Bridge. The farm was almost entirely rough hill grazing land suitable only for raising hardy South Country Cheviot sheep that have been bred to withstand the altitude, poor grazing and inclement weather characteristic of the Southern Uplands and Cheviot Hills of the Scottish Borders. He did most of the shepherding.

The corpus of Douglas's poems that I collected consists of about two hundred items ranging in length from two four-line stanzas to a short epic of nearly 300 lines. They are written in a range of genres. There are pastorals about the landscape and weather of the Borders (e.g. 'The Border', 'The Source', 'Pastoral', 'Watersplash'); there are narrative poems about aspects of border hill sheep farming (e.g. 'Upland Farming', 'To a Border Collie', 'The Chase', 'Wellies and Glaur', 'Woolly Bleaters') and various types of people connected with it (e.g. 'The Country Vet', 'The Fencer', 'The Auctioneer', 'The Lambing Man', 'The Shepherd', 'The College Advisor', 'The Man from the Department'); there are satiric poems that ridicule the foibles of people – Scots, politicians, lawyers, the overuse of acronyms (e.g. 'The Boozer', 'The Forked Tongue', 'Blame', 'The Bigot', 'The Solicitor', 'The Censor', 'The Drunk', 'Initially Idle'); there are elegies composed as tributes to deceased friends and relatives (e.g. 'The Master', 'The Colonel', 'Annie's Song', 'Eric'), and to commemorate happier local events such as the birth of children (e.g. 'The Laddie'), engagements (e.g. 'The Meeting of the Waters'), birthdays (e.g. 'Rob with a Tenner'), weddings (e.g. 'Jenny and Les'), the building of a new porch (e.g. 'Peter's Porch') and the community bus (e.g. 'Ode to a Bus'); and there is one epic poem, 'The Reivers' Last Fling'.

In terms of content, his poems are about a wide range of subjects most of which have a local Borders reference. There are poems about the culture of the Scottish Border regions (e.g. 'First and Last', 'Of Beasts and Men'), about sheep farming (e.g. 'The Gimmer', 'The Dog', 'Henry Dugless'), about Borders landscape (e.g. 'The Border', 'Me Myself and I', 'Pastoral', 'Eildon's Song') including the inclement weather (e.g. 'Winter', 'September Dawn', 'Summertime', 'Springtime', 'The Wet', 'The Flood', 'Sunshine and Shadow') and the dreaded midgies ('Pestilence'), about sport – particularly rugby – (e.g. 'The Roaring Jethart Bull', 'The Day the Lion Roared', 'Requiem'), about Scottish History ('Souden Kirk') and Scottish Nationalism (e.g. 'The Dis-United Kingdom', 'Black is Black', 'Oh Scotland').

Douglas uses a number of literary modes in his poems: satire and allegory to ridicule the human failings (e.g. 'The Bantie Cock', 'Miss Vanity', 'The Odd Laddie', 'The Wild Gimmer', 'Blame', 'The Forked Tongue'); humour as a means of questioning the taken for granted (e.g. 'The Lambing Man's Prayer', 'The Provost's Breeks'); the supernatural – often through the device of dreams – as a means of redressing injustice and bringing morality into the world (e.g. 'The Sheep's Head', 'The Factor's Nightmare', 'Farmer Geordie's Dream', 'The Lambing Man', 'The Factor'); indexicality to link his more general themes to local people (e.g. 'The Reivers' Last Fling', 'Allen of a Thousand Dawns' [commemorating the one hundredth radio programme of *Scottish Farming News*], 'Andy Cant' [a local fiddler]); and irony as a way of evoking the unwelcome contradictions and inconsistencies of life, especially, as we will see, those confronting Scotland and its national identity and 'inciting the moral and political imagination' (Fernandez and Huber 2001: 1) (e.g. 'The Reivers' Last Fling', 'The Dis-United Kingdom', 'The Hero', 'The Publican's Saturday Night').

Tim Douglas and his poetry are widely known throughout the Scottish Borders. Most people I spoke with about local poetry knew of him and many had heard or read his poems. His works have been distributed throughout the Borders and wider Scotland in a number of different ways. Available in bookshops in the main towns of the Borders were a commercial tape of readings of over a dozen of his poems (Douglas n.d. a) and two small booklets of 35 poems altogether, published by local presses (Douglas 1983, 1984); his poems have been read on Radio Scotland; his poems have appeared in the weekly Scotland-wide industry publication, *The Scottish Farmer*; and he is invited to many public events – from formal dinners, radio programmes, to informal small gatherings of friends and relatives – for which he composes poems to be read.

BORDER REIVERS AND BARREN HILLS

As I have mentioned, there are two recurring and historically intercon- nected theme-images – the reivers and landscape of the Borders – in Douglas's poetry about Scotland and its place in the United Kingdom. In using them, he is drawing upon the historical ironies that beset the battles, the raids, the reivers and the landscape of the 300-year Wars of Independence carried out in the Anglo-Scottish borderlands between Scotland and England over Scotland's independence.[7]

Border Conflict

From the accidental death of the Scottish King, Alexander I, in 1286 to the union of the Scottish and English crowns under James I (James VI of Scotland) in 1603, Scotland and England engaged in protracted and profoundly ironic Wars of Independence. During this period, reiving was the Borderers' discriminating response as well as their contribution to these hostilities, so much so that it became the central and defining feature of their way of life. Reiving strictly refers to acts of robbery, raiding, marauding and plundering. Local landowning lairds on both sides of the border recruited raiding parties of 12 to 50 men from among their kin and feudal dependants to engage *en revanche* in armed robbery, arson, kidnapping, blackmail and occasionally murder against their neighbours as well as the enemy over the border. For example, in June 1581, Robin Ellot, Sim Ellot, Clemie Croser, Gawen's Jock and their accomplices raided Thom of the Todhill and his neighbours, dependants of a local laird, Sir Simon Musgrave, stealing 60 cows and oxen, and a horse, and took Thome Rootledg prisoner; in June 1582 'Old Lard of Whitaugh, Young Lard of Whitaugh, Sims Thom, and Jock of Copshawe' stole from 'Mathew Taylor, and the poor widow of Martin Taylor' 140 cows and oxen, 100 sheep, 20 goat, and all their insight (household belongings), £200, and the slaughter of Martin Taylor, John Dodgshon, John Skelloe and Mathew Blackburne (Scott 1817, vol. I: lxxviii)

Reiving was largely a practice of those living in the rural river valleys and hills of the border region. It began as a mode of subsistence in response to the scorched-earth military tactics of Robert Bruce's grandson, the Earl of Carrick, who carried on the Scottish resistance against the military campaigns and political domination by England under Edward in the early years of the fourteenth century culminating in his victory at Bannockburn in 1314 (Fraser 1971: 16–17). Carrick's military tactics included starving the enemy by destroying all potential food sources on the Scottish side of the border through which the English army would have to pass in carrying out its campaign. These tactics were ironic in that their disastrous effects on the livelihoods of people of Carrick's own border region – the borderers whose cause he was fighting for – were not much different from those that the enemy, Edward, wrought upon them. The actions of Edward and Bruce established the paradoxical nature of the conflict that was to continue for nearly 300 years. By the end of the sixteenth century, both London and Edinburgh incorporated reivers and their raiding – the very activity they tried so hard to stamp out – into their military tactics by using local animosities between families and the reivers' ability to attack by stealth to advance their national interests in times of supposed peace.

For London and Edinburgh the most ominous and ironic feature of the Anglo-Scottish border region, its people and their endemic reiving was the confounding of what the Wars of Independence were about: the boundaries separating two kingdoms. London wanted to annul them, Edinburgh to confirm them. Yet, the actions of the governments and reivers negated the very boundaries whose existence and status were the cause of their struggle. This occurred in a number of ways, some of which were self-inflicted – adding another dimension of irony to the Wars of Independence. Under the the Laws of the Marches (*Leges marchiarum*), an accretion of customary procedures for administering the frontier separating the two kingdoms agreed to at a conference of knights from England and Scotland in 1248, the regions on both sides of the border were treated as a single, separate and coherent space with its own character despite the fact that it lay within two kingdoms and societies. In administering the Law, the border zone was divided into six regions, three on each side of the border; a Warden was appointed to maintain law and order in the three Marches within its national boundaries. The Warden was the 'monarch's man' (Fraser 1971: 102) acting on his King's behalf to govern for the benefit of the Borderers by guarding the frontier from incursion, investigating and punishing crimes within his March, pursuing criminal raiding parties across the border, and cooperating with the Warden on the opposite March in keeping the peace.

Wardens were subjected to the same self-inflicted irony as the border region they governed. Like Edward III and Robert Bruce, whose military tactics made no distinction between one's citizens and one's enemy, Wardens confounded the boundary between government authority and resistance to that authority, or between law-enforcer and law-breaker. According to the Law of the Marches, a Warden was supposed to cooperate with the Warden of the opposite March in capturing and punishing reivers. This was a mechanism for unifying and pacifying the Borders. Yet each government strategically directed their Wardens to spy, incite feuds between reiver families or ignore raids on enemies, thereby exacerbating the disputes that they were supposed to stop. The exploits of the English Warden, Lord Dacre, and the Scottish Keeper of Liddesdale, Scott of Buccleuch, are the most celebrated of these 'stirrer' Wardens. For example, Dacre describes his own exploits which are difficult to distinguish from those of the reivers he was appointed to capture and punish:

I have caused to be burnt six times more townys and howsys within the west and middill marshes of Scotland in the same season than is done to us.... The head of Tevyot, Borthwick, and Ale, lyes all every one of them waste now, no corne sawne upon none of the said grounds. (quoted by Oliver 1887: 100)

The final irony of the Wars of Independence was that the outcome did not hinge upon the tactics of the reivers or the political and military strategies of the governments in Edinburgh or London, but rather on the choice of Queen Elizabeth not to marry and produce an heir. The result was that upon her death, the reivers' own Scottish King, James VI, assumed the English throne as James I, joined the two crowns, set about a ruthless quelling of border raiding and thereby nullified all the efforts of the border reivers to resist subjugation to England.

Border Reivers

Not just the Wars of Independence but the reivers themselves are portrayed in historical accounts as ambivalent, ironic characters, embodying what was most cherished and feared. In his *Minstrelsy of the Scottish Borders*, Scott lauded the Douglas clan as 'this race of heroes' (Scott 1931: 57); he applauded the gallant resistance of the Earl of Angus to the unworthy monarch, James III, and of other Border chieftains to tyranny (Scott 1931: 61, 102); he attributed to them honour and moderation even in their rapine (Scott 1931: 110, 120), 'fidelity to their word' (Scott 1931: 122), simplicity and classlessness in demeanour (Scott 1931: 128), and a 'natural pathos' and 'rude energy' (Scott 1931: 160).

Bishop Lesley presents the menacing image of the Borders and its reivers:

> Among all those provinces of Scotland, those which are situated next to England assume to themselves the greatest habits of licence, in which they frequently indulge with impunity. For as, in time of war, they are readily reduced to extreme poverty by the almost daily inroads of the enemy, so, on restoration of peace they entirely neglect to cultivate their lands, though fertile, from fear of the fruits of their labour being immediately destroyed by a new war. Whence it happens that they seek their subsistence by robberies, or rather by plunder and rapine ... nor do they much concern themselves whether it be from Scots or English that they rob and plunder and carry off their booty of horses, cattle, and sheep. (Lesley 1577, in Scott 1817, vol. I, Appendix No. vi.: lxii)

For Lesley, lawless Border reivers not only ignore the social distinctions of citizenship but also of ownership, 'for they have the persuasion that all property is common by law' (Lesley 1577, quoted in Scott 1817, vol. I, Appendix No. vi.: lxv). Fraser makes reference to English and Scottish travellers' accounts in which Borderers are described as 'barbarous, crafty, vengeful, crooked, quarrelsome ... wild and ill to tame' (Fraser 1971: 28–9). He also quotes Camden's parallelism between border landscape, animals and people: 'In the wastes [landscape] ... you may see as it were the ancient nomads, a martial kind of men who, from the month of April into August, lie out scattering and summering with their cattle in little cottages here and there...' (Fraser 1971: 29). For both governments, these images of the border reivers actively resisting their disciplines of ownership, residence and human-ness established the grounds for the violent subjugation that reproduced the conditions for reiving as a mode of subsistence and resistance.

Border Landscape

The conflict itself was carried out in an ironic landscape – loved by Borders people, dreaded by outsiders; and border reivers used this dread as a tactic of their raiding. In a contemporary description of Border life in the sixteenth century, Lesley encapsulates how raiding parties used their intimate knowledge of what to outsiders, like Lesley himself, was the bleak and foreboding character of the border hills to avoid detection and evade capture.

> They leave their frontiers in the night time in troops, going through impassable places, and through many bye paths. In the day time they refresh their horses, and recruit their own strength, in hiding places prepared before-hand, until the

approach of night, when they advance to their place of destination. Having seized upon their booty, they in the same manner return by night, through circuits and bye-ways, to their own habitations. The more expert each leader is in making his way through these dreary places, windings, and precipices, in the darkest night, he is so much more accounted a person of superior ingenuity, and held in greater honour; and with such secrecy can they proceed, that they very rarely allow their prize to be recovered.... (Lesley 1577, in Scott 1817, vol. I, Appendix No. vi: lxvi)

Scott's description of the grim ruins of Hermitage Castle also captures the incongruities of the Borders landscape:

The traveller who first sees it from Nine-stane-rig, with the long and narrow vale of Hermitage [river] in perspective, and the mountains of Westmoreland and Cumberland in the background, is struck with the sublimity of the scene.... After fighting his way through the morasses, along the brink of precipices, and amidst pathless moors ... the first work of man by which the traveller was greeted were the grim towers, distinguished by many a legend, and still haunted ... by the perturbed spirits of those who had done or suffered evil within their precincts. (Scott 1817, vol. II: 168)

While the region includes fertile plains in the coastal districts, 'It is the hills that people remember', writes Fraser (1971: 21), summarising fifteenth- and sixteenth-century descriptions of Border landscape as bleak and ominous, in which the hills were the most potent symbol. In the sixteenth century, for example, Camden described the hills as 'Lean, hungry and waste'. Fraser's own description echoes the same vision of Border landscape:

Along the central part of the frontier line itself is the great tangled ridge of the Cheviot, a rough barrier of desolate treeless tops and moorland with little valleys and gullies running every way ... they are melancholy mountains; probably only the Border people feel at home in them.... (Fraser 1971: 20–1)

And Watson portrays the area in which Teviothead is located: 'In the middle of the Cheviot country ... lies a stretch of upland so stark and empty that the Romans are alleged to have christened it *Ad Fines* – the End of the World' (1985: 24). Thus to outsiders (i.e. the Scottish and English governments), the sparsely populated mountainous topography of the Borders appeared desolate, foreboding and – like the people who lived there – untamed. Reivers and landscape, person and place, are rendered consubstantial, sharing the same qualities – wild, ominous, dangerous – that mock the international boundary.

   This dread of the beautiful Borders landscape is not confined to outsiders. Douglas, himself, evokes a sense of irony in his poetry. On the one hand is the romantic celebration, similar to that found in Scott's collection, of the beauty of the Borders landscape in his poem 'The

Border': 'Have you ever seen the heather/On the blue hills of the border'. A few stanzas later, these hills are explicitly associated with the reivers: 'For these are the hills the reivers rode/In the days of sword and lance'; and, in the final lines, the reivers and landscape together are the crucible of Scotland's distinctive identity as a separate nation: 'Where the hills are a gasp for breath/This was the stage of Scotland's birth/When the play was life or death' (in Douglas n.d. b: 106).

But, on the other hand, he also introduces a note of gloominess and pessimism into the otherwise picturesque landscape. In a reflective piece, 'Me, Myself and I', he opens with a stanza describing a Borders glen, its idyllic burn and the various plants and animals that inhabit the hills.

> A burnie flows amang the trees.
> A briar rose, alive with bees,
> Dips scented petals owre a pool,
> Where water settles, deep and cool.
> Its waters gleam amang the roots
> Wi' pools that teem wi' muckle troots.

As a young man 'That glen was paradise tae me'. But as he grew older, the same landscape, symbolised by the burn, becomes foreboding:

> But, tides maun turn. I've grown sin' syne,
> And cursed yon burn, and changed my mind.
> I canna thole the mass o' weeds,
> The glaury hole o' flukes and reeds.
> ([1981] in Douglas n.d. b: 106)
> (maun = inevitably; sin' syne = since then; thole =
> tolerate; glaury = ooze, slime, sticky mud)

Again, while 'The borders is the finest place on earth' (from 'Kalewater', in Douglas 1984), the beauty of and sense of belonging to the landscape is undermined by its weather. Borders weather is a significant topic in over 25 per cent of his poems. In most (80 per cent) of these poems, rain is the feature of the weather that is emphasised. I found during my fieldwork that for local people rain and its frequency is the most common and remarked upon frustration of Borders climate and Douglas draws upon this shared exasperation in his poetry. In the following stanzas from several of his poems, Douglas juxtaposes the deleterious effects of the awful Borders weather on daily life and upon the spirit of borderers with the sense of belonging that it engenders.[8] In

'The Uplander', rain is a remorseless bane that torments borderers to despair:

> The upland farmer wrestles with varieties of thistles
> That survive as monuments to Man's endeavour,[9]
> And he loses hours of sleep lambing bloody-minded sheep
> In varieties of bloody-minded weather.
> ([1982] in Douglas n.d. b: 170)

There is also a sense of injustice that people of the Borders and Scotland are subjected to the irrational and 'bloody-minded' weather:

> The weather's like a beast that knows no reason
> A psychopathic sadist, bent on fun
> Who sends us, once a year, a rainy season.
> (from 'Rain' [1984] in Douglas n.d. b: 244)

> Almighty God, wha reigns abune,
> Whatever have Thy servants dune
> That ye should hap baith sun and mune
> Wi' rain-grey sky,
> Thus provin' that we canna win
> Whate'er we try?
> (from 'The Flood' [1983] in Douglas n.d. b: 228)

However, the unjust and irrational weather and the misery it engenders –

> Dismal dawns are breaking
> Over hill and glen
> Sullen skies are making
> Miseries for men.
> (from 'Watersplash' [1981] in Douglas n.d. b: 117)

– also builds the distinctive character of Borders people:

> But, damn it all! We should be used to rain.
> There'll come a spell and suns will shine again
> Oh Scotland, you're a granite-hearted place,
> And we must be a stubborn-hearted race.
> (Douglas n.d. b: 117)

Yet, in the midst of this unrelenting ('granite-hearted') misery at the injustice of constant rain, Douglas also suggests that for him – like for other borderers, from the Reivers onward – the weather is an important part of their shared sense of being borderers and their recognition that they would not live in any other place. His lyrical poem, 'The Teri', extols the virtues of the landscape near the Borders town of Hawick and links it to the reivers' sense of belonging and safety in the hills:

> I've heard folk sing of golden sands
> And skies of cloudless blue,
> Of sunlit tropic wonderlands
> Where mist ne're dimmed the view,
> Where sunlight gleams on turquoise streams
> Where blossoms bloom July 'til June
> And life is never hard.
>
> But me, I ken a windswept glen
> Where winter reigns supreme,
> Where months are lost to snow and frost
> And sunlight is a dream,
> Where lashing rain attacks each pane
> And rattles on the roof,
> Where land is turned to porridge, churned
> By sheep or cattle hoof.
>
> Let everyman his homeland praise.
> Our hearts are unalike.
> I toast the hills and banks and braes
> That cradle dear auld Hawick,
> For I have walked the Reiver's way
> When moonlight filled the moor
> And sniffed the scent of meadow hay
> Where Border air blows pure.
> ([1986] in Douglas n.d. b: 289)

The most succinct statement of Douglas's sense of the irony of Borders landscape as articulated in its weather are the following lines of his poem, 'Harvest Thanksgiving': 'In truth we have an equitable climate/And yet we get the most atrocious weather'.

'THE REIVERS' FINAL FLING':
THE INDEXICAL, THE EERIE, THE IRONIC

In 1986, Douglas was invited to be the after dinner speaker for the Border Area National Farmers' Union (NFU) Annual Dinner. This was the occasion when he presented the epic poem, 'The Reivers' Last Fling' (see Appendix). The dinner was held at Dryburgh Abbey Hotel, located in the border town of St Boswells. The name of the hotel, Dryburgh Abbey, itself is of significance to the poem in two ways. First, Dryburgh Abbey located near the town of Melrose is a testament to the border warfare and the reivers. It is a twelfth-century church sacked by the English invaders during the Wars of Independence when the reiving was endemic. Second, Sir Walter Scott, 'the minstrel' in Douglas's poem, 'The Border', is buried in the churchyard.

While the context demanded a light and entertaining performance, the poem had a thought-provoking message about Scottish identity and nationalism. In composing this poem, Douglas incorporated most of the characteristics of his style: the use of images from border history and landscape – including the weather – to express themes of Scottish identity and nationalism; indexicality – making reference to known local persons – to link local people to these broader issues; a touch of the supernatural to portray the political oppression of Scotland by England and the UK and the scope to overcome it; and, most of all, irony to move local people to interrogate the ambiguities and contradictions that Scotland faces as a separate but dependent nation within the United Kingdom. In this respect, the poem intends to excite his readers' and listeners' moral imagination, which, paraphrasing Fernandez and Huber to suit the poetic genre, can be defined as creating as evocative an image or set of images as possible of existing social conditions in their positive and negative aspects along with an image or set of images of one's moral and practical stance towards those conditions (2001: 263).

The poem consists of eight long stanzas of varying length preceded by a listing of the officers of the NFU hosting the dinner, the invited honoured guests – Members of the Westminster Parliament and one Member of the European Parliament – their alternates, and other functionaries supporting the dinner. These people become the main characters in the poem in which Douglas celebrates the heroic – but eventually futile – deeds of the border reivers in their resistance to subjugation by England and uses them as a metaphor for commenting upon the contemporary – and ultimately ironic and futile – debate within Scotland over its identity, independence and sovereignty.

The poem is an epic in a number of senses. First, it celebrates the great deeds of a hero, in this case, Bill Watson, President of the Borders area NFU. While, strictly speaking, the epic genre is about the exploits of a 'legendary hero' (Baldick 2001: 81), Douglas turns the deeds of contemporary leaders of the Borders into legends by likening them to those of the border reivers. Second, such legendary heroes perform 'superhuman exploits ... often saving or founding a nation' (Baldick 2001: 81–2) which as we will see is precisely the nature of 'The Tale' Douglas relates in the poem. Finally, in constructing this poem, Douglas adopts one of the conventions of the Homeric epic: this listing of heroes and combatants (Baldick 2001: 82) which is a major theme of the first four stanzas. Douglas brings together the historical image of the reivers, the landscape and poetic devices that are scattered throughout his earlier compositions to argue the irony of the contemporary Scottish Question.

The period of the 1970s and 1980s was a difficult one for Scotland. Between 1976 and 1987 (when Douglas composed most of the poems in the collections) Scottish industry 'disintegrated with frightening speed' (Devine 2000: 594). Manufacturing declined by almost 31 per cent; one of the worst-hit regions was 'the textile area of the Borders, which lost sixty-four percent of all manufacturing capacity' (Devine 2000: 592). For the people of the Borders and Scotland more generally, there was a bitter irony here because such economic deprivation was occurring at the same time as the UK government was reaping 'fabulous wealth' from oil discovered off the Scottish coast in 1970, a resource that the Scottish National Party claimed would make an independent Scotland economically viable. Thatcher's economic policies and the Westminster Parliament were blamed for the plight of Scotland and the Borders, and the Westminster government (the epithet for England) was accused of favouring the south-east and Midlands, the Conservative-heartland (Devine 2000: 594). Throughout this period, the Scottish conservative vote continually declined. Even at the height of Thatcher's conservative dominance in the 1983 elections, the Scottish Labour Party – the anti-Conservative opposition in Scotland – had almost twice as many MPs in Westminster as the Scottish Conservatives. But this electoral resistance had little effect on Thatcher's economic policies and their consequences for Scotland. Perhaps the most striking example of the political subordination of Scotland was its role as the experimental ground for the introduction of Thatcher's Poll Tax which resulted in the Scottish Conservative Party candidates' poor showing in the 1987 election when they lost 11 of their 21 seats. Despite this electoral dissatisfaction with the unjust treatment from Westminster, Scottish voters 'were hopelessly divided' on the issue of Home Rule (Devine 2000: 586).[10]

Border Reivers (the Indexical)

The title of the poem immediately introduces the historical theme-image of reiving and the reivers' struggle with England over Scottish independence and sovereignty from the fourteenth to the sixteenth century. In the opening three stanzas, Douglas evokes the image of the recruitment of raiding parties by the local lairds of those times, in which the flame beacons on the defensive peel towers of the Borders both warned of an impending attack by a raiding party and called the laird's dependants and kin to join a raiding party. These stanzas project the historical motivations for reiving on to contemporary Scotland through the use of indexicality in identifying the main characters. The President of the Borders area National Farmers' Union, Bill Watson, is Wild Willie Watson, the contemporary local 'laird' recruiting a band of reivers for a final raid on England with the aim of resisting its domination and subjugation and securing its independence, as later emerges in the poem, through stealing England's good weather (compared to that of the Borders). One of the primary forms of indexically identifying the reivers he recruits is in terms of their location in the Borders landscape: its river valleys – Liddesdale, Lauderdale, Eskdale, Ettrick and Yarrow; its rivers – Tweed, Jed and Teviot; and its hills – Lammermuir and Cheviot. He also incorporates reivers from all aspects of Borders society by associating the recruits in terms of their residence in border towns (e.g. Hawick and Galashiels ['Gala']); their border family (e.g. Douglas, Elliot, Armstrong and Scott); their occupation (e.g. farmers, managers, factors and bankers); their sporting prowess, (e.g. cricketers, rugby ['Kelso flankers']); and in general all manner of people in Borders society from peddlers to peers. Finally, Douglas includes the four MPs of Westminster constituencies in the Borders who were invited to the dinner: David Steel (then Leader of the Liberal Party), Archie Kirkwood (Liberal), John Home Robertson (Labour) and Alistair Hutton (Conservative). In the poem, Westminster is a synecdoche for the UK government; Douglas expresses the widespread derogatory view of it directly in two places where he refers to 'the Westminster knaves' and 'the rogues of Westminster'. In addition to local people of the Borders, the reivers invite Scots from outside the Borders region – the Vice-President of the National Farmers' Union of Scotland and a well-known lawyer from Fife – so that the raid is also on behalf of the wider nation of Scotland.[11] This 'wild company, this 'desperate rabble' of characters are also associated with 'illegal' activities, such as poaching salmon and perjury, that are, like the reivers' exploits and their reputed skill at talking themselves out of trouble, signs of cunning resistance to authority.

Rain, Raid and Superhuman Reivers (the Eerie)

In the fifth stanza, the particulars of the modern reivers' raid have not been revealed, but the theme of rain is introduced. As in Douglas's other poems, rain – the symbol of the remorseless, the unjust and the irrational, of being Scottish in a beautiful place – both brings about and signals an exasperation of the Borders reivers with their landscape and it drives the modern reivers in the next stanza to cross the border to begin their raid and wreak havoc and fear on the English. Their plan is revealed. Unlike the reivers of the fourteenth to sixteenth century who stole cattle, sheep, horses and furnishings, they explain to their intended English victims:

> The reivers replied, 'We don't want your lives,
> your money, your houses, your bairns nor your wives.
> We don't want your cattle, nor horses, nor sheep,
> nor cities, nor factories. These you may keep.
> The rain drove us long past the end of our tether.
> We're riding to plunder your climate and weather.'
> ([1986] in Douglas n.d. b: 277)

The reivers steal every seaworthy ship, tie them up to the south of England and 'the whole island tilted around on its axis'; 'Thus Thurso steamed south, as the island turned over/and up to the north went the white cliffs of Dover'; and finally they 'towed Britain down to the north coast of Spain/'til the Borders was more or less opposite Brest'.

The extraordinary character of the raid introduces a supernatural element into the poem. This is a narrative device commonly found in the work of James Hogg (see Simpson 1962; Smith 1980) and in Scott's collection. Douglas's use of it in this and several of his other poems is for similar effects.[12] First, it is only the superhuman efforts of the reivers that can relieve borderers from 'harshness of necessity' of living in the place with 'atrocious weather'. Second, the superhuman is required to expose the injustice of the miserable weather and to bring good weather to the people of the Borders. Third, the superhuman provides those 'oppressed' by the weather scope to overcome its tyranny. Given the nationalistic theme of a number of other poems in which the reivers and/or the weather figure (e.g. 'Souden Kirk', 'The Border', 'The Teri'), the modern reivers' superhuman raid on English weather is an allegory of the Scottish Question: the plight of a subjugated nation living under the miseries of declining manufacturing and increasing unemployment brought about by the unjust policies of an English-dominated Westminster government, which at the same time is raiding the oil wealth of Scotland. In reprisal, the reivers steal the English weather and by turning the island on its axis, subject England to the same misery of a nation subjugated by forces beyond the normal human (electoral) powers to resist. As Simpson says of the use of the supernatural in Hogg's work: 'Riches are given to the deserving, and the wicked are punished' (1962: 61).

The Ironic

The final irony – 'But this great Border raid was to little avail/There's a very sad twist at the end of the tale' (Stanza 7) – is that Scotland cannot be Scotland without its weather. The poem identifies some of the specifics of its identity and economic vitality as a separate nation that depend upon the landscape and climate: its rivers filled with salmon, its hills covered with snow for skiing, the water for its whisky and the toughness of its rugby players. It is in this irony of landscape and identity produced by the superhuman actions of modern-day reivers bringing about what borderers and Scots have always wished for, good weather, that the main persuasion of Douglas emerges. Despite the injustices of being a dependent state, Scotland's distinct identity as a nation is bound up not just with its beautiful landscape and history or resistance but also with its subjugation within the United Kingdom – a political reality that should be preserved despite the injustice it entails. Support for this reading comes from two other poems. In 'Souden Kirk', it is Scotland's status as a separate nation that is highlighted. Douglas opens by alluding to his forebear, James, Earl of Douglas and the Battle of Otterbourne in which he defeated the army of Hotspur in Northumberland but died in the fight. The battle, made famous by Scott's poem, occurred in 1388 during the Wars of Independence in which border Scots were the frontline of the violent resistance to subjugation by the English crown:

> It fell aboot the Lammas tide
> Six centuries lang syne
> That beacons lit the English side
> Frae Otterburn tae Tyne.
> The riders of the Borderland,
> The no-man's land of years,
> Rode south to make Northumberland
> A vale of blood and tears.
> ([1986] in Douglas n.d. b: 293)

   In the next four stanzas, he celebrates the courage and 'grim determination' of the Douglas and his reivers who had no choice but to fight: 'But, desp'rate times breed desp'rate men/and desp'rate deeds are done.' He then reflects upon the present struggle for Scotland's identity and autonomy by juxtaposing it with the time of reiving:

> The cause for which the Douglas died
> Is Scotland's cause no more:
> Men saddle horses and they ride
> For sport but not to war.
> The frontier spans the Border hills
> As ever, west to east
> And, where Jedwater gently spills
> We live our lives in peace.
> ([1986] in Douglas n.d. b: 293)

In these lines, Douglas is pointing out that the frontier separating England and Scotland still exists, but that the cause for which Douglas and the reivers fought – to maintain it, demarcating the Scottish as a separate nation – is no longer necessary. The poem ends, again using the opening lines of Scott's poem to make reference to the reivers and the Battle of Otterbourne, with a claim that the separate identity of Scotland is no longer an issue over which there needs to be a struggle – 'The battle has been won':

> It fell aboot the Lammas tide
> Six centuries lang syne
> That beacons lit the Border side
> Frae Otterburn tae Tyne.
> No more shall Border beacons blaze
> The desperate days are done,
> In peaceful pastures sheep may graze
> The battle has been won.
> ([1986] in Douglas n.d. b: 293)

In the poem, 'The Dis-United Kingdom', Douglas argues for a continuation of the United Kingdom which is founded upon each of the constituent nations maintaining its identity.

> The Welsh pray on their knees, and on their neighbours,
> And sing their Chapel hymns with gay abandon.
> The Scotsman keeps the Sabbath, and he labours
> To keep whatever else he lays his hands on.
> The Irish (most deceiving) hardly know what they believe in,
> But they'll fight for it, with Guinness in their fist.
> So, despite the politicians in their double-faced positions
> A United Kingdom doesn't now exist.
> It's the Englishmen's opinion that the others are dominions

And he wonders where his Empire went.
But from Lerwick down to Swindon
It's a dis-United Kingdom
And the same applies from Donegal to Kent.
The English love to dip through a stiffened upper lip.
They believe they are a race of self-made men,
Thus relieving the almighty
Of the blame for making Blighty,
And relieving him of blame for making them.
Each race is unforgiven, unforgiving,
But keeps its culture, accent, and its soul.
Our differences add colour to our living
And keep this dis-United Kingdom whole.
(in Douglas n.d. b: 37)

Douglas uses satire to make his ironical argument. In the first part of the poem, the separate identity of each of the constituent nations is acknowledged as political reality, but at the same time they are satirised by pointing out the foibles of each – the way each nation looks to itself instead of to the Kingdom as a whole – its self-congratulatory descriptions of its national identity and character. The force of the satire is to highlight that it is the hubris and self-interest of national self-definition that are the causes of the disunity among the constituent nations of the Kingdom, particularly the view of the English that their nation is and should be the dominant one. At the same time, the separate identity of each nation is founded in their relations to the others within the Kingdom. The second part of the poem describes the irony of such disunity. It is in spite of and even because of disunity, of the separate identity and self-interest of each of the nations, that the strength of the dis-united Kingdom continues.

CONCLUSION

In making this argument about Scotland remaining in the Union but simultaneously existing as a separate nation, Douglas re-presents a position about the relation of Scotland to the United Kingdom that has been around for a long time. Since the term 'Home Rule' was coined in the 1880s by the Liberal government, its precise meaning has ranged from devolution – the delegation of some powers to a Scottish Parliament in Edinburgh within the overall sovereignty of the UK state and the Westminster Parliament – to full self-government. The Treaty of Union of 1707, when Scotland became a separate nation within the United

Kingdom, completed the historical process of forming a country fraught with the contradiction of being a unitary but *de jure* multinational state. Since that time, the people of Scotland have held an ambivalent but pragmatic position toward their nested political relations, a position that can be described as political acceptance and cultural resistance. In terms of political acceptance, the advantage of being a subordinate part of the British state was the support Scotland received from the greater financial strength of England and the UK even during those times when, as in the Thatcher years, Scotland bore the brunt of harsh economic policies. For example, Devine points out that in Victorian Scotland, while some Scots 'were deeply concerned about aspects of the union relationship .... The Association [The National Association for the Vindication of Scottish Rights] took the view that there were weaknesses in the union but wanted to improve it rather than repeal it' (2000: 287); in 1931 the Scottish Trade Union Congress abandoned its support for Home Rule because of the advantages of being a member of the Union during the harsh economic climate (2000: 324); during the Labour government of Harold Wilson elected in 1964:

Scotland was gaining from the union as public revenues were channelled north in the form of massive regional assistance and other benefits. Ross [the Secretary of State for Scotland under Wilson] had demonstrated that ... the union relationship could be maximised to Scottish advantage. (2000: 580)

Even in the 1970s when the SNP was experiencing its greatest electoral successes, there is evidence (see note 1, p. 44) that voting for the SNP was more to do with getting the Westminster government to give Scotland more support than genuine backing for the party's policy of Scottish independence (Devine 2000: 578, 586). In terms of cultural resistance, Scotland could continue to view itself as a separate nation with its own civil institutions of law, education and religion, and to celebrate its distinctive culture and history of resistance to English subjugation.

Douglas's poetic spin on Scotland's incongruous position within the dis-United Kingdom is to render it ironic. It is the device he uses to enhance the power of his poetry, as Abu-Lughod argues for Bedouin poetry, to move people emotionally and to transform their attitudes (1986: 242) in a number of possible ways. First, as Scoggin suggests, irony can express an 'intractable ambiguity' (2001: 146). Here she is referring to the effect of irony of leaving its victim – the reader or listener – to wonder over the meaning and intent of the event. There is a hint of such intractable uncertainty in Douglas's poetry: the reader is left to wonder, is he expressing his view of what Scotland's relation should be, is he exposing the hypocrisy of the relation and those who accept it, and/or revelling, like the reivers, in the Scottish national sport of tormenting the English?

Second, in such a relation of inequality and uncertainty, irony can also be used to challenge and bring discomfort to a superior, as Herzfeld describes in his encounter with a Greek villager who exaggerates a conventional form of addressing a superior.[13] The image of the reiver is a particularly good vehicle for such a discomforting challenge: they themselves were ironic in raiding both neighbour and enemy; they were a constant thorn in the side of both Edinburgh and London, resisting their discipline but at the same time being co-opted into it as both governments used them to carry on the war in times of peace. Likewise, the image of the Borders landscape – bleak, wild, and foreboding – where the reivers carried out their raids and used their knowledge of it to avoid capture by the authorities has the poetic effect of hurling a discomforting challenge at the government in London. In 'The Reivers' Final Fling', this discomfort of raiding by the weak is transposed to the contemporary situation.

Third, Herzfeld also suggests a possible meta-irony in such unequal relations: 'Note, however, that the problem of whether we can speak of resistance where no obvious, lasting effects are evident is precisely that of irony' (2001: 74–5). For all the reivers' efforts, during the fourteenth to the sixteenth century, and in the twentieth century, there was no lasting effect on the situation of Scotland. In the former historical time, there was the irony of a Scottish King and the union of the crowns he embodied undermining the effort of the reivers to ensure Scotland's independence; in the latter poetic time, even when the reivers are successful in stealing England's weather and subjecting the English to Scotland's miserable climate, they find their national identity – founded in its landscape and weather – subverted, so they re-rotate the island and return to the ambiguous status quo weather-wise and politics-wise.

Fourth, in the poem 'Dis-United Kingdom', Douglas as a border Scot engages in self-irony as a means of 'exciting the moral imagination' (Fernandez and Huber 2001: 263) of the status quo. In describing the distasteful attributes of the national identities of the constituent nations – including his own Scotland – of the United Kingdom, Douglas parodies the tendency of each nation to take itself too seriously as the basis of self-government. Simultaneously, he mocks the political 'meta-narrative' of each nation being able to maintain a distinctive identity: while it is meant as an opiate to repress resistance to and to maintain the Union, it foments dis-unity within it. Douglas's final line – 'And keep this dis-united kingdom whole' – has final and intractable irony: Who has the last laugh? The Scots, the British or the poet?

APPENDIX

'The Reivers' Final Fling'
(for the Borders Area National Farmers' Union Annual Dinner)
Dramatis Personae:
    Bill Watson, Upper Kidson, Peebles, President
    Willie Phillips, Hyndlee, Bonchester Bridge, Vice-President
    Bob Noble, Duns, Secretary
    Hamish Steven, Branch secretary
    David Syme, Branch secretary
    Peter Gardiner, Branch secretary
Speakers:
    Sir Henry Plumb, DL, MEP
    John Hay, Angus, Vice-President NFU Scotland
    Nicholas Fairbairn, QC, MP
    (reserve) John Read, St Boswells (veterinary surgeon)
Guests:
    David Steel, MP
    Archie Kirkwood, MP
    John Home Robertson, MP
    Alistair Hutton, MEP
    (reserves) Willie Swan, Lord Lt Berwickshire
    Jimmy Stobo, NFU
    Alex Trotter, Nature Conservancy
Entertainers:
    Alan Anderson, piano
    Iain Girvan, voice
Scribes:
    Victor Robertson, *The Scotsman*
    Gordon Anderson, *Tweeddale Press*
    Dan Buglass, *Scottish Farmer*, Radio Tweed etc.

And a cast of thousands

'The Tale'
[Stanza 1]
    Wild Willie Watson, the scourge of the Tweed
    was greatly in need of a dram and a feed
    so he lit all the beacons on Peel Tower and fell
    and summoned the Borders to Dryburgh Hotel.
    By Landrover, Rangerover, battered old truck,
    trusting in providence, fortune or luck:

By limousines, taxis and clapped-out old heaps,
stinking of collies and silage and neeps,
the reivers rolled in from the East and the West,
laundered and groomed in their go-to-kirk best.
Bill Watson had plans that would solve all our trouble.
He summoned his trusty lieutenant, Bob Noble,
to gird up his loins and to roll up his sleeves
and to round up a troop of the Liddesdale thieves:
To travel each track, be it broad, be it narrow,
and rouse all the rogues of the Ettrick and Yarrow;
political rogues to include in the deal,
Archie O'Kirkwood and Davie The Steel.
(But due to the dirt the bold Tarzan has stirred
the Westminster knaves gave Wild Willie the bird
and now that she's flying, they're trying to catch her.
What happens to-night may be crucial to Thatcher.)
He summoned such rogues as e'er fled from the cops,
filthy Hawick wingers and coarse Gala props:
Dubious horse dealers, hard of the fist,
jockeys and trainers and Oliver Twist:
Hunters and poachers and peddlers and peers,
crooked contractors and bent auctioneers:
The dregs of the hills and the plunderers worse
that are found in the grain-wealthy lands of the Merse.
Where the Winters are cold, but the Summers are hotter,
he gathered a Stobo, a Swan and a Trotter.
(A Swan's better off at a Dryburgh feed
than drowning in diesel at Berwick-on-Tweed.)
Farmers and managers, factors and bankers,
Manderston cricketers, coarse Kelso flankers:
Feeders of beef and of pork and of mutton:
John O'Home Robertson, Alistair Hutton:
(Just glance at Wild Bill as he flexes his muscles
and curses the rogues of Westminster and Brussels.
'The Government's mother,' says Bill, 'is a spinster,'
and most of his curses are aimed at Westminster,
for Messrs. Home, Robertson, Kirkwood and Steel
have turned down the chance of an excellent meal.)
[Stanza 2]
'Musicians,' said Bill, 'will be greatly required
to keep the wild company keenly inspired.'
A light-fingered Anderson tickled the keys

and played the piano with style and with ease,
while, ready for song as for pillage and slaughter
was bold Iain Girvan, the voice of Kalewater.
Meanwhile, noble Bob was obeying Bill's orders
and searching for refuse all over the Borders.
From Tweedmouth to Solway, where Heaven's wide arch is
spread windy and wet oe'r the land of the Marches,
he gathered the worst of the Jed and the Teviot,
Lammermuir, Lauderdale, Eskdale and Cheviot:
All who had strayed from the straight and the narrow –
Wee Willie Phillips, the Hyndlee Cock Sparrow:
Douglases, Elliots, Armstrongs and Scotts,
and such desperadoes as Forsters and Stotts:
Villains from Alewater, Kalewater, Meigle,
who, even to name, would be almost illegal.
As desp'rate a crew as e'er swore at a Parson
or perjured themselves out of murder and arson:
As evil a bunch as e'er cleikit a salmon
or boasted a two hundred plus per cent lambing:
As crooked a crew of degenerates' sons
as boasted a crop that exceeded four tons.

[Stanza 3]

But before all the plans had been settled and sealed,
he gathered some reivers from further afield.
Putting names to the faces of such a huge force
would be of enormous importance of course.
In Angus, quite close to the toun o' Carnoustie,
there dwelleth a bachelor, sturdy and trusty,
a capable chiel, who can kindle strong flames,
John Hay has a knack of remembering names.
A guide was required by the villainous band
so they wouldn't get lost in the Sassenach's land,
so a strong European, Sir Henry, has come,
as bold as a knight and as ripe as a plum.
A man with the gift of the gab was sore needed
as over the Border the rabble proceeded,
to talk the raid out of all trouble and strife
and just such a character dwelleth in Fife –
An advocate dapper, of intellect tricky,
that silver-tongued orator, Fairbairn-the-Nicky.
(But Nicky's another political sinner
who turned down the chance of an excellent dinner.)

Yet Wild Wille Watson was not beaten yet.
'If we can't find a lawyer, we'll try for a vet.
A vet can aye carry a claymore and targe
and he'll charge just as well as a lawyer can charge.'
So Nicky's ill fortune brings luck to John Read,
who joined in the raid for the price of a feed.
[Stanza 4]
Wild Bill was aware of potential alarms.
There were sure to be needed some sergeants-at-arms
to keep such a desperate rabble in order
as soon as it mounted and made for the Border.
He summoned a Steven, a Gardiner, a Syme,
as ugly a bunch as committed a crime.
He told them to discipline those in the raid
and to gather subscriptions that hadn't been paid.
[Stanza 5]
The plans were well laid. The time would be soon
but a reiver must ride by the light o' the moon.
It rained for a month through a curtain of mist.
As they waited for moonlight the reivers got pissed.
And led by the wizard of old Kirkton hill
they tackled their task with both spirit and will
and word filtered out, through the cloud cover dense,
to the man in command of the nation's defence.
George Younger, however, was in on the plot
for, unlike swinging Tarzan, stout George is a Scot.
So George gave the forces six weeks of paid leave
and the plot of the reivers received a reprieve.
There were chiels taking notes of the reivers' bold plan –
Andersons, Robertsons, Desperate Dan.
They listened, recorded and printed the tale
but the words that they wrote were to little avail,
for, apart from the sport and the stories of rapers
no-one believes what they read in the papers.
They were lost in Westminster's political fever
and anyway, who would pay heed to a reiver.
A wind of good fortune blew down from the North
and swept up the mist from the Clyde and the Forth.
The moon blossomed bright o'er the whole countryside.
It was time for the Borders to saddle and ride.
As Distillers await the bold Gulliver's travels,
so Westminster quakes as the story unravels.

[Stanza 6]

The reivers all mounted their horses and rode.
Their regiments vast, like the Amazon flowed.
They galloped past Hadrian's Wall and its forts.
They made for the harbours. They made for the ports.
The English lay trembling behind every dyke,
crying, 'Spare us, but steal just whatever you like.'
The reivers replied, 'We don't want your lives,
your money, your houses, your bairns nor your wives.
We don't want your cattle, nor horses, nor sheep,
nor cities, nor factories. These you may keep.
The rain drove us long past the end of our tether.
We're riding to plunder your climate and weather.'
They stole every ship that the nation could float
from the QE2 down to a wee fishing boat,
from Cornwall to Lewis, from Kent to the Skerries,
submarines, lifeboats and cross channel ferries.
Half of them steamed to the coast of Caithness
and to Cornwall and Devon, they hijacked the rest.
To the coasts of these places, the vessels were chained,
then they opened the throttles. They heaved and they strained.
With a strain that was worse than the Chancellor's taxes,
the whole island tilted around on its axis.
It turned with a crack, loud, dramatic and frantic
and Wales walloped Ireland across the Atlantic.
Thus Thurso steamed south, as the island turned over
and up to the North went the white cliffs of Dover.
They unhitched the ships and they yoked up again
and towed Britain down to the north coast of Spain,
'til the Borders was more or less opposite Brest
and close to Bordeaux was the coast of Caithness.
The islands were carefully gathered and most
were planted conveniently close to the coast.

[Stanza 7]

But this great Border raid was to little avail.
There's a very sad twist at the end of the tale.
'Though the climate was grand for the crops and the soil,
they travelled too far from the rigs and the oil.
The oilfields were closer to Norway than us
which created a mighty political fuss.
To the South and the West lay the Tweed and the Spey
and the swift-running salmon got lost on the way.

The snow swiftly thawed from Cairngorms and Glenshee
and despite the facilities, no-one could ski.
Professional clubs of French rugby seduced
the cream of the players the Borders produced,
and sad were the hearts that the rainfall in Biscay
was found to be useless for putting in whisky.
So,

[Stanza 8]

They yoked all the ships to the island once more,
transported it back to its place as before.
They never found Ireland. It foundered and sank
somewhere across by the Newfoundland Bank.
Thus Headmistress Maggie was mightily chuffed
that the problem of Ulster was finally stuffed
and Wild Willie Watson, the record records,
was offered a seat in the House of Lords.
'But the raid, I'm afraid,' said Wild Bill,
'was a failure. I'd sooner be transported out
to Australia and live out my days in the heat o'
the sun, for Peebles for pleasure can be overdone.'
Hawick for forrits and Kelsae for backs
have no sunny beaches to lie and relax.
Drouth is where dust is — Sahara or Spain,
Jethart for Justice and lashings of rain.
It's sun for the just and it's rain for the sinner.
It's Soho for lust and it's Dryburgh for dinner.

NOTES

1. There is evidence that Douglas's political position as formulated in his poetry has wider acceptance. Devine notes that opinion polls throughout 1974 'revealed that, while a third of the Scots had voted for the SNP in that year, only 12 percent supported independence' (1999: 578)

2. 'Jed' refers to the Jedwater, one of the rivers flowing through the Borders and associated with the town of Jedburgh.

3. Some examples: 'The Battle of Otterbourne', 'The Sang of the Outlaw Murray', 'Johnnie Armstrong', 'Jamie Telfer of the Fair Dodhead', 'The Raid of Reidswire', 'Kinmont Willie', 'Jock o' the Side and Hobbie Noble'.

4. Two examples of Hogg's prose are: 'The Shepherd's Calendar: Tales and Sketches Illustrative of Pastoral Life, Occupations, and Superstitions' and 'The Siege of Roxburgh: A Legend of the Wars of Scotland and England, in the Reign of Robert II'. An example of his poetry is a miscellaneous collection of his early ballads, *The Mountain Bard* (Hogg 1872).

5. In an early action prior to the main battle, the Earl of Douglas was mortally wounded. Before he died, he instructed his troops to 'conceal my death, defend my standard, and avenge my fall!' (Scott, 1931: 124).

6. Douglas, as we saw in the poems about the Battle of Otterbourne, is an important clan in the history of the Borders.

7. 'On a recent period of fieldwork in the Borders, I was struck by two tangible indications that reivers were becoming a prominent symbol of a distinctive Borders regional identity. First, The Borders Regional Council – representing Borderers of town and country – has erected signposts on all the main roads leading into the region announcing to travellers that they were entering "The Borders". These signposts contained a striking logo depicting the distinctive "steel bonnets" of the reivers. Second, in Teviothead on the main A7 road from Edinburgh to Carlisle that runs through the major Border towns of Galashiels, Selkirk, Hawick and Langholm, a small commercial museum recently opened. Its name is the Johnnie Armstrong Museum and it portrays the exploits of this most [in]famous of Border reivers, who was betrayed, captured and hung "tradition has it" (Watson 1985: 94) at Caerlanrig Farm in Teviothead and buried in the nearby church yard' (Gray 2000: 43).

8. In a small number of poems, Douglas uses rain as a metaphor for sadness at the passing of a friend or relative as in the elegy, 'Garry': 'The Autumn rain/proclaims a cold tomorrow'; or for dramatic effect as in 'Farmer Geordie's Dream': 'The whisky ran like rain.'

9. Note the irony here in calling thistles, weeds that destroy good grazing ground, 'monuments to Man's endeavour'.

10. It was not until the elections of 1997, when Scotland became a 'Conservative-free zone', that devolution received the support of the Scottish people in a referendum. Even here, for the Scottish National Party, the outcome left Scotland in an incongruous situation as a separate nation/dependent state.

11. Sir Henry Plumb, future president of the National Farmers Union and currently Member of the European Parliament was also invited and mentioned in the poem: 'A guide was required by the villainous band/so they wouldn't get lost in the Sassenach's land'.

12. 'The Sheep' Heid', 'Farmer Geordie's Dream', 'The Lambing Man', 'A Factor's Nightmare'.

13. I witnessed the same kind of irony during my fieldwork on hill sheep farms in the Scottish Borders with the over-obsequious doffing of the cap I saw a shepherd perform to his farmer boss.

REFERENCES

Abu-Lughod, L. (1986) *Veiled Sentiments: Honour and Poetry in a Bedouin Society*. Berkeley: University of California Press.

Baldick, C. (2001) *The Concise Oxford Dictionary of Literary Terms*. Oxford: Oxford University Press.

Cameron, D.K. (1987) *The Ballad and the Plough: A Folk-History of the Scottish Farmtouns*. London: Victor Gollancz Ltd.

Caton, S.C. (1990) *'Peaks of Yemen I Summon': Poetry as Cultural Practice in a North Yemeni Tribe*. Berkeley: University of California Press.

Devine, T.M. (1999) *The Scottish Nation, 1700–2000*. London: Penguin Books.

—— (2000) *The Scottish Nation, 1700–2000*. London: Penguin Books.

Douglas, T.G.O. (1983) *Country Places: Scenes from the Scottish Borders*. Gatehousecote, Bonchester Bridge.

—— (1984) *Borderline Ballads*. Gatehousecote, Bonchester Bridge.

—— (n.d. a) *Poems from the Scottish Countryside* (Cassette tape), introduced by Charlie Allan and read by Allan Wright. Ardo 103: Ardo Pedigree Cattle.

—— (n.d. b) *Border Rhymes* (poems written between 1970 and 1986), unpublished collection.

Fernandez, J.W. and M.T. Huber (2001) 'Introduction: The Anthropology of Irony', in J.W. Fernandez and M.T. Huber (eds) *Irony in Action: Anthropology, Practice, and the Moral Imagination*. Chicago: University of Chicago Press.

Fraser, G.M. (1971) *The Steel Bonnets: The Story of the Anglo-Scottish Border Reivers*. London: Pan Books Ltd.

Gray, J.N. (2000) *At Home in the Hills: Sense of Place in the Scottish Borders*. New York: Berghahn Books.

Herzfeld, M. (2001) 'Irony and Power: Towards a Politics of Mockery in Greece', in J.W. Fernandez and M.T. Huber (eds) *Irony in Action: Anthropology, Practice and the Moral Imagination*. Chicago: University of Chicago Press.

Hogg, James (1872) *The Works of the Ettrick Shepherd*. Edinburgh: Blackie and Son.

Oliver, J. Rutherford (1887) *Upper Teviotdale and the Scotts of Buccleuch: A Local and Family History*. Hawick: W. and J. Kennedy.

Reed, J. (1991) *Border Ballads: A Selection*. Manchester: Carcanet Press Limited.

Riddell, Henry Scott (1871) *Poetical Works*, edited by James Brydon, MD. Glasgow: Maurice Ogle and Co.

Scoggin, M. (2001) 'Wine in the Writing, Truth in the Rhetoric: Three Levels of Irony in the Chinese Essay Genre', in J.W. Fernandez and M.T. Huber (eds) *Irony in Action: Anthropology, Practice and the Moral Imagination*. Chicago: University of Chicago Press.

Scott, Sir Walter (1817) *The Border Antiquities of England and Scotland Comprising Specimens of Architecture and Sculpture, and Other Vestiges of Former Ages, Accompanied By Descriptions* (vols I and II). London: Longman, Hurst, Rees, Orme, and Brown.

—— (1931) *Minstrelsy of the Scottish Borders*. London: George G. Harrap and Company Ltd.

Simpson, L. (1962) *James Hogg: A Critical Study*. London: Oliver and Boyd.

Smith, N.C. (1980) *James Hogg*. Boston: Twayne Publishers.

Strathern, A. and P.J. Stewart (2001) *Minorities and Memories: Survivals and Extinctions in Scotland and Western Europe*. Durham, NC: Carolina Academic Press.

Watson, G. (1985 [1974]) *The Border Reivers*. Warkworth, Northumberland: Sandhill Press.

3   CÉIDE FIELDS: NATURAL HISTORIES OF A BURIED LANDSCAPE

Stuart McLean

'Is it a quagmire, then? or like a quicksand?'

'Like either, or both. Nay! It is more treacherous than either. You may call it, if you are poetically inclined, a "carpet of death!" What you see is simply a film or skin of vegetation of a very low kind, mixed with the mould of decayed vegetable fiber and grit and rubbish of all kinds which have somehow got mixed into it, floating on a sea of ooze and slime – of something half liquid half solid, and of an unknown depth. It will bear up a certain weight, for there is a degree of cohesion in it; but it is not all of equal cohesive power, and if one were to step on the wrong spot – ' He was silent.

'What then?'

'Only a matter of specific gravity! A body suddenly immersed would, when the air of the lungs had escaped and the rigor mortis had set in, probably sink a considerable distance; then it would rise after nine days, when decomposition began to generate gases, and make an effort to reach the top. Not succeeding in this, it would ultimately waste away, and the bones would become incorporated with the existing vegetation somewhere about the roots, or would lie among the slime at the bottom.'

'Well,' said I, 'for real cold-blooded horror, commend me to your men of science.'

(Bram Stoker, *The Snake's Pass*, 1890)

WHAT IS A PEAT BOG?

What is a peat bog? The question – at once obvious and opaque – engages an age-old philosophical, political and scientific conundrum: that of the dynamic between 'nature' and 'history', along with its various permutations – the history of nature, the nature of history, historical nature, natural history. This perennial puzzle, its contemporary ramifications and its implications for the anthropological study of the present, will form the subject of this chapter. The focus of my discussion is Ireland, more particularly north County Mayo and the stretch of coastline between the town of Ballycastle to the North and the Erris peninsula to the South. I begin, however, with a further definition.

According to the men of science who inspired such horror in Stoker's narrator, a peat bog consists of two layers: a thin upper layer, consisting of a soft carpet of living vegetation, mostly sphagnum mosses, and, underlying it, a much thicker layer of peat, made up of the compacted remains of plants and animals, accumulated over hundreds or thousands of years. Water passes rapidly through the upper layer, but is retained by the lower, through which it moves at a much slower rate. Despite the appearance of its surface, a bog can consist of between 85 and 98 per cent water – that is, it may contain a lesser proportion of solids than does milk.

Geographers like to distinguish between the raised bogs of the Irish midlands (formed around 10,000 years ago at the end of the last Ice Age, from lakes left behind by the northward retreat of glaciers) and the so-called blanket bogs occupying much of the uplands and West Coast, which are believed to date from the period of early human settlement, some 5,000 years or more before the present. In the region of north-west County Mayo, so the story goes, the first farmers set about clearing areas of forest to make way for grazing land. They cut down trees, divided fields and erected stone walls and farmsteads. With the trees gone, increasing rainfall caused minerals to wash down through the soil, forming a water-resistant iron pan. Peat accumulates in waterlogged soils deficient in the oxygen needed by the micro-organisms that assist in the breakdown of plant matter. The surface growth of plants such as sphagnum moss increases the acidity of the water, making it still less hospitable to micro-organisms and thus adding to the build up of plant remains. Here, the result was that the adjacent ground became buried under a layer of acidic peat, forcing the farmers to relocate. Already abandoned (and thus, in a sense, already a ruin) the field system was eventually overrun by the newly formed peat-bog, which, as it expanded, engulfed everything in its path – field walls, houses, outbuildings, tombs, along with their contents – all preserved intact by the acidic and anaerobic conditions below the bog's surface (Aalen et al. 1997: 108–11, 117–21; Foss and O'Connell 1997: 184–6; Mitchell 1997: 144–8, 202–11). Did the farmers initiate or just accelerate the sequence of events leading to the loss of their fields? Would climatic change have accomplished the same result unaided? The men (and women) of science decline to answer, pleading insufficient evidence. It is only the re-emergence of the buried traces of this remote past that engages what is, in appearance at least, a more unambiguously human history.

The practice of cutting peat, or turf, for fuel is mentioned in the earliest written records. Turbary rights, the right to cut turf from a designated section of bog, were a common feature of leasehold agreements between landlords and tenants throughout the colonial period.[1] They survive to the present alongside the mechanised extraction of peat by *Bord na Móna* (Turf Board), a state corporation set up in 1946 to develop Ireland's peat resources on a fully commercial basis (Mitchell 1997: 334–7).[2] It was in 1930, during peat-cutting in the village of Belderrig, situated on a remote stretch of coast to the south of Ballycastle, that a series of stones were uncovered beneath the bog's surface. A local schoolteacher, Patrick Caulfield, was the first to realise that the stones formed an ordered pattern and pre-dated the formation of the bog. Excavations began in 1934, conducted at first by volunteers and subsequently with the support of the Irish state and University College, Dublin.[3] They eventually unearthed an extensive field system, stretching across more than 1,000 hectares and opening onto a high cliff coastline, 375 feet above sea-level, together with farmsteads and a number of tombs, buried beneath up to 4 metres of bog. Now known by the name Céide Fields (from the Irish *céide*, meaning a flat-topped hill) and administered by the Office of Public Works, the site has since been the subject of intensive research, including excavation, pollen analysis and radio-carbon dating, which has set the construction of the field walls in the Early Neolithic period, between 3700 and 3500 BCE (Caulfield et al. 1998; Cooney 2000: 25–9).

Today, excavations have ceased and part of the site is open to the public, along with a visitors' centre completed in 1993.[4] The section of the site accessible to visitors is set back from the coastal road and surrounded by a low fence. Beyond the fence is an area, off limits to the public, where research continues. Further inland, stretching beyond the summits of the nearby hills, is an expanse of undisturbed bog whose secrets remain as yet intact. A similar interplay of revelation and concealment is manifested on a smaller scale within the visitors' enclosure. Gravel pathways connect fields, houses and animal enclosures laid bare by decades of archaeological excavation. At the same time, the layout of the site serves as a reminder of the implacable presence of the bog, from which these discoveries have been wrested. In several places, it is possible to step off the path and onto the bog itself. The ground feels soft and yielding to the tread, although (here, at least) firm enough to bear up one's weight. Move your foot and a waterlogged imprint remains, the moisture disappearing gradually below the surface as the imprint fades. A further reminder of the bog's elusive materiality comes at the conclusion to the guided tour that departs hourly from the visitors' centre. The tour, which includes a brief history of the site, its rediscovery and subsequent exploration, ends with a demonstration of the archaeological method of sinking a metal probe to determine the whereabouts of buried field walls, a technique formerly employed by local farmers to locate fossilised bog timber for use as fuel. Visitors are invited to 'have a go'. A pool of ooze forms around the base of the metal shaft as it descends through the soft, spongiform ground, down through 50 centuries.

The bog might be thought of as an archive of sorts, recording the material after-traces both of the processes of its own formation and of the generations of human settlement with which its history is intertwined. In which case, it might be asked, how does it serve to link the various human histories successively enacted on and around its surface to the more expansive geophysical temporalities that have shaped the surrounding landscape? Certainly, the bog affords a repository of sedimented pasts, which are no less valuable a resource for contemporary articulations of place and nationhood, a point illustrated by continuing state subsidy of the site and by the 50,000 visitors who make their way here annually in the absence of public transport. Yet the latter-day resurfacing and appropriation of these pasts seems linked indissolubly both to their prior immersion in the bog's occluded depths and to the ongoing transformation of the landscape itself. Accordingly, it is to the bog's emergence as a figure of the archaic past and to its paradoxical yet necessary relation to histories of progress, that I now turn.

EUROPEAN MARGINS AND COLONIAL TOPOGRAPHIES

Consider, first of all, the extent to which the story of that mythified yet world-historically efficacious entity called 'Europe' has been one of protracted struggle against the abject, waterlogged expanses marking its own inner and outer frontiers: the Mediterranean plains with their malarial swamps, blocking the inland expansion of human settlement, the reclamation of which for agricultural use was achieved only at the cost of numerous lives and not completed, in some instances, until the nineteenth century; the fens of eastern England, an area of marsh and scrub, prone to inundation by the North Sea, where large-scale drainage operations began only in the late sixteenth century (Braudel 1972: 66–84; Darby 1940: 1–22, 23–82; Dobson 1997).[5] These accursed places, situated ambivalently between land and water, liquid and solid, have spawned a proliferating image repertoire: miasmas, marsh fevers, outlaws and brigands, will o' the wisps, witches and goblins; a set of associations given one of its most enduring expressions in Dante's depiction of the fifth circle of Hell as a 'dreary swampland, vaporous and malignant', where the souls of the damned are mired in perpetuity (quoted in Giblett 1996: 28).[6]

In Ireland, during the early Christian and medieval periods, including the Anglo-Norman invasions of the twelfth century, despite the continued practice of turf-cutting, bogs remained largely resistant to colonisation and settlement. Early modern maps of Ireland continue to depict them as obstacles to agriculture and transport (including the movement of troops) and as a refuge of outlaws. Like other wilderness spaces in Western Europe, bogs appear to have been associated too with a variety of supernatural manifestations, including apparitions of the dead. Historian Jean-Claude Schmitt has suggested that these tended to take the form in such settings, not of individualised revenants, but of an undifferentiated mass (Schmitt 1998: 184–5). One sixteenth-century map (now in the Greenwich Maritime Museum) showing the border between counties Sligo and Leitrim includes a description of fairy armies sighted on a nearby bog: 'In this bog ... there is every whott [hot?] summer strange fighting of battles, sometimes at foot, sometimes wt horse, sometimes castles seen on a sudden, sometimes great store of cows driving and fighting for them' (quoted in Andrews 1997: 202).

It was only with the consolidation of English power during the late sixteenth and early seventeenth centuries, when these spectral hosts had been joined by an all-too substantial English military presence, that the hitherto unrealised agricultural potential of boglands became apparent to a further wave of English settlers (Mitchell 1997: 315–27).[7] At the same time, the newly emergent natural sciences were busily reconfiguring the category of 'nature' itself as a distinct object of knowledge, governed by its own laws and classificatory principles (Chappell 1992; Shapin and Schaffer 1989; Thomas 1983). The earliest publications dealing with bogs date from the mid-seventeenth century, when substantial areas of land in Ireland had already been forcibly cleared to make way for estates and plantations. Gerard Boate's *Ireland's Natural History* (1652) was among the first of such studies. Boate, a Dutch physician in the employ of Oliver Cromwell, wrote from the combined perspectives of coloniser and scientific observer. He described bog-formation as a recent phenomenon, attributable to 'the retchlessness of the Irish who let daily more and more of their good land grow boggy through their carelessness' (1652: 112). Along with descriptions of bogs, their flora and fauna, he included detailed accounts of methods to be employed in their drainage, a task he saw as falling to the English as the 'introducers of all good things in Ireland' (1652: 114). Another seventeenth-century writer concerned with the reclamation of bogs was William King, an Anglican cleric and future Archbishop of Dublin, whose paper 'Of the Bogs and Loughs of Ireland', presented to the Royal Society in 1685, identified the presence of bogs, in Ireland and elsewhere in northern Europe, as the hallmark of 'every barbarous ill-inhabited country'. King noted both the disadvantages of bogs (that they prevented the consolidation of land-holdings, impeded transportation, posed a danger to cattle and offered a refuge for thieves and outlaws), along with what he termed their 'conveniences', including their capacity to act as a barrier to invasion and conquest, their importance as a source of fuel, following the destruction of much of Ireland's native woodlands, and, no less strikingly, their preservative properties, as illustrated by butter, timber and human bodies retrieved from their depths – 'a Turf-Bog preserves things strangely' (1685: 954).

During the late eighteenth and early nineteenth centuries, the reclamation of bogs was facilitated by a programme of road building throughout Ireland, joining remote areas to ports and market towns (including the present-day coastal road linking Ballycastle and Belderrig to Belmullet and the Erris peninsula). One result was an increase in the potential value both of existing agricultural land and of adjacent areas of as yet undrained bog. Following the Act of Union of 1800, which formalised Ireland's incorporation into the larger British polity, the reclamation and commercial exploitation of bogs became a matter of increasing concern to both landowners and politicians, a point illustrated by the setting up in 1809 of a government appointed commission to inquire into peat-bogs and their uses (Foss and O'Connell 1997: 192). The Commission's reports, published between 1810 and 1814, included details of the formation, morphology and vegetation of bogs, along with maps and drawings, and, inevitably, advice on drainage and reclamation. The reports suggest too that, during the years in question, actual reclamation was for the most part carried out by small tenant farmers, under the dual pressure of population increase and the desire of landlords to maximise their income from rent on land used for the cultivation of commercial crops, thus forcing their smaller tenants to reclaim areas of bog in order to meet their own subsistence needs (Connell 1950–1). Where landlords were directly supportive of reclamation schemes, these were often used to introduce new farming methods or new patterns of land tenure. Lord George Hill, who held estates near Dunfanaghy in County Donegal, supported the drainage and enclosure of large areas of bog, seeking at the same time both to regularise working hours among his tenants by introducing a system of wage labor and to encourage land consolidation. On his estates as elsewhere, reclaimed land was let as individual holdings, rather than, as previously, in the form of scattered strips. Visiting Dunfanaghy during the summer of 1849, the Scottish essayist and historian Thomas Carlyle praised the efforts of Lord George and other local landowners to subdue the 'abominable bog', although he feared that their efforts were, as he put it, 'all swallowed up in the surrounding chaos', which, he noted, remained chaotic still (Carlyle 1882: 240).

Carlyle's characterisation of the landscape of West Donegal was echoed by many nineteenth-century commentators (both English and Irish) who continued to view Ireland's boglands as unproductive wildernesses, needing to be drained or otherwise rendered commercially profitable. If the demographic disaster of the Great Famine of the 1840s removed one source of pressure on bogs as potential agricultural land, the decades immediately preceding and following nonetheless witnessed a bewildering array of proposals, varying in scope and practicality, for the commercial exploitation of bogs. In addition to reclamation schemes and efforts to employ turf as an industrial fuel, attempts were made to utilise turf as fertiliser and animal litter, and in the manufacture of brown paper, hardboard, candles and fire-lighters, made from dipping hardened turf into inflammable liquid (O'Gráda 1994: 321–4). By 1887, Robert Dennis (author of the study *Industrial Ireland*) was able to observe that: 'There is hardly any natural substance the use of which has been made the subject of so much experiment as peat' (quoted O'Gráda 1994: 323).

At the same time, the drainage of bogs and wetlands resulted in the uncovering of increasing numbers of buried or submerged artifacts. In Ireland, by the mid-nineteenth century, reclamation projects had brought to light not only the remains of prehistoric settlements, but also an assortment of weaponry, household objects and other items, fuelling an upsurge of amateur and scholarly interest in wetland archaeology (Coles and Coles 1980: 9–31). Nor were inanimate objects the only finds associated with drainage and reclamation schemes. In Ireland, as throughout northern and western Europe, bogs were a plentiful source of human remains, mostly Iron Age or later, preserved in the depths in the oxygen-free waters by a process analogous to tanning. These bog-corpses, variously interpreted as burials, executions or sacrificial offerings to a (usually feminised) earth deity, have since found wider fame through the writings of the serendipitously named Danish archaeologist P.V. Glob and, latterly, through the poetry of Seamus Heaney, who drew a series of analogies between ancient sacrificial and mortuary practices and the state and paramilitary violence besetting his native Northern Ireland in the 1970s (Glob 1998; Heaney 1976).[8] Although the best-known of them (the Tollund Man, the Grauballe Man) hail from the vicinity of

Jutland in southern Denmark, Ireland has produced more than 80 bog people in the period between 1750 and the present (Glob 1998: 18–36, 37–62, 101–18). As the population (and with it the extent both of peat-cutting and of agricultural encroachment on boglands) increased during the early decades of the nineteenth century, so did the frequency of such finds. The best-preserved of them was found at a depth of nine and a half feet at Gallagh, near Castleblakeney, County Galway, in 1821. Having been disinterred several times for the benefit of visitors, it is now displayed in Dublin in the National Museum of Ireland (O'Floinn 1988; Raftery 1994: 188).[9]

Much has been written on the importance of archaeology, including studies of the Celtic past, for the formulation of national identity claims, both official and oppositional, in present-day Europe (Dietler 1994; Graves-Brown et al. 1996). I wish to focus here, however, on a different aspect. If reclamation schemes aimed to domesticate and thus, in a sense, to further disenchant the landscape, much archaeological scholarship from the mid-nineteenth century onward appears to have contributed to a very different view, recasting the bog both as an implicitly feminised space and as a site, not of economic production, but of sacrificial expenditure.[10] Bodies and artifacts were widely interpreted as offerings to a sanguinary earth goddess, while the bog itself was portrayed both as the resting place of the prehistoric dead and as the supposed habitation of a variety of in-dwelling supernatural presences, many of them indifferent or downright hostile to humans: the *huldre*, a malevolent fairy, described by Glob as luring travellers to a watery death and lending her name to Huldre Fen in Jutland; or her Irish counterpart of sorts, the *pooka*, a protean, shape-shifting, trickster-spirit, capable of assuming a variety of forms and associated in particular (according to army colonel and amateur antiquarian William Gregory Wood-Martin) with bogs and other waterlogged places, whose amorphous character it appears to share (Glob 1998: 79; Wood-Martin 1902: 55).[11] Alongside the potential space of counter-imagining opened by these accounts, what seems crucial is the way in which archaeological and folkloristic specu-lations regarding nature spirits and pagan sacrifice were enabled, in the most practical sense, by a series of human interventions aimed at rendering boglands more fully integrated into the industrial and commercial present.

THE SNAKE'S PASS

The dual character with which the nineteenth-century imagination invested bogs is manifested in striking fashion in Bram Stoker's novel *The*

Snake's Pass, first published in 1890 and set in a fictional rural community in the vicinity of north County Mayo, close to the present-day location of Céide Fields.[12] At the centre of the novel's imagined topography is the so-called 'shifting bog', situated on land acquired by the local gombeen man (money-lender) 'Black Murdock'. The exchange quoted at the beginning of this chapter takes place between the novel's aristocratic English narrator, Arthur Severn, and his childhood friend, Richard Sutherland, who is engaged in surveying the land on which the shifting bog is situated. The bog is identified explicitly as a repository of the ancient past, including, according to local legend, the crown of the King of the Snakes, who vowed to return and reclaim it after St Patrick banished the snakes from Ireland, an incident commemorated, it is said, in the name of the adjacent mountain – *Knockcalltecrore* (Hill of the Lost Crown of Gold). An alternative explanation of the name refers to an episode in more recent history – the 1798 French landing at Killala Bay, in support of the rising of the United Irishmen, and to a treasure chest hidden (allegedly) by French soldiers when it had become apparent that the rising was a failure (Stoker 1990: 18–31).[13]

It is in pursuit of the treasure chest that Murdock engages Sutherland's services as a surveyor and undertakes a series of increasingly hazardous excavations in and around the shifting bog. The bog comes, finally, to furnish his nemesis, as he and his house are engulfed by it when it shifts for the last time and its accumulated mass of liquid and debris pours out through the Snake's Pass (the *Schleenanaher*, through which the King of the Snakes is reputed to have made his exit) and into the sea. The final catastrophe is witnessed by Severn and his fiancée, Norah Joyce, the daughter of a local farmer, who lives with her father on land adjacent to Murdock's:

The sound of the waves dashing on the rocks below, and the booming of the distant breakers filled the air – but through it came another sound, the like of which I had never heard, and the like of which I hope, in God's providence, I shall never hear again – a long, slow gurgle, with something of a sucking sound; something terrible – resistless – and with a sort of hiss in it, as of seething waters striving to be free.

Then the convulsion of the bog grew greater; it almost seemed as though some monstrous living thing was deep under the surface and writhing to escape.

By this time Murdock's house had sunk almost level with the bog. He had climbed on the thatched roof, and stood there looking towards us, and stretching forth his hands as though in supplication for help. For a while the superior size and buoyancy of the roof sustained it, but then it too began slowly to sink. Murdock knelt, and clasped his hands in a frenzy of prayer.

And then came a mighty roar and a gathering rush. The side of the hill below us seemed to burst. Murdock threw up his arms – we heard his wild cry as the roof of the house, and he with it, was in an instant sucked below the surface of the heaving mass.

Then came the end of the terrible convulsion. With a rushing sound, and the noise of a thousand waters falling, the whole bog swept, in waves of gathering size, with a hideous writhing, down the mountain-side to the entrance of the *Schleenanaher* – struck the portals with a sound like thunder, and piled up into a vast height. And then the millions of tons of slime and ooze, and bog and earth, and broken rock swept through the Pass into the sea. (1990: 229–30)

The following morning reveals a transfigured landscape: a rocky ravine with a stream running along its bottom, occasionally broadening into pools of varying depths and issuing into the sea at the Snake's Pass. The unblocking of the ravine discloses too the Frenchmen's treasure chest (along with the skeletons of the soldiers entrusted with its care) and an 'ancient crown of strange form', secreted in a cave (1990: 239–42). The evacuation of the shifting bog serves also as a prelude to the further remaking of the surrounding landscape, to be realised in the form of a new house and estate laid out by Sutherland for Severn and Norah to occupy on their return from their honeymoon.

Stoker's portrayal of the shifting bog is notable for its explicit linking of the bog as colonial topography – a space of wildness and excess needing to be reformed and domesticated – with its significance as the receptacle of submerged pasts, including both historical events and the nebulous before-time of pagan myth, evoked through the legend of the King of the Snakes. The description of the final catastrophe suggests that it is precisely the eruptive manifestation of the bog's wayward and transgressive materiality, its dissolution of surfaces and boundaries into a mobile and amorphous mass, which enables both the orderly refashioning of the landscape (subsequent to the bog's final shifting) and the retrieval of the buried artifacts formerly consigned to its depths, recalling both the thwarted revolutionary aspirations of the 1790s and the longer-vanished world of pre-Christian Ireland.

Equally significant is the gratuitous and unsolicited aspect of this process, revealed most tellingly in the unpredictability of the bog's periodic self-transmutations. Here is a history which, much as it may elude human intentionality or design, appears nonetheless as their unacknowledged precondition, the imagined before-time of material flux, from which both images of the past and teleologically driven projects of societal transformation are distilled, yet which, through its successive historical articulations, is produced as a constitutive excess threatening the epistemic boundaries of such projects. Written at the tail end of a self-styled century of progress, Stoker's novel reveals the extent to which, both in the Irish context and elsewhere, such a vision of the natural environment, here exemplified in the formless substance of the bog, is at once tied to and threateningly subversive of the ensemble of transformations that have been taken to constitute (in this case, European) modernity. The catastrophic resurgence of such an other time-scale affords one guise in which the project of modernity, impelled by the logic of its own unfolding, revisits the scene of its founding exclusions and repudiations – past epochs, geophysical temporalities, the returning dead – affording, at the same time, a glimpse of a different kind of history, no longer concerned with a sovereign and centred human subject as its source and referent. In the case of Ireland's colonial relationship with its once powerful neighbour, such a history affords both a space of dissolution, in which understandings of time and place appear disconcertingly malleable, and a conduit for the resurfacing of all that the present proclaims itself to have displaced, conjuring not only an image of the past in the instant of its foreclosure, but also the ebb and flow of a life anterior and indifferent to human agency, in the process, perhaps, pointing the way to consideration of other pasts and other futures.

THE MODERN CONSTITUTION

Stoker's conjoining of a mythic time of origin with the events of the more recent colonial past, seems, no less than that other origin scene enacted by the first farmers, to depend upon a reiterated slippage between conventionally separate domains: nature/society; natural history/human history. Such a distinction, as Bruno Latour reminds us, has acquired a singular force and urgency within the self-designated time-frame of modernity, where it has served to organise not only the latter's dominant self-images (what Latour terms the 'modern constitution'), but also the relationship between what have come to be constituted as discrete fields of knowledge: the natural sciences here, the social and historical sciences there; nature on the one side, society, history and the human subject on the other. At the same time, the separation thus instituted can be seen to have facilitated the repeated transgression of the very boundaries it purports to establish. The technological appropriation of nature is enabled to proceed on an unprecedented scale precisely to the degree that the resultant nature-society 'hybrids' are not acknowledged as such at the level of modernity's sanctioned self-representations (Latour 1993: 13–48). Herein, perhaps, lies the public secret of the modern: the boundaries between nature and society are scrupulously maintained at the level of discourse, precisely in order that they might be repeatedly crossed in practice.[14]

The results can be seen along the coastal road from Ballycastle to Belmullet, where the peat laid down over centuries and millennia is cut away in cross sections and stacked to dry in fields by local farmers.[15] Further inland, at Bord na Móna's peat extraction works at nearby Oweninny, turf-harvesting machines cut a brown, rectilinear swathe across the landscape.[16] As successive layers are stripped away, animal and vegetable remains are processed into a commercial product, dried and compacted and packaged as the standardised peat briquettes on sale in every supermarket in Ireland. Five miles distant in the direction of Belmullet is the peat-fuelled power station at Bellacorrick, which, together with seven others of its kind, currently produces more than a tenth of Ireland's electricity. The spongiform wilderness evoked by earlier writers seems finally to have been subdued to human purposes. Or has it?

Despite Ireland's much vaunted commercial and foreign-investment boom of the past decade (the so-called 'Celtic tiger' economy), north Mayo remains an area of higher than average unemployment, as high as 55 per cent in the nearby town of Belmullet, on the edge of the Erris peninsula. Meanwhile, more recent efforts to turn the adjacent bog to profitable use have often proved no more successful than many of their nineteenth-century counterparts. In 1994 the Norwegian-based multi-national Norsk Hydro announced a new venture to produce peat-based smokeless solid fuel briquettes on a site near Bangor Erris, surrounded by 1,100 acres of uncut bog. Construction work began on what was described as a 'highly automated, state-of-the-art facility' (*Irish Times*) along with a recruitment drive for 50 employees, the number to double once the plant became fully operational. The project was hailed in enthu-siastic terms by planning and development agencies and received coverage in the national press. Five years later, in 1999, with the new plant yet to go into production, Norsk Hydro pulled out, with the loss of 43 jobs. Press coverage of the closure cited stories from former employees regarding unsuitable equipment and harvesting methods. There were problems too with the peat itself. Despite protracted research and repeated adjustments to the production process, the water content of the briquettes remained, it was alleged, too high, making them impossible to dry and thus unsuitable either as domestic fuel or for use by the Bellacorrick power station, one of the plant's envisaged customers. The venture, previously touted by one government spokesperson as likely to produce a 'phenomenal' impact on the local economy, collapsed amid recriminations and threatened law suits as *Údarás na Gaeltachta*, the state development agency, refused to subsidise a proposed rescue package. Since its inception, the scheme had absorbed £26 million in foreign capital and a further £3 million in state funds. Not a single saleable briquette had been produced.[17]

Developers, it appears, continue to come and go, but the bog remains, at least for the present. Even so, in its seeming capacity to endure, the landscape bears the all-too-evident signatures of a continuing human presence: the alternation of intact and cutaway bog, creating a tiered and chequered expanse of green and brown, along with the secrets retrieved from the bog's depths, inventoried and displayed in museums and on the pages of scholarly journals. Indeed, is it not just such projects of transformation and classification that appear to precipitate the resurgence of an insurrectionary and intransigent nature, and that precisely to the degree that such a nature is already comprehensively humanised?

What happens, then, when the modern constitution begins to falter, when the human appropriation and transformation of nature reaches an extent such that it can no longer be contained (or disguised) by the terms of a preconceived opposition between nature and society, when nature itself becomes constituted as a new kind of political object? Recently, these questions have impelled both a reinvigorated ecological anthropology and the nascent field of science and technology studies to reformulate the relationship between the natural and the social as a reciprocally constituting, rather than an oppositional one, a move necessitating, at the same time, the elaboration of new analytic vocabularies and new models of social scientific explanation. Against this backdrop, however, a further and no less pressing problem emerges. How, in the context of this changing present, is one to think about, first, the historical fate of a nature that is at once thoroughly socialised and yet relegated by definitional fiat to a status of radical exteriority in relation to the social, and, second, the continuing implication of that same nature in a range of practices and institutions that have hitherto tended to be aligned exclusively with the side of society?

NATURAL HISTORY

I call the attempt to engage this question 'natural history', a term borrowed, in the first instance, from Theodor Adorno's essay of that name of 1932 and referring both to the instituted separation between nature and history and to the human domination of a dehumanised and instrumentalised nature enabled by it. The task of natural history (defined as the 'dialectical overcoming' of the nature–history opposition) was understood by Adorno as twofold. On the one hand, it required the rehistoricising of so-called 'first nature', that is, of the 'nature' studied by the natural sciences and conceived of as the domain of impersonal laws, operating independently of human intention or design. On the other, it entailed the re-awakening and transfiguration of the life dormant in the 'second nature' of social convention, which, to the degree that it had become habituated, had taken on for its onetime human creators the appearance of permanence and fixity (Adorno 1984).

Adorno saw the project of re-awakening as exemplified most strikingly in the work of Walter Benjamin, who himself likens the task of the cultural critic explicitly to that of the archaeologist digging through successive strata to uncover what lies buried beneath. In Benjamin's case, the site of excavation was, pre-eminently, language: 'It is the medium of that which is experienced, just as the earth is the medium in which ancient cities lie buried' (Benjamin 1999a: 576). Such a view implies that the past is never fully past, but remains rather subliminally contemporaneous within the present in the guise of these buried traces. In the case of language, the experience to be retrieved was, not least, that of a hypothetically lost or superseded relation to the natural world. Its passing was registered as humanity's supposed 'fall' out of an originary language of names, predicated upon the coincidence and consubstantiality of words and things, into a condition of 'over-naming', whereby the link between the linguistic sign and its referent came to appear a merely arbitrary one (Benjamin 1996). If language thus appeared exiled from an earlier state of bodied immediacy, the implied loss was not to be seen as absolute. Like the remnants of the remote past preserved in the bog, intimations of an older intimacy between signifiers and signifieds were to be found within and alongside the semiotic order of language in the form of magical correspondences and 'non-sensuous similarities' and of the mimetic faculty ('the once powerful compulsion to become or behave like something else') as a capability existing, crucially, both in nature and in such forms of human practice as dance, ritual, music and, of course, language (Benjamin 1999b, 1999c). If mimesis appeared to traverse both sides of the opposition between nature and history, the modes and degrees of its social presencing were, nonetheless, to be understood as historically mutable. Benjamin could thus point to the attenuated status of the mimetic faculty in the present, as compared to earlier ages when humans were more fully aware of living in a mimetically charged universe. Even so, modern man remained susceptible to being moved by the vestiges of this once prodigious capability, whether as revived by the new representational technologies of film and montage, or whether 'on southern moonlit nights when he feels alive within himself mimetic forces that he had long since thought dead, while nature, which possesses them all, transforms itself into the likeness of the moon' (Benjamin 1999d: 685).

Natural history, understood thus, necessitates grasping not only the historicity of the seemingly natural, but also the covert persistence of disavowed nature within the contrastively defined domains of society, history, language and subjectivity. Such a task differs from the syntheses of 'culture' and 'nature' proposed by sociobiology and, more recently, evolutionary psychology in so far as it seeks not to explicate the former by way of the latter, as is arguably the case with these approaches, but to explore the possibilities of a foundational instability taken to inhabit the very terms of the binary, such that they can neither be maintained in their distinctness nor simply collapsed into one another. In tracing a movement across the received terms of the nature–history opposition, natural history lays claim to a space already traversed by a variety of contemporary currents: actor-network theory, science and technology studies, the new ecologies and the philosophical work of, amongst others, Michel Serres (Barnes et al. 1996; Biersack 1999; Crumley 1994; Latour 1999; Law and Hassard 1999; Serres 1995). Where it differs, arguably, from these is in its greater willingness to credit retrojected nature with a disruptive or critical potential within the designated realm of the social and in its explicit linking of the resurfacing of the present-past (whether through medium of language or of landscape) to contemporary projects of transformation and renewal. These might include both the re-imagining of human–nature interactions and, following Benjamin, the quest for a linguistic mode in which material nature would be implicated rather than merely named. Natural history thus engages other recent attempts to formulate such an idiom of contagion and corporeal inter-connectedness: Kristeva's pre-symbolic *chora*, Artaud's and Deleuze and Guattari's 'body without organs', with its attendant logic of rhizomatics and becoming-other, Giorgio Agamben's inferred realm of pre-subjectival 'infancy', understood as one of pure non-signifying linguistic possibility from which all discourse emerges and to which it invariably returns (Agamben 1993; Deleuze and Guattari 1983; Kristeva 1984). As in Benjamin's theorisation of the mimetic faculty, what is sought is both a displacement of subjectival privilege in the name of alternative modes of experiencing and knowing, and a critically expanded understanding of the human, with an attendant blurring of conceptual boundaries between the social and the natural. What secures such an undertaking against charges of essentialism is the acknowledgement that its own conditions of possibility are given in the very bifurcation of languages that these thinkers, like Adorno and Benjamin, set out to overcome. It is only the social fact of the separation of the domains of nature and history (as established in its current form) that permits the recognition of their actual and continuing inter-involvement and imbues that recognition with a subversive potential in the present.

THE PRESENT AND FUTURE OF IRISH PEAT BOGS

What then might constitute the preconditions for such a rethinking in the present? In Ireland since the 1980s conservationist arguments have depicted the bog primarily as an endangered natural habitat, a view finding support in an ever-growing scientific literature concerned with the flora and fauna of Irish peatlands. The Irish Peatland Conservation Council, established in 1982, has reiterated such a vision in successive publications, pointing to Ireland's unique position in Western Europe by virtue of its having preserved intact substantial areas of bogland and warning that the survival of Ireland's bogs is threatened both by large-scale mechanical extraction and by the continued practice of hand turf-cutting.[18] In response to appeals by conservation groups and to European Union environmental legislation, the Irish government has agreed to restrictions on turf-cutting (including the scaling-down of operations by Bord na Móna) and to the establishment of bog conservation areas, including five sites in north Mayo.[19] Opponents of these proposals have emphasised instead the bog's continuing importance as a source of domestic fuel. The Irish Farmers' Association has campaigned against recently introduced bans on turf-cutting in designated conservation areas, claiming that such bans represent a threat to their members' livelihood and demanding either financial compensation or access to alternative (non-designated) sources of turf, while an alliance of conservation area action groups, formed in 1998, has petitioned central government, demanding turf-cutting be treated as a historically sanctioned right.

   Wilderness or resource? Nature or history? From both sides, the stakes appear intimidatingly high. Rather than accept the terms of the choice, let me conclude by turning to a particular case. In many areas of Ireland's west coast, including north Mayo, centuries of hand-cutting and, latterly, mechanical extraction have wrought a further and startling transformation upon the landscape, once more bringing the traces of the forgotten past to light. Centuries after the abandonment of the Céide Fields system, when the growth of the bog was still in its early stages, Ireland's climate appears to have become temporarily warmer, causing the bog to dry out in places, with the result that secondary forests of Scots pine began to take root on its surface. In the centuries following, as the climate became once again colder and wetter, the trees died and the bog began to expand once more, eventually engulfing the pines now covering parts of its surface. Today, peat-cutting on the blanket bogs of north Mayo, including the stretch of coast between Céide Fields and Belmullet, has uncovered the fossilised remains of these ancient forests. In places, along the coastal road, where successive layers of peat have been stripped away, the trees formerly growing on the site can be seen in clumps, their trunks and branches protruding from the ground, sometimes to a height of several feet. The ghost-like pallor of the dead wood, sometimes visible across an entire section of cutaway, affords an unsettling contrast to the green-brown patchwork of the surrounding landscape. These spectral trees afford not only a visual jolt to the passer-by, but also a palpable impediment to the further cutting away of the bog by hand or machine: as though the archaic past were obtruding itself in protest upon the commercial hubris of the present. Yet the past thus conjured is not that of the pristine nature sometimes appealed to in contemporary conservationist discourse. Instead, what is evoked in these wayside scenes is a reminder of a bygone, but all-too-human history, in which the Neolithic farmers of Céide Fields and their successors are complicit, no less than the impersonal rhythms of rainfall and climatic change. If the boglands of Ireland's west coast have fuelled successive literary and other imaginings of a chaotically resurgent wild nature, at odds with the trajectories of agrarian modernisation and industrial progress, these long-buried forests appear more akin to Adorno's sterile and desiccated 'first nature'. As such, theirs is an apparitional death-in-life, flickering between a vision of alienated nature and a no-less-estranged world of human practice, at once affirming and calling into question the fact of their continuing separation.

One of these pines, uncovered during turf-cutting at Belderrig, forms the centrepiece of the entrance lobby of the Céide Fields visitors' centre.[20] Reaching from ground to mezzanine level, its dry trunk shows a succession of secondary roots marking the bog's incremental rise. Some 4,000 years old, and yet post-dating the last human occupation of the Céide Fields site, it casts a defamiliarising light both on the monument itself and on the modern trappings of the visitors' centre. If the centre's displays and audio-visual presentations tend, like the site itself, to convey an impression of continuity between the past and present communities of north Mayo, the presence of such a specimen of the vanished yet contemporaneous past suggests that things are never so simple. Such a juxtaposition of ancient and modern evokes less the linear time-scale of progress and cumulative human advancement (by which Ireland, in the past, has so often been judged and found wanting) than a stubbornly recursive other-time, resolutely non-linear, in which the social and the natural, as conventionally designated, are no longer sharply distinguished. As a focal point of the nature–society assemblage constituted by the site and its environs, the tree trunk serves to render both the history of nature and the nature in history simultaneously and disconcertingly legible. The human project of refashioning a definitionally silenced nature here provides the precondition for that same nature's re-emergence in the uncanny guise of a secret familiar, implicating and threatening the boundaries of the humanly assigned orders of significance instituted in contradistinction to it.

The term 'natural history' refers here to the search for a vocabulary adequate to the delineation of that secret familiarity, a vocabulary that continues in many ways to remain elusive. If the reflections of Adorno and Benjamin help us to sense more clearly the magnitude of the problem at hand, neither should be seen to offer a ready solution. The method of 'negative dialectics' propounded in Adorno's later work scarcely seems an advance in this respect, advocating as it does a constant critical shuttling between the twin poles of nature and history, which suggests less the projected dialectical overcoming of the terms of the opposition than recognition of its continuing intractability (Adorno 1973). For Benjamin too, the sought-after idiom of mimetic interconnectedness between words, persons and things remains for the most part a prospect to be glimpsed or gestured toward, rather than attained. Perhaps both thinkers remain, in Latour's sense, too modern, too invested in radical breaks and great transformations and therefore unable, finally, to make explicit the multiple linkages that their own analyses, no less than the modern constitution itself, both affirm and deny. Could it be that the sought-after idiom is destined to remain unthinkable, even in our present and much advertised state of ecological emergency?

The bog itself, which has formed the real subject of this chapter, appears no less recalcitrant. Reviewing the histories and prior uses, along with the contemporary controversies surrounding the future of Irish boglands, one is led to reflect not only on their shifting human significances, but also on their grossly substantial and yet maddeningly elusive materiality. Liquid or solid? Raw nature or human artifact? Like some monstrously recalcitrant *Ding an sich*, the bog appears to move further away with each successive attempt to explain and classify. Yet in doing so, it offers a no less emphatic reminder that its history is inextricably intertwined with centuries of human action and imagining, never more so than in the early twenty-first century, when the competing claims of local residents, developers, researchers and conservationists have turned boglands into an object of often bitter controversy. Yet it is perhaps the very ontological instability disclosed by this clash of agendas and definitions, as much as any litany of ecological disasters, that affords the medium through which a once disenfranchised nature can be seen to reassert itself in the present with unsettling force. Such a reassertion, however (if, indeed, it can be called that), far from suggesting a possible resolution, threatens to make the historiographical and conceptual dilemmas posed by the study of Irish boglands appear all the more acute. Faced, on the one hand, with the inscrutable facticity of vegetable debris, ooze and slime, and, on the other, with the multiple and asynchronous human pasts (colonial, pre- and post-) materialised and rendered visible through it, can received forms of thought and language do any more than acknowledge their own insufficiency? In place of a conclusion therefore, I end by affirming my own continuing perplexity: what have I been talking about?

NOTES

1. Although bog conditions and thus methods of working vary greatly from place to place, peat is generally cut with a special spade (*sleán*) from a vertical bank down almost to the underlying mineral soil. Prior to cutting, the upper layer of fibrous sod is usually trimmed off, or may be spread below the bank for dry footing (in time the sods accumulate so that grazing can develop on the cut-away at a lower level). The wet sods of newly cut turf are wind-dried in small stooks on the pared surface and may shrink considerably. As they dry they are moved into progressively larger piles until finally they are removed from the bog and stacked in or near farmsteads. Turf may be transported either in willow baskets, or 'creels', carried on the back of a donkey or on a wooden sled, or 'slipe' (Aalen et al. 1997: 120).

2. Bord na Móna eventually acquired a total of 80,000 hectares of bogland, making it the largest single owner of peatland in Ireland today. Its operations are concentrated mainly on the raised bogs of the Irish midlands, with a number of smaller production centres on the west coast. In 1990, Bord na Móna's output was approximately 8 million tons of peat, more than half of this being used for the generation of electricity. Peat is sold in the form of dried sods and briquettes for domestic and industrial consumption and fertilised peat and horticultural peat products are marketed internationally. The success of Bord na Móna prompted the establishment of a number of smaller peat production companies, often with grants made available under a 1981 Turf Development Act (Foss and O'Connell 1997: 191–2).

3. Caulfield's son, Seamus Caulfield, now a Professor of Archaeology at University College, Dublin, is currently director of excavations at the site.

4. Designed by architects at the Office of Public Works, Dublin, the visitors' centre is administered by *Dúchas*, the Heritage Service. The building itself is a pyramidal structure, part limestone and part peat-clad, set into banked earth and topped by a glass observation platform overlooking the site on one side and the adjacent coast on the other.

5. Darby cites a description of the inhabitants of the fens from William Camden's *Britannia*, which first appeared in 1586 and was translated into English in 1610. According to Camden, the fenlanders were: 'a kind of people according to the nature of the place where they dwell rude, uncivill and envious to all others whom they call Upland-men' (quoted Darby 1940: 23).

6. Economic historian Sidney Pollard has written a comparative overview of marginal lands and their role in the economic and political history of Europe (Pollard 1997).

Margaret Anne Doody describes at greater length the literary associations of 'marshes, shores and muddy margins' (Doody 1996: 319–36).

7. Leyburn notes that during the seventeenth century, much bog clearance, in the northern province of Ulster and elsewhere, was carried out by English and Scottish settlers who had acquired lands in Ireland as a result of the dispossession of Gaelic landed families (Leyburn 1962: 110–15).

8. Some of Heaney's most striking explorations of this theme are to be found in a series of poems in the 1975 collection, *North*, which apostrophises both the peat bog corpses of Ireland and Scandinavia and the bog itself as a preserver of persons and objects that it finally regurgitates both as the stuff of poetry and as a strange, yet disconcertingly familiar presence among the living (Heaney 1976; see also McLean 2003).

9. Eight years after its initial discovery, the body was given to the Royal Dublin Society where it was displayed for a number of years, before passing to the Royal Irish Academy (later the National Museum) in 1860. It was never conserved and is now in a shrunken and shrivelled state with few of the details originally present surviving. Analysis of the tissues has suggested a date in the early Bronze Age (Raftery 1994: 188). Raghnaill O'Floinn has suggested that the two sharpened stakes found placed at an angle at either side of the body indicate that this was a deliberate burial rather than an accidental drowning and, further, that the band of hazel rods described in contemporary reports as fastening at the neck the tunic in which the body is clothed may have served as a garrote, used to strangle the victim. Unfortunately, the band has not survived and there is no medical evidence to support such a hypothesis (O'Floinn 1988: 94–7).

10. Of the bog bodies of northern Europe, Glob writes: 'At the beginning of the era of the bog people it was not a male but a female god that was dominant; and her servant, who fulfilled the role of the male deity, had to be sacrificed at the completion of the journeyings so that the cycle of nature might be supported and helped forward' (Glob 1998: 190). Although such an interpretation by no means exhausts archaeological scholarship concerned with bog-related finds, much of which has been concerned equally with settlement history and the development of agriculture, the sacrificial hypothesis remains current. A recent study of Iron Age Ireland notes that rivers, lakes and bogs were identified by the Celts as sacred sites and that objects retrieved from them can therefore be understood as votive offerings, while the bodies retrieved from Irish bogs can likewise be viewed as executions or human sacrifices (Raftery 1994: 182–5).

11. Wood-Martin writes that: 'the Pooka is especially connected with bogs, marshes and water, and is in general represented as shaking the dripping ooze from his hairy hide' (Wood-Martin 1902: 55).

12. Bram Stoker (1847–1912), a Trinity College educated Protestant from the middle-class north Dublin suburb of Clontarf, was to spend most of his adult life in London as secretary and manager to the Victorian actor and theatrical impresario Henry Irving. Stoker is of course best known for *Dracula*, first published in 1897, a novel that achieved its greatest popularity only after his death.

13. Theobald Wolfe Tone, a Protestant trained as a lawyer, helped to found the Society of United Irishmen in Belfast in 1791, with a further branch being established in Dublin in the same year. Inspired both by the French and American Revolutions, and by older traditions of liberalism, it aimed at Parliamentary reform and the ultimate removal of English influence in Irish affairs. The Society operated, initially, as a radical club, disseminating propaganda through publications such as the *Northern Star*. Following the suppression of the Dublin Society in 1794, the Belfast contingent reconstituted itself as a clandestine organisation dedicated to armed insurrection. Tone visited Paris in 1796 to elicit support, with the result that an expeditionary force consisting of 36

ships was dispatched, arriving at Bantry Bay, County Cork, having weathered a severe storm, but no landing was attempted. The following year, a campaign of counter-insurgency resulted in the arrest of many members of the Society. A series of risings finally took place in 1798, beginning with outbreaks in Dublin, Kildare and Meath on 23–4 May, spreading to Carlow the following day. Further risings took place in the northern province of Ulster (Counties Antrim and Down) and in the westernmost province of Connacht, spurred by the arrival of another French force of 1,019 men, which landed at Killala Bay, County Mayo, on 22 August. The French were joined by local volunteers, and succeeded in establishing a provisional government, before being encircled and forced to surrender at Ballinamuck, County Longford, on 8 September. The French were allowed to return to their ships; 2,000 of their local supporters were massacred. The principal focus of the insurrection was, however, Wexford, where the insurgents' main camp at Vinegar Hill, near Enniscorthy, was successfully stormed on 21 June by a force of 10,000, commanded by General Lake, who had superintended the counter-insurgency campaign of the previous year. Tone was tried and sentenced to be hanged, but cut his own throat while awaiting execution (Whelan 1998).

14. The term 'public secret' is Taussig's and refers to 'that which is generally known, but cannot be articulated' (Taussig 1999: 5).

15. The visual appearance of the landscape is, in many cases, further altered by the use of black plastic bags to protect drying peat from the rain, creating what has sometimes been called a 'rubbish tip' effect. I thank the editors, Andrew Strathern and Pamela Stewart, for reminding me of this phenomenon.

16. Technologies employed in mechanised peat extraction vary in accordance with the scale of the operation. In the case of the tractor-driven, lightweight fuel-peat machines in widespread use in Ireland, peat is extruded onto the surface of the bog in 'sausages' taken from slits in the ground by a metal disc or chainsaw. In good weather, the peat is soon dried by the sun, but in wet weather it often cannot be collected and suffocates the surface vegetation, which has already suffered damage from the weight of the tractor. Bord na Móna employs large turf-harvesting machines to collect milled peat that has been laid out in linear ridges. In the harvesting process, the ridges are transferred to a massive, longitudinal stockpile, where the peat is stored until it is required for the manufacture of commercially sold peat briquettes or else for burning in power stations (Aalen et al. 1997: 111–12).

17. Details of the venture and its collapse can be found in a series of reports published in the *Irish Times*: 23 August 1997; 18 May 2000; 29 May 2000 <http://www.ireland.com/newspaper/archive>.

18. The Council's proposals for peatland conservation are outlined in its *Irish Peatland Conservation Plan 2000*, published in 1996 (Foss and O'Connell 1996). For further discussion of conservation issues relating to bogs, see Cross (1989) and O'Connell (1987).

19. The European Union's policy on nature conservation within its territories comprises two pieces of legislation: the Directive on the Conservation of Natural and Semi-Natural Habitats of Wild Flora and Fauna (Directive 92/43/EEC), which aims to establish a European network of Special Areas of Conservation (SACs), among them 155 peatland areas in the Republic of Ireland and 21 in Northern Ireland, and a Directive on the Conservation of Wild Birds (Directive 79/409/EEC), which aims to safeguard the habitats of bird species through the creation of Special Protection Areas (SPAs), to include 73 Irish peatlands. Together, the directives aim to establish an EU-wide network of protected areas known as 'Network 2000' (Foss and O'Connell 1996: 13–15).

20. Visitors to the centre find themselves at first in a circular space, the walls of which feature paintings by local artists featuring scenes from the history of the site, including

the period of early settlement. It is flanked to the right by an audio-visual room, showing images of the site and the surrounding coast, and to the left by the main, walk-through display area. One display shows the growth of the bog across the intervening centuries by means of cross-sections, illustrating the increasing depth of peat (1.5 metres at present), alongside painted illustrations juxtaposing views of the vanished pre-bog forest – oak, hazel, birch – with the present-day landscape, together with photographs of flowering plants, mosses and insects. Next comes a life-size recreation of a Neolithic house found beneath a group of megalithic tombs at Ballyglass, near the eastern limit of Céide Fields; replicas of furniture (modelled after similar examples from Skara Brae, in the Orkney Islands); a child grinding grain; and an elderly woman in bed (referred to by staff at the centre as 'the granny'). The accompanying text points out that the original Céide Fields community must have been organised (able to carry out planned projects), numerous (able to clear large areas of forest and divide up the land thus cleared with stone walls), and possessed of 'spiritual beliefs' (inferred from the presence of tombs and houses for the dead). The texts evoke a peaceful community (as evidenced by unprotected and scattered family dwellings and the absence of fortifications) with a mainly pastoral economy based on year-round grazing. Continuities with the present are emphasised through reference to settlement patterns and the continued practice of cattle rearing and by a quotation from Seamus Heaney's poem 'Belderg', reproduced in the final wall panel: 'A landscape fossilized/Its stonewall patternings/Repeated before our eyes/In the stonewalls of Mayo' (Heaney 1976: 13). A further display, at mezzanine level consists of a geological exhibition, with views of nearby Downpatrick Head and samples of rocks, including basalt (originating 350 km below the earth's surface), sandstone, quartz, together with rocks from Céide cliff rocks identified as 350 million years old. The Céide rocks are accompanied by a 'Time-Line of the Universe,' from the Big Bang to the present, and by more painted images illustrating the phases of climate change: polar bears amid glacial landscapes, giant Irish deer roaming prehistoric woodlands. Accompanying texts point out that evidence of these changes is to be found in the deltas near Ballycastle, in marine muds containing shells laid down under the ice at Belderrig harbour and in the post-glacial fossil soils underlying the bog itself.

REFERENCES

Aalen, F.H.A., K. Whelan and M. Stout (eds) (1997) *Atlas of the Rural Irish Landscape*. Toronto: University of Toronto Press.

Adorno, T.W. (1973) *Negative Dialectics*. E.B. Ashton trans. New York: Continuum.

—— (1984) [1932] 'The Idea of Natural History', Robert Hullot-Kentor trans. *Telos* 60: 111–24.

Agamben, G. (1993) *Infancy and History: Essays on the Destruction of Experience*. Liz Heron trans. London: Verso.

Andrews, J.H. (1997) 'Paper Landscapes: Mapping Ireland's Physical Geography', in J.W. Foster (ed.) *Nature in Ireland: A Scientific and Cultural History*. Dublin: Lilliput Press, pp. 199–218.

Barnes, B., D. Bloor and J. Henry (1996) *Scientific Knowledge: A Sociological Analysis*. Chicago: University of Chicago Press.

Benjamin, W. (1996) 'On Language as Such and the Language of Man', in M. Bullock and M.W. Jennings (eds) *Selected Writings, vol. 1, 1913–1926*. Cambridge, MA: Belknap Press, pp. 62–74.

—— (1999a) 'Excavation and Memory', in M.W. Jennings, H. Eliand and G. Smith (eds) *Selected Writings, vol. 2. 1927–1934*. Cambridge, MA: Belknap Press, p. 76.

—— (1999b) 'The Doctrine of the Similar', in M.W. Jennings, H. Eliand and G. Smith (eds) *Selected Writings, vol. 2. 1927–1934*. Cambridge, MA: Belknap Press, pp. 694–8.

—— (1999c) 'On the Mimetic Faculty', in M.W. Jennings, H. Eliand and G. Smith (eds) *Selected Writings, vol. 2. 1927–1934*. Cambridge, MA: Belknap Press, pp. 720–2.

—— (1999d) 'On Astrology', in M.W. Jennings, H. Eliand and G. Smith (eds) *Selected Writings, vol. 2. 1927–1934*. Cambridge, MA: Belknap Press, pp. 684–5.

Biersack, A. (1999) 'Introduction: from the "New Ecology" to the New Ecologies, Contemporary Issues Forum. Ecologies for Tomorrow: Reading Rappaport Today', *American Anthropologist* 101(1): 5–18.

Boate, G. (1657) *Irelands Naturall History: Being a True and Ample Description of its Situation, Greatness, Shape, and Nature, of its Hills, Woods, Heaths, Bogs, of its Fruitfull Parts, and Profitable Grounds*. London: Samuel Hartlib.

Braudel, F. (1972) *The Mediterranean and the Mediterranean World in the Age of Phillip II*, vol. 1. New York: Harper and Row.

Carlyle, T. (1882) *Reminiscences of My Irish Journey in 1849*. London: Sampson, Low, Marston, Searle.

Caulfield, S., R.G. O'Donnell and P.I. Mitchell (1998) 'C Dating of a Neolithic Field System at Céide Fields, County Mayo, Ireland', *Radiocarbon* 40(20): 629–40.

Chappell, V.C. (1992) *Seventeenth-century Natural Scientists*. New York: Garland Publishing.

Coles, B. and J. Coles (1980) *People of the Wetlands: Bogs, Bodies and Lake-Dwellers*. London: Thames and Hudson.

Connell, K.H. (1950–1) 'The Colonization of Waste Land in Ireland, 1780–1845', *Economic History Review* (2nd Series) 3: 44–71.

Cooney, G. (2000) *Landscapes of Neolithic Ireland*. London: Routledge.

Cross, J.R. (1989) *Peatlands: Wastelands or Heritage? An Introduction to Bogs and Fens*. Dublin: Wildlife Service.

Crumley, C.L. (ed.)(1994) *Historical Ecology: Cultural Knowledge and Changing Landscapes*. Santa Fe, NM: School of American Research Press.

Darby, H.C. (1940) *Draining the Fens*. Cambridge: Cambridge University Press.

Deleuze, G. and F. Guattari (1983) *Anti-Oedipus: Capitalism and Schizophrenia*. R. Hurley, M. Seem and H.R. Lane trans. Minneapolis: University of Minnesota Press.

Dietler, M. (1994) 'Our Ancestors the Gauls: Archaeology, Ethnic Nationalism and the Manipulation of Celtic Identity in Modern Europe', *American Anthropologist* 96(3): 584–605.

Dobson, M.J. (1997) *Contours of Death and Disease in Early Modern England*. Cambridge: Cambridge University Press.

Doody, M.A. (1996) *The True Story of the Novel*. New Brunswick, NJ: Rutgers University Press.

Foss, P. and C. O'Connell (1996) *Irish Peatland Conservation Plan 2000*. Dublin: Irish Peatland Conservation Council.

—— (1997) 'Bogland: Study and Utilization', in J.W. Foster (ed.) *Nature in Ireland: A Scientific and Cultural History*. Dublin: Lilliput Press, pp. 184–98.

Giblett, R. (1996) *Postmodern Wetlands: Culture, History, Ecology*. Edinburgh: Edinburgh University Press.

Glob, P.V. (1998 [1965]) *The Bog People*. London: Faber and Faber.

Graves-Brown, P., S. Jones and C. Gamble (eds)(1996) *Cultural Identity and Archaeology: The Construction of European Communities*. London: Routledge.

Heaney, S. (1976 [1975]) *North*. New York: Oxford University Press.

Irish Times. Dublin. (http://www.ireland.com/newspaper/archive).

King, W. (1685) 'Of the Bogs and Loughs of Ireland', by Mr William King, Fellow of the Dublin Society, as presented to that Society. *Philosophical Transactions of the Royal Society* 15: 948–60.

Kristeva, J. (1984) *Revolution in Poetic Language*. M. Waller trans. New York: Columbia University Press.

Latour, B. (1993) *We Have Never Been Modern*. C. Porter trans. Cambridge, MA: Harvard University Press.

—— (1999) *Pandora's Hope: Essays on the Reality of Science Studies*. Cambridge, MA: Harvard University Press.

Law, J. and J. Hassard (1999) *Actor-Network Theory and After*. Oxford: Blackwell.

Leyburn, J.G. (1962) *The Scotch Irish: A Social History*. Chapel Hill, NC: University of North Carolina Press.

McLean, S. (2003) (in press) *The Event and its Terrors: Ireland, Famine, Modernity and the Limits of Historiography*. Stanford, CA: Stanford University Press.

Mitchell, F.G. (1997) *Reading the Irish Landscape*. Dublin: Town House and Country House.

O'Connell, C. (ed.)(1987) *The IPCC Guide to Irish Peatlands*. Dublin: Irish Peatland Conservation Council.

O'Gráda, C. (1994) *Ireland: A New Economic History, 1780–1939*. Oxford: Clarendon Press.

O'Floinn, R. (1988) 'Irish Bog Bodies', *Archaeology Ireland* 10(1): 93–7.

Pollard, S. (1997) *Marginal Europe: The Contribution of Marginal Lands Since the Middle Ages*. Oxford: Clarendon Press.

Raftery, B. (1994) *Pagan Celtic Ireland: The Enigma of the Irish Iron Age*. London: Thames and Hudson.

Schmitt, J-C. (1998 [1994]) *Ghosts in the Middle Ages: The Living and the Dead in Medieval Society*. Teresa Lavender Fagan trans. Chicago: University of Chicago Press.

Serres, M. (1995 [1982]) *Genesis*. G. James and J. Nielson trans. Ann Arbor: University of Michigan Press.

Shapin, S. and S. Schaffer (1989) *Leviathan and the Air Pump: Hobbes, Boyle and the Experimental Life*. Princeton, NJ: Princeton University Press.

Stoker, Bram (1990 [1890]) *The Snake's Pass*. Dingle, County Kerry: Brandon.

Taussig, M. (1999) *Defacement: Public Secrecy and the Labor of the Negative*. Stanford, CA: Stanford University Press.

Thomas, K. (1983) *Man and the Natural World: Changing Attitudes in England, 1500–1800*. New York, Oxford: Oxford University Press.

Whelan, K. (1998) *Fellowship of Freedom: The United Irishmen and 1978*. Cork: Cork University Press.

Wood-Martin, W.G. (1902) *Traces of the Elder Faiths of Ireland: A Folklore Sketch; A Handbook of Irish Pre-Christian Traditions*, vol. 1. London: Longmans, Green and Co.

4 LANDSCAPE REPRESENTATION: PLACE AND IDENTITY IN NINETEENTH-CENTURY ORDNANCE SURVEY MAPS OF IRELAND

Angèle Smith

In the nineteenth century the British Ordnance Survey undertook an intensive mapping project of the whole of Ireland at a scale of 6 map inches to every mile on the ground. In doing so an army of soldier-surveyors was unleashed into the local landscape. In every part of the country, the colonial presence dressed in bright red coats could not be ignored. This mapping project was unprecedented for its detail and for its systematic process of documenting the landscape. Field boundaries, roads, villages, isolated houses, even individual trees were included in this national cartographic artifact. It was an act of colonial domination – mapping was a means for Britain to maintain colonial control over Ireland, making the landscape, its people and past known and quantifiable.

Landscape research, both in historical and current contexts, recognises that there are multiple ways of seeing and understanding landscapes (Baker 1992; Bender 1993, 1998; Hirsch and O'Hanlon 1995; Layton and Ucko 1999; Tilley 1994). Maps, as representations of landscape, are political tools for controlling the sense and meaning of that landscape by claiming authority in the presentation of one perspective and heralding it as 'real' and 'true' (Black 1997; Harley 1989; Kain and Baigent 1992). Colonial maps make obvious this act of appropriation of landscape perception, manipulating landscape images to create a sense of a colonial landscape of control and order.

The act of colonising is a process of physical occupation and formal governance over a piece of landscape, but it is also a matter of the politics of perception, experience and representation. By controlling the images of places, people and their past, colonial administrations are able to control the knowledge of these. While the Irish had their own means of remembering places and events in the landscape, there are no known early native Irish-made maps of Ireland. It is the outsider who requires a map in order to occupy and own the local landscape and the image of that landscape.

While maps have traditionally been regarded as 'objective', and mapping considered as a scientific exercise of accurately describing the 'lay of the land' (Thrower 1996; Tooley 1978), more critical analysis of maps recognises their cultural subjectivity (Monmonier 1991; Pickles 1992; Wood 1992a, 1992b). Representations of landscape are culturally determined, dependent on who is doing the 'seeing'. But in mapping this cultural understanding of the world (the perception of the map-maker), what is recorded on the map is justified and legitimised while also influencing and reinforcing what is seen (or not seen) in the actual landscape. Thus maps are powerful images that helped to shape and reinforce the colonial view by authorising control and appropriating the land through its representation.

But landscape representations are not uncontested. Maps are the sites of interaction – in the case of nineteenth-century Ireland, between the surveyors in the field and the Ordnance Survey officials in Dublin; and among the surveyors, the local Irish population and their Anglo-Protestant landlords. There are multiple ways of perceiving and understanding the landscape as well as the social memories and meanings that are encoded in the landscape. Therefore maps are also the sites of cultural negotiations in which competing perceptions and experiences of the landscape and its social history are manipulated.

In this chapter, I will illustrate the colonial process of mapping in nineteenth-century Ireland and how the map becomes an artifact of the complex negotiation of identity and place within the landscape. The mapping project is a colonial tool of power initiated to know and control the local landscape and the people. But it is a process that involves social interaction and relations that are contested at the international (colonial), national (Irish nationalist) and local level. The contested nature of documenting the landscape and the social memories and histories embedded within it, is part of the mediation that constructs and is represented on the final map.

MAPS OF MEANING, MEMORY AND IDENTITY

Maps, as the representations of landscapes, are complex artifacts of the negotiation of identity and place. These artifacts attempt to represent the memories, meanings and sense of belonging as well as the process of social relations and interactions. The spatiality represented in the maps is both produced by and helps to produce social relations of power (Foucault 1984; Soja 1989), by encoding and depicting space that is simultaneously physical, social and ideological.

Maps are artifacts of the physical space that is inhabited, moved through and contested. They are artifacts of the social space between different actors within the landscape, including those persons involved with the on-the-ground mapping; those whose lands are being mapped; and those who control the administration of the mapping project. Finally, maps are artifacts of the ideological space that inform individuals of their understanding of the landscape, whether that understanding is rooted in the shared memories, shared access to, and practice in places; or in how the landscape is controlled and power exercised through it.

All maps are political. They control knowledge, claiming authorship and ownership of knowledge about landscapes, people and their past. Maps aim to dictate how to 'see', 'remember' and make sense of the world. As a representation, maps do not, indeed can not, mimic the 'real' world. Mark Monmonier (1991) argues that all maps representing a three-dimensional world in two-dimensional form, *must* lie and distort reality by simplifying, omitting, selecting and making choices about what and what not to record. What is marked on the map exists; what is not marked does not. What is named is considered significant; what goes un-named is not. How names are recorded (in what language, in what type of script they appear on the map) is also a process of choice and selection, as is the curve of the lakeshore, or the scale that is decided upon.

Maps cannot accurately portray the 'real' landscape (there are too many 'real' landscapes to represent). Rather, maps are representative of the 'imagined' landscape of the map-maker. In this way, the map is an excellent artifact of the cultural perceptions of the surveyor. Situated within the socio-historical and political context of the map-making, the map is an artifact of how the 'imagined' landscape influences people's understanding and interpretation of the 'real' world around them. Therefore, maps are a powerful means of manipulating and re-shaping the physical, social and ideological space.

But creating the 'image' of landscape is a complex process that engenders contestation. Landscapes are fundamental to a person's or community's sense of belonging and identity through shared experiences and events, shared memories and histories (Lovell 1998; Platt 1996). The act of remembering (naming places where experiences have 'taken place'), is an act of ritualisation. The practice of returning to a place, remembering a place, is practised ritual and therefore in one sense makes place sacred in the shared memories of the community. It is not surprising then that the representation of landscape is imbued with contestation that is heavily charged, emotionally, socially and politically.

In the following case study of nineteenth-century Ordnance Survey maps of Ireland, I illustrate how these landscape representations are the sites of social interaction and cultural negotiation of place, memories and meanings. First, I will situate the survey in its socio-historical and political context to outline why and how the mapping project was undertaken. I then offer specific examples to illustrate how different landscape perspectives are scripted into the maps.

NINETEENTH-CENTURY ORDNANCE SURVEY MAPS OF IRELAND

To situate this mapping survey, it must be recognised that this was just one act in the long colonial history linking Ireland to Britain. Other mapping projects had been initiated by the colonising British in Ireland prior to the nineteenth century. Always, surveys of the land coincided with periods of political uncertainty and instability (Andrews 1985, 1997; Hayes McCoy 1964). Earlier mapping projects usually accompanied military operations resulting in vast land clearances, and the re-writing of the landscape to make it 'British space' (Foster 1988; P. Robinson 1984; Stout and Stout 1997).

The Ordnance Survey mapping in the nineteenth century differed in that it was not part of a land clearance project. It was not, strictly speaking, a military map, although it can be argued that military control was still at issue with this new survey of the country. Even though the Napoleonic Wars (1800–15) were over, the British still feared French invasion along the Irish coast (Moody and Martin 1994). Thus an accurate coastal map was required. Perhaps even more pressing was the growing awareness of rural unrest and the formation of Irish secret societies (Boyce 1991; Crossman 1996). Internal control could be maintained through a mapping project which required an army of soldier-surveyors to plot the landscape. This meant that for a prolonged time the presence of the British army in all parts of the Irish countryside was a constant reminder of colonial rule. The final map meant that the landscape and its people were documented in close detail.

The official impetus for establishing the British Ordnance Survey of Ireland in 1824, was to produce a national map to re-evaluate the county tax (which paid for many of the country's roads and bridges and much of its local government machinery) (Close 1969; Seymour 1980). The map was an administrative mechanism of the state, the aim of which was better economic and political control of the local-level landscape and the access through it. Given the scale of 6 inches to the mile and the unprecedented detail it allowed, the map aided in valuing the land at a local level. But the system of land tenure in Ireland often meant that it was not clear who (landlord, middleman lessor or the occupier) was obliged to pay certain taxes (Andrews 1975). Therefore, even though taxation was based on the value of the land, it was imperative to know who lived on the land and under what kind of arrangements. The maps did this by reducing to mathematical exactness the number of the people, and where and how they lived on the landscape. The map documents were a quantitative and official means of management.

While ultimately controlled by the London Office, the Survey in Ireland was operated by its own administrative hierarchy from Mountjoy House in Dublin under the direction of Superintendent Colonel Colby. Five district parties comprised of Royal Engineers and the lower-ranking Royal Sappers and Miners systematically mapped the country, starting in the north and advancing steadily southward. Along the way, these parties recruited assistants for short periods from local civilians (Andrews 1975; Seymour 1980).

Data, extensively recorded in field and placename books, was sent back to the Dublin office to be verified and produced in the final map sheets. In order to be 'verified' the Assistant Superintendent, Lt Larcom, established a Placenames and Antiquities Department which was responsible for providing accurate and definitive spellings for placenames (Andrews 1983). Through extensive archival research and field work to collect local information, this department also recorded cultural information in the form of local stories about monuments and places as part of the 'Memoir' (a social survey) meant to accompany the final map document.

The maps were a compilation of knowledge. They were official tools of administration and created colonial images of control. However, they also recorded a local Irish sense of place, identity and belonging. In the following examples, I will illustrate that different landscape perspectives, different memories and histories, are scripted into the maps in the representations of gentlemen's estates; state, colonial and historical buildings; local placenames; and sacred places such as hilltops. These examples are based on analysis of the first edition 6-inch maps of 1837 for the area of Carrowkeel–Lough Arrow in southern Co. Sligo, situated in the northwest of Ireland (Smith 2001).

MAPPED ESTATES

One of the most notable features on the black-and-white Ordnance Survey maps is the estates and 'big houses' of the landed gentry class. Especially prominent on the 6-inch maps, these estates were highlighted, shaded gray against the otherwise stark white backdrop of the landscape. They were clear focal points on the maps also because they were treed landscape parks.

The Irish landscape in the nineteenth-century was relatively bare of woods or tree cover of any kind (Wood-Martin 1880). When they did occur, far from being 'natural' features of the landscape, trees and woods represented social hierarchy. Irish woodlands had long since disappeared and peasants burned turf in lieu of wood for fuel. Where trees were scarce, they were a valued commodity and an indicator of wealth and status. Only the gentry could afford to have woods or tree-lined avenues. That the trees were marked by dark symbols had the effect of highlighting them on the maps and marking the presence of wealth and status.

Estates such as Hollybrook (in my study area) were also conspicuous on the map because they had named houses. In the case of Hollybrook, the main house is represented as a large rectangular building with many out-buildings and stables, and is labelled 'Hollybrook house'. As the seat of the landed gentry, the Ffolliott family's house at Hollybrook had great influence over the local population in this area. These dominant houses were especially noticeable on the maps because they contrasted with the cabins and small fields of the tenantry living either in dispersed and isolated farmsteads, or in small clustered settlements called clachans. These clachan settlements were unlike the classic English village: they had no church, pub, school or shops (cf. Aalen et al. 1997: 79–85). Although most of the Irish population lived in clachans on marginal lands, the maps did not represent them in close detail – despite the fact that the scale of the map permitted it. The effect of highlighting the big houses and estates of the gentry was to change the function of the survey 'from marking the land, to bearing witness to its ownership' (Hamer 1989: 197). Thus the map succeeded in depicting and thereby reinforcing the social class structure within the nation, emphasising that local-level control was in the hands of the Anglo-Protestant gentry class, and stressing a history that was colonial.

In Britain, local-level control and order was recognisable in village life, the centre of which was the church. The church spire represented a sense of authority and rule. The Irish countryside did not offer such easy symbolism of power. It is not surprising that only eight years after the Catholic Emancipation (1829), which essentially legalised the practice of Roman Catholicism in Ireland, there were few formal Catholic churches (Taylor 1995). There were, however, a small number of churches depicted on the maps. The map of Ballymote town near Carrowkeel–Lough Arrow, shows a 'Church' which represents the Church of Ireland. In an area predominantly populated by Roman

Catholic Irish, designating only this Church of Ireland church as 'Church' sends the message of its supremacy: there was only one 'Church', one official religion of the state.

In the relative absence of markers of power and control on the landscape, the estates of the Anglo-Protestant gentry class were even more important for reinforcing (creating?) an image of colonial rule and authority. It must be remembered that this was a time of significant turmoil in the countryside, with secret societies challenging colonial governance. Therefore it was necessary, through the mapping project, to gain information about the people and the landscape through a close 'gaze', but it was also important to portray an image that silenced the unrest and depicted a landscape of order and control. Yet, the estates of the landlord class are not the only colonial images of control represented in the mapped landscape.

MAPPED STATE CONTROL AND COLONIAL/HISTORICAL BUILDINGS

State control was also portrayed through the meticulous mapping and labelling of public buildings that represented state institutions, for example, the above-mentioned Protestant churches, as well as National schools. National schools were first established in 1831 (Proudfoot 1993) to systematise and promote the English language in more remote areas. These labelled public buildings representative of state control, stood out on the maps in the absence of any Irish institutions – because Irish gatherings were illegal, and thus were invisible to the British map-maker. In the second half of the 1800s, constabulary barracks dot the mapped landscape indicating still more state control at the local level. Other public buildings that were featured on the maps include the Corn Mill, Pound and Kiln, structures with far-reaching importance, as well as tax value.

Also mapped were historical structures. These sites were often emblems of colonial history, marking sites of conflict between the Irish and British forces. In the area of Carrowkeel–Lough Arrow in Co. Sligo, the maps record the structures of Ballinafad Castle, Bricklieve Castle and Castlebaldwin – all British-built and each a mark of colonial conquest (Fairbanks 1998). Each of these was depicted on the map as if it was standing, an intact building, still wielding colonial power over the local landscape. This was not the case, however; in reality they were in a ruinous state.

Today all that remains of Bricklieve Castle is a single upright wall in the middle of a field. In 1837, the site's depiction on the Ordnance Survey map does not suggest its ruinous state, nor is it labelled 'in ruins', which was common practice for non-Anglo unoccupied and decrepit structures. Either much more of the structure existed at the time of the survey, or it was not considered expedient to call attention to its dilapidated state. Or it might also be that sites of Anglo colonisation were never marked as 'in ruins', thereby reaffirming the continuing control over the land. This was also the situation with the seventeenth-century house site, Castlebaldwin. The structure itself appears on the map as an L-shaped building. It is not labelled as 'in ruins', though the local story recounts that the house was set on fire by the servants while Captain Baldwin was away on a hunt. It surely was 'in ruins' in 1837 when the surveyors mapped it, as it is today. Further, each of these historical colonial sites was labelled with its 'proper name', suggesting its importance to the map-maker.

These two examples illustrate the re-writing of local identity, sense of place and social history into a strictly colonial narrative. Conversely, the *mediation* of local identity is seen in the mapping of placenames and sacred places, such as hilltops.

PLACENAMES: MAPPED MEMORIES

The placenames were meticulously recorded by the Ordnance Survey antiquarians of the Placenames and Antiquities Department (O'Maolfabhail 1992). Placenames on maps reflect the culturally meaningful landscape of the local population. They are mnemonic codes for local stories and traditions, recognised by and part of the shared memory of the local community (Basso 1996; T. Robinson 1996). Sometimes the stories were recorded in the placename books (written down by the surveyors and antiquarians in the field) as translations and interpretations of the placenames. However, unlike the maps, these books, while official, are not public documents. Therefore, the placename would not register the same history for the British surveyors and administrators as it would for those who live in the named landscape. While the maps do appropriate and control, they also (unwittingly) encode a sense of identity and belonging in the landscape from a local perspective. Multiple meanings and memories were being reified in the maps.

Townlands, parishes and baronies were the main geopolitical units marked and named on the maps. These were standardised, defined and fixed on the maps in a way they had never been before. Through the choice of script style of the placename, linework marking the boundary and the actual fixing of the boundary itself, the Ordnance Survey was able to create an official and administrative landscape. Today, for example, townlands still define the land division for such state institutions as the Department of Agriculture (for keeping track of veterinary service and, more recently, the spread of foot and mouth disease). Townlands are the basis for recording the national census and form the boundaries of electoral wards (Canavan 1991; Dallat 1991). Measuring and fixing the townland boundary sometimes resulted in altering that townland, by combining smaller townlands or by dividing larger townlands. But while the Ordnance Survey fixed these boundaries on the maps for administrative purposes, local social meaning and histories were also being scripted in the maps.

Baronies correspond closely to the old Gaelic *Tuath* or tribal division and it was upon this land division unit that taxes were levied during the seventeenth and eighteenth centuries. Parishes (many dating from the twelfth century) were a religious division of land over which local clergy had jurisdiction. But it was the townland that was (and is) the distinguishing, albeit invisible, landscape feature of Ireland. Many townland names are of great antiquity and they are important not just because they became the unit for administration during the nineteenth-century on the Ordnance Survey maps, but because townlands are the centralising focus of social identity in rural Ireland. 'Centuries old, they have not only defined the land but the people' (Canavan 1991: 49). They are imbued with memory and tradition through local knowledge of events or experiences that occurred at that place. They locate where one lives, linking one's identity to belonging in land and home (Lovell 1998).

As O'Maolfabhail (former head of the modern Ordnance Survey Placenames division) writes:

The names of the townlands of Ireland are living links with our past and although the mapping and valuation of the nineteenth century have frozen in suspended animation, so to speak, the townlands which until then had been a living organism, the names themselves have always had and still have an independent vitality of their own. (in Dallat 1991: 9)

Although mapping boundaries and placenames (of the townlands, parishes, baronies, as well as some physical features such as mountains or valleys) fixed them on paper, from the perspective of the local people, the maps could be viewed as verifying and validating their sense of dwelling and belonging on the landscape.

However, like the boundary lines, placenames on the nineteenth-century maps were sometimes manipulated and altered. The names were simplified and standardised. For example, the different spellings (and pronunciations) provided for the Irish word meaning 'a ridge' – *Drum*, *Drim*, *Drom* – were standardised to 'Drum'. Likewise, *Derry* and *Dirry* (an 'oakwood'), became 'Derry'. Some placenames were even anglicised on the map. Some were transliterated (witness the townland named *Ardraigh* in Irish is re-named with the more English spelling 'Ardrea'). Others were translated, the meaning of the Irish translated into English; for example, *Lis na Muc* meaning literally 'Fort of the Pigs', became 'Swinefort' on the map. Other places were simply re-named altogether. Although there is debate about how much the placenames were standardised and anglicised (O'Maolfabhail 1978, 1992), their presence on the maps was culturally meaningful for the identity of the local community.

In the study area of Carrowkeel–Lough Arrow, families are linked to the landscape in such townland placenames as *Ballymullany* ('O'Mullany's or Hugh Mullany's town'), *Treenmacmurtough* ('MacMurtogh's third of land') or in the townland *Ballyhealy* ('Healy's town') referring to the chief family that ruled this area prior to the English conquest and the establishment of the Ffolliotts as landlords. In other cases, stories of events and experiences are embedded in placenames. The translation of townland name *Carrickhawna* is given as 'all hallowtide rock' and it is recorded that: 'a little before November [at the festival time of Samhain], the old men, time out of mind, used to assemble here to settle their little affairs for the ensuing half-year' (Ordnance Survey of Ireland 1837). Elsewhere the townland of *Aghanagh* is translated as 'a short prayer or petition' and it is here that the Placename Books recount the story of O'Roark's Ford, where Saint Fintane Monem prayed that the chief O'Roark might never topple the monastery that Monem built on this site (Ordnance Survey of Ireland 1837). This story is retold through the placename on the map. Only those familiar with the story and the place would draw meaning from the name and, from that meaning, a sense of their own identity and belonging and attachment to this landscape.

Clues to religious meaning and sacred places are also found in placenames, as seen above where the placename serves as mnemonic marker for the acts of Catholic saints. Folklore and myth are also encoded in many placenames, such as *Cuilsheeghary*, meaning 'wood of the fairies'. In another example, the townland Mullaghfarna (*Mullac fearna* in Irish) means 'hilltop of the Alder'. On the 1837 map, no woods are depicted but the name suggests that there may have been trees here in earlier times. Trees were often considered sacred and, according to Celtic lore, the first woman was a rowan tree and the first man an alder (Pennick 1996). Perhaps this indicates that the hill marked a significant religious place.

MAPPED RITUAL SPACE: HILLTOP FESTIVALS

The mapping of placenames and the stories they encode illustrate how the local understanding of the landscape was recorded on the Ordnance

Survey maps. Hilltops were places rich with legend and ritual. Most mountain and hilltops were named. Examples in my study area include the hills *Crockanaw* (meaning 'hill of the oxen') and *Crocklosky* (or 'hill of the burning'). These names are recorded in the Ordnance Survey field books (Ordnance Survey of Ireland 1837), but they are not found on the map itself, even though the upland topography was poorly mapped and thus there would have been space on the map to record these placenames. Mountain and hilltops were important to the daily and ritual life of the local community. Thus by not including the placename on the map, the place was made no less sacred to the local people. In fact, some (cf. Bender 1998; Chidester and Linenthal 1995) might argue, by systematically attempting to re-write the hilltop landscape with a colonial history only, the contested and therefore sacred significance of the place is increased by the mere depiction of the (even un-named) hill on the mapped landscape.

For the local inhabitants, these mountain tops were important in their daily life. There was a long history of the pastoral Gaelic society practising transhumance: grazing their cattle in the uplands during the summer months (Aalen et al. 1997). Also, turf for fuel was cut from mountain-top bogs. As the first part of the nineteenth-century was a period of unprecedentedly high population densities, some poorer tenants and squatters even had small isolated cabins and farms in these marginal uplands (Campbell 1995; Connell 1950).

Mountain and hilltops were also important places for keeping alive rituals, customs and seasonal festivals. These were significant gathering places. At the Lughnasa festival, traditionally held on the first day of August, the local people gathered to celebrate the first harvest. The events of this ancient ritual are described in detail:

In very many localities the chief event of the festival was not so much the festival meal as the festive gathering out of doors. This took the form of an excursion to some traditional site, usually on a hill or mountain top ... where large numbers of people from the surrounding area congregated, traveling thither on foot, on horseback or in carts and other equipages. Often the gathering place was somewhat remote, to be reached by climbing hill tracks or scrambling over rough country. For the young and active this added to the enjoyment of the outing .... It also meant that the older people and the smaller children, not able to travel the rugged ways, did not join in the outing. This meant less restraint on the merriment of the robust and energetic. Many of the participants came prepared to 'make a day of it' bringing food and drink and musical instruments, and spending the afternoon and evening in eating, drinking and dancing. The young men engaged in tests of skill and strength, in sport and games. The girls picked wild flowers and made them into garlands and nosegays. Almost always there were wild berries to be picked and enjoyed ... [and] in the evening a great bonfire was lit. (Danaher 1972: 168–70)

In *The Festival of Lughnasa*, Máire MacNéill (1962) investigates the widespread popularity of the celebration as well as its origins, thought to date far back in antiquity, suggesting that: 'such customs as the offerings of flowers and fruit ... may possibly be survivals of pre-Christian religious ceremonies' (Danaher 1972: 177). Indeed, the tradition of hilltop bonfires at harvest time is significant for cementing for the community their sense of identity with the long history of their ancestors' place in this landscape. As Marquardt and Crumley argue: 'the fires connect local, familiar landscapes to knowledgeable, capable, and powerful pre-decessors. In short, the fires mediate between people and the landscape' (1987: 378).

In the Carrowkeel–Lough Arrow area, these celebrations still take place on the hilltops. The second last Sunday of July is known as Bilberry Sunday (keeping with custom, it is still a time for berry-picking), and the last Sunday is now called Garland Sunday (young women still weave garlands of flowers). Although the name has changed, the same ritual activities take place: climbing Kesh Corran mountain, playing games, dancing, feasting on picnics, and lighting bonfires at night is still tradition. The meanings of these rituals may have been modified but they have continued to take place over a long history.

These festivals would have taken place in the nineteenth-century as the landscape was being mapped by the British soldier-surveyors. Indeed, the first edition Ordnance Survey map of the Carrowkeel–Lough Arrow area was surveyed during the spring and summer of 1836, with the surveyors beginning in March and moving out of the area in September (Ordnance Survey of Ireland 1836). These surveyors would have witnessed the hilltop rituals of Lughnasa; if not participating themselves, they could not have avoided seeing the bonfires on each hill in the area as evening fell. These places were (and still are) meaningful for local people: they were named places and part of the social memory and the identity of the community, linking both the landscape and the people to the past. Despite this, the hilltop names were not recorded on the Ordnance Survey maps.

Why were these hilltop names not represented on the mapped landscape? Mountain tops were places of interaction between competing knowledges and understandings of the landscape. How 'place' was defined, and its significance, was understood differently: as a place with a name; as a sacred or ritual site; or as a trigonometric station. The maps silenced many of these knowledges. The message was: no history existed here prior to the survey (and colonial rule). In fact, what the maps do, by silencing the past in the landscape, is *re-make* history – re-writing it as a colonial narrative.

Chidester and Linenthal (1995) argue that places are made sacred where there are ritualised practices associated with a landscape; multiple interpretations of the meaning and significance of that landscape; and, finally, contestation of the polyvalent meanings. Hilltops can be understood as sacred places because there are ritual hilltop bonfires, as at the Lughnasa festival; multiple interpretations held by the local community and the soldier-surveyors; and because these contradictory understandings collide on the map. Thus the hilltops of the local landscape are mapped as negotiated contested space. These places are the site of struggle over the legitimate ownership of sacred symbols: for the local community there is the sense of their social memory anchored to the place; and for the British soldier-surveyors (or, more correctly, for their superiors in Dublin) there is the sense of colonial control, military might and the 'superiority' of science witnessed in the mapping process itself. The maps attempt to appropriate the hilltops by excluding the local sense of belonging and memory through the act of silencing the local social praxis and social meaning of their landscape. This act of domination is not wholly (nor could it ever be entirely) successful, but is always resisted through the persistence of the locally remembered placenames (itself an act of making sacred and memorialising the landscape) and the rituals practised annually on the hilltops at the beginning of harvest. The silence on the maps has had little effect on the local sense of identity and place.

DISCUSSION: LANDSCAPE REPRESENTATIONS OF IDENTITY AND PLACE

Maps are political tools that attempt to control knowledge. In the case of the nineteenth-century Ordnance Survey maps of Ireland, these colonial artifacts aim to control the knowledge of the local landscape for economic, political and militaristic security and gain. The local landscape and people's place within it shape their sense of identity. Thus the maps aimed also to control the knowledge of place and identity, defined by social memory and historical perceptions. This was achieved in part through the very process of mapping the entire country in close detail by British soldier-surveyors. It was also accomplished, to some degree, in the representation of the mapped landscape. Examination of the final maps illustrates colonial control at the local level by highlighting the estates of the Anglo-Protestant gentry class, thereby reinforcing and emphasising the social hierarchy of power relations in the rural landscape. Anglo-Irish state control was also underscored through the depiction of state institutional buildings and the representation of colonial buildings that symbolised control (castles and stronghouses) as fully intact, thus exerting a sense of colonial peace and order in the countryside.

But this colonial domination met with resistance and contestation. This counter-hegemonic force opposing the appropriation and control over the people and their landscape was subtly recorded and can be read from the maps themselves. Thus maps are the site of interaction of many social relations of power in operation, and reflect the process of negotiation. While acting to *control*, in fact the maps *mediate* the voices of multiple actors, representing multiple understandings of the landscape, and reflecting multiple experiences and knowledges. Maps are sites of interaction, contestation and cultural negotiation on the different yet overlapping levels of the local, national and international scales.

At the international scale, it is recognised that these maps were colonial maps that linked Ireland to Britain, the colonised with the coloniser. The deployment of a vast army of soldier-surveyors in the Irish countryside sweeping from north to south reflects the militaristic tone of the whole of the survey process. Further, the survey method of linking Irish coordinates into the existing British triangulation system (Andrews 1975), sent a message that Ireland was part of Britain, that its lands were British. The representation of colonial control and order in the rural landscape has been detailed in the examination of the maps. In all of these ways, it is clear that the maps represent the material culture of colonial ties with Ireland on an international scale.

At the same time, I would argue that the Ordnance Survey can also be understood at the national scale of interaction and negotiation. Representing the local landlords' estates in detail can as easily be interpreted as the state (equated with a commonly landless urban administrative class) keeping a watchful eye on the power exerted by the rural gentry class. Remembering that the mapping project was administrative in origin, with the aim of re-assessing the county taxation system, it may well have affected the local gentry class and their ability to make their own tax payments to the state. Mapping state institutions alongside the estates negotiated a desired balance between local control in the hands of the Anglo-Protestant landlords and the urban-administered state.

The maps can be understood at the national level of negotiation in yet another way. These maps were colonial, made by and for colonial administrative control, yet they were employed by the members of the nationalist movement parties (e.g. The Young Irelanders) as symbols of national pride (Cairns and Richards 1988; Duffy 1880). This is a strategy of inversion, whereby the colonial tool of domination becomes the nationalist tool of resistance (Smith 1998). The maps and what they represented – the Irish landscape, the people, and their past in the form of placenames and ancient monuments – were offered as symbols of Irish nationalism. The contemporary political newspaper *The Nation* popularised the maps and encouraged the Irish to use the new Ordnance Survey maps. Public attention was drawn to the monuments on the maps and the Irish people were challenged (in a foreshadowing of the political Celtic Revival movement of the late 1800s) that:

it becomes us all who do not wish to lose the heritage of centuries, nor to feel ourselves living among nameless ruins, when we might have an ancestral home ... to aid in or originate a series of efforts to save all that remains of the past ... [with the] faith that Ireland could and should be great again by magnifying what she had been. (Davis 1842: 42–53)

The popularisation of the maps was used and manipulated through the machinery of nationalism. This strategy subverted the colonial production of the maps to further increasing nationalist sentiment. Chidester and Linenthal write: 'In the production of sacred space and places, meaning and power coalesce; the national question is answered in the ritualization of memory and the divination of a shared future' (1995: 31). That placenames and ancient monuments on the maps were stressed in the nationalist rhetoric suggests that social memory was ritualised for political goals at the national level.

Finally, and perhaps most obviously, maps can be understood as sites of negotiation of multiple meanings of landscape, place and identity at the local level. It is at the local level that 'interactions' are most numerous and diverse. The field surveyors 'interacted' with the landscape they mapped. The local Irish inhabitants also 'interacted' with and knew that landscape with a deep sense of familiarity and belonging to the place that shaped their sense of individual and community identity. There were many contradictory ways of understanding the landscape among the British soldier-surveyors in the field, the antiquarians and orthographers, and those people who lived in the local landscapes. Even among these local inhabitants, there were multiple vantage points, including the Anglo-Protestant landlord class and the Irish tenant farmers. Others too, contributed to the maps and were part of the mediation at the local level. For example, Protestant clergymen were often sought out by the surveyors and antiquarians as trustworthy sources of information for placenames. Further, it must be recognised that, within any of these groups of actors, there was not one single but rather many ways of knowing the landscape. While acting to silence and re-write many of these local knowledges of the landscape, the maps also acted to 'preserve' the meanings and shared memories of the landscape for the local population. For those who could read the subtext on the maps which represented placenames and sacred or ritual places (such as the mountain and hilltops), it meant that the maps also encoded local perspectives of the landscape.

The local-level landscape is also the site of complex social interactions between these many different interested parties (even some of whom were never physically present in the local landscape but still played a role in these relations of power). Although more obscured in the documentary evidence than the administrative operations in the Dublin offices, the local-level landscape was where different groups of people came face to face (sometimes in conflict) to produce the cultural mediation of the landscape, the social memories and histories represented on the maps.

The social production and efficacy of the sense of place and identity is defined by social memories and historical perceptions of the local landscape. In nineteenth-century Ireland, the colonial process of mapping the countryside undertaken by the British Ordnance Survey attempted, and was partially successful, at re-writing the images of the Irish landscape and its people. This political project, however, was contested at the international, national and local level. The contest between British colonialism and Irish nationalism for the control of the land, the people and their past, was played out through these maps. The competing perceptions of the landscape shape the artifact of the map as the site of social interaction, contestation and cultural negotiation of identity and place within the landscape.

REFERENCES

Aalen, F.H.A., K. Whelan and M. Stout (eds) (1997) *Atlas of the Irish Rural Landscape*. Cork, Ireland: Cork University Press.

Andrews, J.H. (1975) *A Paper Landscape: The Ordnance Survey in Nineteenth-century Ireland*. Oxford: Oxford University Press.

—— (1983) 'Thomas Aiskew Larcom, 1801–1879', *Geographers' Bibliographical Studies* 7: 71–4.

—— (1985) *Plantation Acres: An Historical Study of the Irish Land Surveyor and His Maps*. Omagh, Co. Tyrone: Ulster Historical Foundation.

—— (1997) *Shapes of Ireland: Maps and Their Makers 1564–1839*. Dublin: Geography Publications.

Baker, A. (1992) 'Introduction: On Ideology and Landscape', in A. Baker and G. Biger (eds) *Ideology and Landscape in Historical Perspective: Essays on the Meanings of Some Places in the Past*. Cambridge: Cambridge University Press, pp. 1–14.

Basso, K. (1996) 'Wisdom Sits in Places: Notes on a Western Apache Landscape', in K. Basso and S. Felds (eds) *Senses of Place*. Albuquerque: University of New Mexico, pp. 53–90.

Bender, B. (1993) 'Introduction: Landscape – Meaning and Action', in B. Bender (ed.) *Landscape: Politics and Perspectives*. Providence, RI: Berg, pp. 1–17.

—— (1998) *Stonehenge: Making Space*. Oxford: Berg.

Black, J. (1997) *Maps and History: Constructing Images of the Past*. New Haven, CT: Yale University Press.

Boyce, D.G. (1991) *Nineteenth-century Ireland: The Search for Stability*. Savage, MD: Barnes and Noble Books.

Cairns, D. and S. Richards (1988) *Writing Ireland: Colonialism, Nationalism and Culture*. Manchester: Manchester University Press.

Campbell, S. (1995) *The Great Irish Famine*. Strokestown, Roscommon: Famine Museum.

Canavan, T. (1991) 'Townlands in Ulster Today', in T. Canavan (ed.) *Every Stoney Acre Has a Name: A Celebration of the Townland in Ulster*. Belfast: Federation for Ulster Local Studies, pp. 49–52.

Chidester, D. and E. Linenthal (1995) 'Introduction', in D. Chidester and E. Linenthal (eds) *American Sacred Space*. Bloomington: Indiana University Press, pp. 1–42.

Close, Col. C. (1969) *The Early Years of the Ordnance Survey*. New York: Augustus M. Kelley, Publishers.

Connell, K.H. (1950) *The Population of Ireland, 1750–1845*. Oxford: Clarendon Press.

Crossman, V. (1996) *Politics, Law and Order in Nineteenth-century Ireland*. New York: St Martin's Press.

Dallat, C. (1991) 'Townlands: Their Origin and Significance', in T. Canavan (ed.) *Every Stoney Acre Has a Name: A Celebration of the Townland in Ulster*. Belfast: Federation for Ulster Local Studies, pp. 3–10.

Danaher, K. (1972) *The Year in Ireland: Irish Calendar Customs*. Cork: Mercier Press.

Davis, T. (1842) *Literary and Historical Essays from the Nation and The Dublin Monthly Magazine*. Dublin: J. Duffy.

Duffy, C.G. (1880) *Young Ireland: A Fragment of Irish History, 1840–1850*. London.

Fairbanks, K. (1998) 'Ballinafad Castle', *The Corran Herald* 31, Ballymote Heritage Group, Sligo, p. 13.

Foster, R.F. (1988) *Modern Ireland, 1600–1972*. London: Penguin.

Foucault, M. (1984) 'Space, Knowledge and Power', in P. Rabinow (ed.) *The Foucault Reader*. New York: Pantheon, pp. 239–56.

Hamer, M. (1989) 'Putting Ireland on the Map', *Textual Practice* 3(2): 184–201.

Harley, J.B. (1989) 'Deconstructing the Map', *Cartographica* 26(2): 1–20.

Hayes McCoy, G.A. (ed.) (1964) *Ulster and Other Irish Maps, c. 1600*. Dublin: Stationery Office for the Irish Manuscripts Commission.

Hirsch, E. and M. O'Hanlon (eds) (1995) *The Anthropology of Landscape: Perspectives on Place and Space*. Oxford: Clarendon Press.

Kain, R. and E. Baigent (1992) *The Cadastral Map in the Service of the State: A History of Property Mapping*. Chicago: University of Chicago Press.

Layton, R. and P.J. Ucko (1999) 'Introduction: Gazing on the Landscape and Encountering the Environment', in P.J. Ucko and R. Layton (eds) *The Archaeology and Anthropology of Landscape: Shaping Your Landscape*, One World Archaeology Series. London: Routledge, pp. 1–20.

Lovell, N. (1998) 'Introduction', in N. Lovell (ed.) *Locality and Belonging*. London: Routledge, pp. 1–24.

MacNéill, M. (1962) *The Festival of Lughnasa*. Oxford: Oxford University Press.

Marquardt, M. and C. Crumley (1987) 'Feux Celtiques: Burgundian Festival as Performance and Process', in C. Crumley and M. Marquart (eds) *Regional Dynamics: Burgundian Landscapes in Historical Perspective*. New York: Academic Press, pp. 361–84.

Monmonier, M. (1991) *How to Lie with Maps*. Chicago: University of Chicago Press.

Moody, T.W. and F.X. Martin (eds) (1994) *The Course of Irish History*. Dublin: Mercier Press.

O'Maolfabhail, A. (1978) 'Keep Townland Names Alive', *Ulster Local Studies* 3(2): 3–5.

—— (1992) 'The Placenames of Ireland in the Third Millennium', in *The Proceedings of a Seminar 28 February 1992*. Dublin: Ordnance Survey for the Placenames Commission.

Ordnance Survey of Ireland (1836) *Monthly Progress Reports*, District B, 1836, OS 1/12. Dublin.

—— (1837) *Field NameBooks, Co. Sligo*. Dublin.

Pennick, N. (1996) *Celtic Sacred Landscapes*. London: Thames and Hudson.

Pickles, J. (1992) 'Texts, Hermeneutics and Propaganda Maps', in T.J. Barnes and J. Duncan (eds) *Writing Worlds: Discourse, Text and Metaphor in the Representation of Landscape*. London: Routledge, pp. 193–230.

Platt, K. (1996) 'Places of Experience and the Experience of Place', in L.S. Rouner (ed.) *The Longing for Home*. Notre Dame, IN: University of Notre Dame Press.

Proudfoot, L.J. (1993) 'Spatial Transformation and Social Agency: Property, Society and Improvement, c. 1700 to c. 1900', in B.J. Graham and L.J. Proudfoot (eds) *An Historical Geography of Ireland*. London: Academic Press, pp. 219–57.

Robinson, P. (1984) *The Plantation of Ulster: British Settlement in an Irish Landscape, 1600–1670*. Dublin: Gill and MacMillan.

Robinson, T. (1996) *Setting Foot on the Shores of Connemara and Other Writings*. Dublin: The Lilliput Press.

Seymour, W.A. (1980) *A History of the Ordnance Survey*. Folkestone, Kent: Wm. Dawson and Sons Ltd.

Smith, A. (1998) 'Landscapes of Power: The Archaeology of 19th-century Irish Ordnance Survey Maps', *Archaeological Dialogues* 5(1): 69–84.

—— (2001) 'Mapping Cultural and Archaeological Meanings: Representing Landscapes and Pasts in 19th-century Ireland', Unpublished PhD dissertation. Amherst, MA: University of Massachusetts at Amherst.

Soja, E. (1989) *Postmodern Geographies*. London: Verso.

Stout, G. and M. Stout (1997) 'Early Landscapes: From Prehistory to Plantation', in F.H.A. Aalen, K. Whwlan and M. Stout (eds) *Atlas of the Irish Rural Landscape*. Cork: Cork University Press, pp. 31–63.

Taylor, L. (1995) *Occasion of Faith: An Anthropology of Irish Catholics*. Philadelphia: University of Pennsylvania Press.

Thrower, N. (1996) *Maps and Civilization: Cartography in Culture and Society*. Chicago: University of Chicago Press.

Tilley, C. (1994) *Phenomenology of Landscape: Places, Paths and Monuments*. Oxford: Berg Publishers.

Tooley, R.V. (1978) *Maps and Map-makers*. New York: Crown Publishers, Inc.

Wood, D. (1992a) *The Power of Maps*. New York: Guilford Press.

—— (1992b) 'How Maps Work', *Cartographica* 29(3): 66–74.

Wood-Martin, W.G. (1880) *Sligo and the Enniskilleners, 1681–1691*. Dublin: Hodges and Figges.

5   MEMORIES OF ANCESTRY IN THE FORESTS OF MADAGASCAR

Janice Harper

The forested regions of Madagascar are internationally famed for their exceptional – and critically endangered – species diversity.[1] From the perspective of many Westerners, tropical forests are near mythic landscapes, reflecting the natural history of non-human life. From the perspective of those who live in the forests, however, they reflect not natural history, but social history. In this way, they are viewed as symbols of shared histories of collective empowerment and resistance to outside control. As conservation policies promote the creation of protected areas and national parks in these forests, residents counter that the forests are the land of the ancestors, and as ancestral land, they are valued and revered as sacred, and their appropriation is regarded as theft.

In order to understand contemporary issues regarding the 'ancestral' lands of the forest, it is important to understand how people came to live in the forest in the first place and how the surrounding land came to be cast as ancestral. At the same time, processes of reorganising land and agriculture in Madagascar, as elsewhere in Africa, have been specifically tied to changing ethnic identities. Combined processes of economic change, migration, and changing social identities, had profound influence on how people lived in and near the forest. While conservation policy in Madagascar assumes an ethnic element shaping land tenure and agricultural practices, residents themselves value ancestry and access to material resources as more salient social divisions. These internal social differences may supersede the boundaries of ethnicity, and thereby form the core of social identity for forest residents.

To demonstrate how concepts of the forest as historically contested terrain are differently understood by forest residents and by conservationists, I draw from my experience living in a village adjacent to a national park in the south-eastern forests of Madagascar. I first discuss

89

the establishment of the park and a conservation and development project intended to facilitate agricultural modernisation. The project administrators presumed that agricultural practices were based on ethnic identities and 'traditions', which I suggest was misguided. In contrast, oral histories detail the founding of the village by members of two lineages. As members of the different lineages gained or lost prestige and power with the social changes of the twentieth century, conflicting histories of the village unfolded. As one lineage gained power, their ancestry was recast as one of nobility, while the ancestry of those who lost power and forest land was recast as a lineage of slaves, an historical revision that, I argue, was used locally to legitimate rising social inequality. These social divisions were not, however, absolute. As the forests surrounding them took on new meanings through the creation of the national park, the shared history of resistance to outside control over local resources and livelihoods contributed to social alliances that have transcended community differences.

THE ISLAND OF MADAGASCAR

The geographical terrain of Madagascar includes tropical, cloud, and montane forests, grasslands and desert. The island is distinguished by a spine of mountains running longitudinally down its centre. The southern regions of the island are dry, barely fertile desert. In other parts of the island, shifting cultivation, primarily of rice, but also of manioc, maize, beans and other crops, has been practised with varying intensity since early settlement, combined with pastoral production. Irrigated rice production has also been practised for many generations, but land suitable for wet-rice production is limited throughout much of the island. Along the coast, fishing supplants agriculture as the primary economic practice.

Although Madagascar is noted for its forest environment, not all Malagasy live in forests. People live in crowded cities, as well as small towns, tiny hamlets, deserts and coastal fishing villages. The island is peppered with small, seemingly isolated villages that are scattered throughout the mountainous terrain and cut off by barely navigable rivers or blazing deserts of cactus and sand. Major transportation routes more often resemble a slow-bouncing lunar terrain than the smooth-riding ribbons of concrete Westerners enjoy. The difficulty of traversing the island has led many visitors, both foreign and urban-based Malagasy, to conclude that villagers live lives cut off from the outside world, a geographical isolation that some believe goes hand in hand with a cultural seclusion. Yet, no matter how remote a village, its inhabitants have ridden in cars, listened to radios, maybe even watched television sets.

They have all seen well-dressed Asians, Europeans, and Americans packing cameras, notebooks, computers, tape recorders or Bibles. Most rural residents engage in economic exchange of one sort or another with people from other regions, countries or continents. The concept of 'remote' is therefore a bit tricky, as a person can be cut off from roads and communication during certain rainy months of the year, constrained by old age or affliction from going to town for supplies all through the year, and yet at the same time be economically dependent upon market prices in a town they haven't seen in years or even decades.

Despite the diffusion of villages, towns, and cities, human habitation has been characterised more as an intrusion upon the idyllic Garden of Eden so frequently conjured in images of Madagascar. Harrison (1992: 74, 75) provides a characteristic summary of how human culture is regarded as a threat to the island's non-human ecology:

The past serves a clear warning. Within the past two thousand years giant lemurs roamed the mosaic of forest and wooded savannah that once cloaked the plateaux. There were dwarf hippos and a giant tortoise with a shell well over a metre long. And huge elephant birds like the towering *Aepyornis*, chest like a wine barrel, thighs like a horse's, egg big as a football: probable source, through sailor's tales, of the legendary Roc that carried Sinbad off in its talons.

The plateaux are now bare and increasingly barren. The bones are all that remain of the creatures that once lived there. A row of twelve sad skulls in a glass cabinet in Tsimbazaza zoo commemorates the extinct lemurs. The skeletons of *Aepyornis* and dwarf hippo, and the shell of giant tortoise, stand beside them. No major climatic changes occurred that could explain their disappearance. But, some time during the first centuries of our era, longboats sailed over from South East Asia, by way of southern India and East Africa, bringing the first humans to the island.

Within a thousand years of their coming, no land vertebrate heavier than 12 kilogrammes survived. Their habitat, the plateau forest and savannah, was destroyed by fire, turned into pasture for the longhorned, humpbacked Zebu cattle which the settlers brought over, and rice paddies in the valley bottoms. The survivors were hunted to extinction for their meat.

A new wave of extinctions may be imminent. The main threat is the clearance of the rainforests to provide farmland for growing populations.

In many such accounts, whether popular or policy-oriented, the people are not counted as among the island's 'wealth', they are not a part of the island's 'treasure trove'. They are, at best, 'friendly', 'poor', 'uneducated'. At worst, they remain fixed in superstition and ignorance, as the following comments of a well-known travel writer attest:

While pregnant, Ruth had been advised by her local friends to take extra care as some *ombiasa* [diviners], far out in the bush, still like to get hold of unborn babies; the sun-dried heart and eyes of the unborn are added to their necklaces as par-

ticularly powerful charms. This sounds like an extract from one of the more
luridly heathen-bashing chapters of the Reverend Matthews or the Reverend
Ellis. Yet when I recall the faces of a few of those Mahafaly herdsmen it seemed
not entirely impossible that in certain areas such customs survive. (Murphy
1985: 153)

these seemingly easy-going, cheerful, friendly Malagasy are so constrained by a
complicated system of beliefs and prohibitions (superstitions, to us) that fear is
one of their dominant emotions – even in the 1980s. (Murphy 1985: 89)

Fortunately casual travelers only need to know that they are dealing with a
society far more complex than it looks and to remember that they may be seen
as potential dangers because *vazaha* [foreigners] are ignorant of local taboos and
could possess mysterious powers to which the Malagasy have no antidotes.
(Murphy 1985: 60)

The stereotyping of Malagasy as hopelessly fixed in traditions of
ancestor worship, divination and irrational fear of outsiders, has been
used to separate contemporary forest farmers from the recent history and
political economy of their regions, including a pre-colonial autocracy
and forced labour, colonial rule, and postcolonial resource appropriation. Just as Murphy could explain Malagasy codes of conduct regarding
foreigners as a superstitious fear of their 'mysterious' power, with no
mention of the history of the three centuries of foreign authority over
their land and lives, so too can conservation and development managers
explain agricultural practices as 'tradition' (RNPP 1994), or one can find
in *Sierra* magazine the following explanation for why the people who live
in the forested Ranomafana region do not have enough food:

As in much of the tropics, the people living in the Ranomafana rainforest of
southeastern Madagascar are the forest's worst enemy, slashing and burning
huge swaths of trees to clear land for crops. Plowing the soil would help them
raise more food on a single plot of land and let them stop roaming so destruc-
tively through the forest, but just teaching people to plow is not the answer here.
For the people of Ranomafana, plowing is taboo because it turns the earth's back
on God. (Knox 1989: 81)

Knox's suggestion that Malagasy do not plough the land because they
regard it as a taboo is not only inaccurate, it is consistent with prevailing
themes in development discourse which explain indigenous economies
as based more on ignorance than experience. But viewing the economic
practices of forest residents as destructive, tied to tradition and in need
of control by outsiders, is not just a view of non-Malagasy. Indeed, urban-
based, educated Malagasy are frequently among those who most
strongly condemn the practices of their rural compatriots. In the
following quote, written by a Malagasy for a World-wide Fund for Nature
(WWF) Report, swidden, or 'slash and burn' agriculture is not only

viewed as destructive, it is also viewed as a result of the state 'giving' forest residents access to the land, an open access regime regarded as innately unmanaged.

Madagascar's enormous biodiversity is extremely important from a scientific point of view. Traditionally our Queen regulated the balance between Man and Nature, deciding on distribution and utilisation of natural resources through a feudal system, whereas the French colonialists laid down clear regulations, but this was no real guarantee of conservation. At independence in 1960 government had strong control of the resources, but in the 1970s people were given free access, which led to severe deforestation and grass burning with resultant soil erosion. (Rabetaliana n.d.: 1)

This quotation illuminates how the forest, and its use, are viewed by the Malagasy state as a national resource to be managed by the state. Conversely, international environmental organisations generally operate under the impression that forests are a 'global' resource. By suggesting that species deemed of scientific or economic value must be protected, the 1973 US Endangered Species Act has legislated the rights of US citizens to manage forests outside the boundaries of the United States; this legislation grants Western conservationists the moral authority to intervene in the land management of other countries on behalf of 'science' (see Zerner 1996 for a discussion of such conservation narratives). One such effort toward this objective has been unfolding in the south-eastern forests of Madagascar, near the village I call Ranotsara.

After Western scientists discovered the existence of rare lemur species in the forests of south-eastern Madagascar in the late 1980s, the national government of Madagascar established the Ranomafana National Park (RNP) in 1990, with funding from USAID, the World Bank and a number of other private donors. The lemurs' habitat was dwindling due in large part to the destruction of the forest cover, as farmers cut and burned the forests to plant rice. The USAID-funded Ranomafana National Park Project (RNPP) was responsible for administering the park during the first six years of its inception, and it launched development strategies aimed at encouraging expanded irrigated rice production to replace the indigenous method of swidden rice production, more commonly referred to by the Malagasy term, *tavy*. *Tavy* farming was regarded by local residents and development planners as a cultural 'tradition', although it had only been practised in the region for a few generations. Prior to that time, much of the region was uninhabited, but the population increased as irrigated rice farmers migrated from the high plateau to the hilly terrain, where flat lands suitable for irrigated rice farming were limited, and swidden production more efficient and productive. Although ecologically suitable to the terrain, *tavy* farming is not without its limitations.

Following two or three seasons of production, soil fertility declines and the land must be left in fallow for ten to fifteen years. Thus, *tavy* farming requires continuing expansion into the forests, but with the establishment of the park, residents were prohibited from further expansion. Indeed, residents were prohibited from entering the forests completely except to bury their dead, while researchers, urban-based Malagasy, Europeans and Americans, and tourists, were ushered in.

Like many similar conservation and development projects and national parks, and unlike projects and parks which are more participatory in practice, the residents of the Ranomafana forests were completely excluded from the debates on proprietorship of the land, despite public rhetoric to the contrary.[2] Moreover, local views of how the forest might be managed were completely disregarded in favour of preservationist views which regard biodiversity as morally superior to the human lives in the forest ecosystem. These images are difficult for many Americans and others, concerned with the very real and rapid devastation of the earth, to dismiss. Nevertheless, an understanding of how residents view themselves in the context of their land, and how they conceptualise their exclusion from it, may illuminate the ongoing tensions between residents and others that lead to continued depletion of the island's resources.

CONCEPTUALISING ETHNICITY

Prior to and during its first phase of the project (1990 to 1993), project administrators sought to gain cultural understandings relative to health care through the collection of sociocultural baseline data. Hanson (1997) alleged that it was in the methodology of this data collection effort that categories of ethnicity became set in stone. The region was characterised as comprised of two ethnic groups, 'Betsileo' and 'Tanala'. Hanson (1997) suggested that attempts to accumulate data on 'households' were based on assumptions of what constituted 'typical' 'Betsileo' and 'Tanala' households.

In almost every one of these studies, resident peoples were first constructed along ethnic lines. Thus, people were defined as being of either the Betsileo or Tanala ethnic group.... Building upon this ethnic basis, a set of standard sociological categories were used to further define the household, its occupants, and their role in local and more global markets. (Hanson 1997: 90)

Internal divisions in Ranotsara, discussed below, forged its social identity as 'Tanala', as rising economic and social inequalities led to intensified *tavy* production. Contrary to the belief that, by encouraging the expansion of wet-rice fields, *tavy* production would decrease, it was found that *tavy* was not abandoned at all; it was merely augmented by increased wet-rice production (Ferraro 1994). In Ranotsara, it was those who had been provided with agricultural assistance by the project who most rapidly expanded their *tavy* fields, because they had been economically empowered to hire labourers and rent *tavy* fields from their less advantaged kin and neighbours.

The increasing impoverishment of the majority of residents served to reinforce an *image* of poverty, by way of visible markers such as inadequate and ragged clothing, dilapidated housing, and poor health and nutrition. This image of poverty was perceived by many outsiders as evidence of backwardness, ignorance and laziness. The solidifying of a 'Tanala' ethnic identity, which I believe was brought about in part by internal divisions in the village and in part by the project reifying nineteenth-century stereotypes, contributed to the project abandoning the community as a pilot village.

Hanson (1997: 24, 245), writing about a similar village a few kilometres from Ranotsara, points to future conceptualisations of 'Tanala' needs and the link between social identity and health:

With the turn of the twenty-first century, the RNPP will in all likelihood be deeply involved in the lives of Ambodiaviavy residents. The question at this point is not whether RNPP planners will be able to introduce and define what they believe to be the true needs of the Tanala. This much is certain. Rather, the important consideration now is to what extent, the Tanala people of the Ranomafana region will be able to participate in this definition and interpretation process. This is no small matter. If we assume that a medical center, for example, is defined by the Project as a Tanala need, it will make a good deal of difference for the Tanala as to whether they decide who would staff the center, whether medical teams from the center reach Ambodiaviavy on a monthly basis, or whether the medicines within the center are offered to Tanala individuals free of charge or distributed to lineage leaders.

Hanson's concern for the 'Tanala' residents of Ambodiaviavy is also a concern for the residents of Ranotsara. While Ranotsara is considered a 'Tanala' village by the residents, most of whom describe themselves as descended from 'Betsileo' ancestors, it has been identified in early project documents as a 'Betsileo' village, which at the same time ranked the 'Betsileo' heritage as superior to a 'Tanala' ancestry. 'To have both a Betsileo father and mother was a sign of distinction' (RNPP 1989). In contrast to the project's finding, not one of the residents I interviewed suggested that either ethnicity was superior to the other or that any distinction was conferred by having two 'Betsileo' parents as opposed to one or none.

Although regarded in project documents as a 'Betsileo' village, Ranotsara was routinely described by project workers as a 'Tanala' village during my residence there. The reason it was originally listed as a 'Betsileo' village was that most of the residents, when asked their ethnic identity, were asked questions such as '*Inona no ny fokonao?*' which, roughly translated into English, is 'What is your descent?' or 'Who are your people?' As such, they would indicate that they were 'Betsileo' because their ancestors were. Still, they persisted in practising *tavy*, thus conveying the 'Tanala' status to project management. Moreover, as stated previously, the descent to greater and greater impoverishment has burned an image of backwardness and hopelessness into the eyes and hearts of project administration such that Ranotsara can now only be understood as 'Tanala' to these outsiders.

A STORY OF AN ISLAND VILLAGE

The village of Ranotsara is located in the south-eastern montane rain forests of Madagascar, where the altitudinal gradient ranges from 600 to 1,200 metres, with an annual precipitation rate of approximately 2,900 mm (Ferraro 1994). While the climate is very hot and dry from about October to the end of December, from January to March heavy, constant rains begin, including one or more cyclones every year. Such cyclones commonly destroy crops, homes, and even kill people. The threat of cyclones, therefore, is very real to the residents of Ranotsara, who must work daily in the thundering rain, with few clothes for protection, and can still face serious loss should a cyclone destroy their homes or fields. From March through September, the rains continue, gradually becoming much gentler, with intermittent sunny days.

From a distance, Ranotsara is a lovely, quiet hamlet of thatch and tin-roofed homes made of mud, resting amongst banana, coffee and jack-fruit trees in the centre of vast wet-rice fields, often shimmering with the brilliant green of swelling rice. Surrounding these fields rise stony, forested hills, reaching to the celebrated forests of Madagascar, just a 10- to 20-minute walk away. The eerie cries of lemurs echo through the village every morning and every evening – the residents readily discern a species just from the sounds it makes as it plays. Children play just as joyfully, and their laughter enlivens the peaceful village, while the rhythmic beating by dozens of women and girls pounding rice, bananas and coffee provides a steady percussion to mark the time of day.

Reaching the village, a different view envelops the visitor. The people are poor – most wear shredded, filthy rags for clothes; a few wear brightly coloured new clothes imported from the West – Beverly Hills 90210 t-shirts for the boys, frilly acrylic dresses for the girls, one or two digital watches on the wrists of young men. Nearly everyone is at once both scrawny and strong – while some men are obviously robust and muscular, others are barely heavier than their bones. Yet, regardless of the fat on their flesh, they are all active – hauling wood, beating rice, planting crops, and carrying children.

Virtually every child has some visible health problem – bellies bloated with worms, noses running, ears oozing white or yellow pus from infection, skin encrusted with scabies lesions, huge boils protruding from legs and arms. Most are coughing or wheezing. A public health survey of the region found that 69 per cent of the children under the age of 10 were underweight and 11 per cent were wasted (having low weight for height) and the parasite load of children was 97 per cent (Kightlinger 1993). Their parents and grandparents are often as sick, and yet they defy the stereotypical image of lethargic, malnourished Africans. Instead, all, young and old, scrawny and robust, hungry and sated, are working, playing, interacting.

The profoundly poor health of the people in an area of such 'species rich' forests struck another observer as well. Visiting the newly-established Ranomafana National Park in the early 1990s, journalist Paul Harrison noted of Ambodiaviavy, one of the park's model villages and about 10 kilometres from Ranotsara:

The health of Ambodiaviavy's people is among the worst I have seen in seventeen years of travel throughout the Third World. Half the children were infected with malaria, though only one in six had had fever in the past fortnight. The children delouse one another in lines or circles of four or five. The village is riddled with fleas. It took me three days to get rid of the ones I caught. One in six children has scabies lesions on their hands. One in three has lesions from the jigger flea. The female eats her way into flesh, covers herself with a cyst, and converts herself into a living brood chamber, bloated with her swelling eggs. The hatched larvae eat their way out. Locals pick the cysts out with a pin – but the sore often gets infected.

There are internal parasites. Over 90 per cent of the children have an average of six roundworms, as big as a medium sized garden worm, living in their stomach. One child had a hundred, with a combined weight of 2 kilos. Half have whipworm as well, and a third have hookworm. These parasites consume much of the limited food that the child eats. This contributes heavily to child malnutrition. So does diarrhoea – one person in three has an attack in any given fortnight. Almost six out of ten children are malnourished – one in ten severely so.

There are the bleak cases like forty-eight-year-old Fambelo, who hobbles around on a stick, no longer able to dig his fields, with swollen, aching throat and back pains. He has been seriously ill for a year but hasn't seen a doctor, because he's afraid of the cost in drugs and hospital charges. Blind, landless Miray can afford no treatment or help, but supports his five children working on others' fields, feeling his way. (Harrison 1992: 86)

Harrison's description of sickness in Ambodiaviavy is not much different than one encounters in Ranotsara, where just as 'blind, landless Miray' supports his children by working in the fields of others, forgoing the health treatment he so badly needs, others confront both similar and differing fates and obligations shaping their health in multiple ways. While such health problems are not new, many suggest the prevalence has increased over time; others express outrage that their children are continuing to die from diseases that are now curable, but their deepening poverty has made it impossible for them to purchase the medicines or the food they need to restore health. Moreover, the poverty associated with illness and early death is not shared by all, but is instead, an outcome of local histories and tensions.

HISTORICAL OVERVIEW

During the late eighteenth century, the ruler of a small highland kingdom, Andrianampoinimerina, seized control of the central highlands and instituted a series of land and labour policies aimed at strengthening his kingdom and expanding his rule. These strategies included dividing the island into administrative areas in order to facilitate tax collection, the imposition of forced labour to build the kingdom and associated infra-structure, and the creation of social identities tied to the land in an effort to foster social cohesion and loyalty to the king (see Harper 2002 for a more detailed summary of these measures). The forging of ethnicity in the highlands was most notably marked by the creation of a 'Merina' identity, in which people were encouraged to identify themselves as Merina, invest in the building of elaborate ancestral tombs tying them to the land and fixing them in place, thereby marking their allegiance to the king (see Larson 2000 on Merina ethnicity). In addition, the king promoted a caste-system, in which people were identified as *andriana* (noble), *hova* (free) or *andevo* (slave). One could be forced into slavery through a number of mechanisms, including non-payment of taxes, allegations of sorcery (commonly levied against wealthier people, whose property was then seized by the king), or birth. *Andriana* status could be conferred for loyalty or service to the king, while *hova* took on differing meanings in different parts of the island, but generally applied to those regarded as neither noble nor enslaved.

Among the administrative divisions the king created was the southern highland group identified as 'Betsileo'. Due to the flat topography of the highlands, people living in the 'Betsileo' region had become adept at irrigated rice agriculture; their agricultural skills facilitated their economic prosperity, which in turn attracted the attention of the king who, along with his successors, promoted educational and administrative opportunities for many in this region.

While the highlands provided suitable terrain for expansion of the kingdom, the value of the forests to the monarchy was considerable. Although Andrianampoinimerina's reign never extended to the south-eastern forests that comprise the Ranomafana region, his land policies did have significant impact on the forested terrain of the highlands, and his social policies fostered considerable migration into the south-eastern forests. Several authors have pointed to the magnitude of forest destruction during the development of the Merina empire (e.g. Boiteau 1982; Tacchi 1892; Verín 1990). In order to build up the empire and promote international trade, a massive industrialisation crusade using forced labour was initiated under Andrianampoinimerina; it included construction of a massive hydraulics system, as well as roads and railways from Antananarivo to the eastern coast. These projects, which continued during the reign of Andrianampoinimerina's successors Radama I and Ranavalona I, destroyed enormous expanses of forests, particularly between the capital city of Antananarivo in the central highlands and the eastern port of Tamatave on the coast. Indeed, Bloch (1989), Hardenbergh (1992) and Verín (1986) have suggested that the Merina expansion and development of waterworks caused total deforestation throughout much of the eastern forests in this region.[3]

While there was considerable resistance to Merina rule, open resistance led to public persecution, incarceration or death. Thus, covert resistance became commonplace. The primary form of covert resistance was to relocate to deeply forested lands, particularly the south-eastern forests, where the new laws of the Merina kingdom were unenforceable. Such relocation, however, had serious costs. Malaria was far more prevalent, and the lands were less fertile. But even the minimal existence afforded by living in these steep and densely forested terrains provided many with a greater chance of survival than they would have under servitude to the Merina kingdom. It was in these forested regions that people began to identify themselves as 'Tanala', or People of the Forest, to signify the forest lifestyles they came to embrace.

With the onset of colonial rule in 1895, taxation and forced labour continued. In addition, the colonial government launched a series of policies intended to increase the labour pool, including the creation of hospitals and clinics to increase reproductive fitness, and taxes imposed on unmarried men and women (see Harper 2002 for more detailed discussion). Another important administrative measure taken to increase the agricultural labour supply was to promote *tavy* production. Concerned with declining agricultural production, the colonial state took the position that tying people to land would promote agricultural production:

Owing to the rapid formation of roads practicable for carriages, porters' work will gradually be less needed; and it will be desirable to increase the number of natives who hold land. In all cases, however, holders must be obliged to cultivate. (*Antananarivo Annual* 1898: 248)

At other times and in other places, however, the colonial administration banned *tavy* production, which was viewed as a threat to the timber interests of European industries, which sought exotic woods for export.

The political and administrative policies of the colonial government to augment the labour pool proved effective and the population increased. By 1941, however, the increasing population contributed to rice shortages because reproductive control of men and women, accompanied by the introduction of Western drugs, vaccines and health clinics, brought larger families and lower mortality. At the same time, a focus on cash-crop production left less land available for subsistence rice production. To offset the impoverishment associated with the rice shortages, *tavy* production was intensified in the Ranomafana forests (Hanson 1997).

HISTORICAL MEMORIES OF RANOTSARA

The village of Ranotsara was established sometime at the end of the nineteenth century, when the French colonial government expelled the Merina autocracy and gained power. While oral histories are vague on the exact reasons for migration to Ranotsara, it appears that the ancestors of the current village leaders migrated to the area to avoid taxation and forced labour. Two families are regarded as having established the village, the first family was of the Zafindraraoto lineage, which is regarded throughout the Ranomafana region as *hova* caste. The second family to settle the area is of the Zafinaraina lineage, regarded by village residents as *andriana*. The founding Zafindraraoto were regarded by members of both lineages as excellent *tavy* farmers, and were labelled *tompontany*, or 'masters of the land'. They taught the Zafinaraina how to farm the steep hillsides, and the Zafinaraina taught the 'masters of the land' how to farm the flat lands by flooding the fields and planting rice. In gratitude, it is said, the Zafindraraoto or 'masters of the land' gave several parcels of flat lands to the Zafinaraina.

Within two generations, the lineages began to intermarry and their children and grandchildren are now the elders of the village, along with the grandchildren of the founding members, who maintain distinct identities tied to their lineages. Throughout the first half of the twentieth century both lineages are said to have prospered, but it was with the colonial introduction of cash-crop production in the mid-twentieth century that residents suggest economic inequality began.

One of the men born to the first couple to intermarry was selected by colonial officers, for reasons that remain unclear to me, to receive coffee and banana trees for cash-crop production. These concessions not only provided him with greater land to control, but they increased the cash available to him, enabling him to purchase many cattle and to hire migrants from the highlands (now termed 'Betsileo') to work his fields. His eldest son, whom I call Koto,[4] received the best irrigated flat lands from his family, lands which had been conferred by both the Zafind-raraoto and by the colonial administration. He managed these lands with care, along with many head of cattle that he had inherited from his father. He also cleared his own *tavy* fields and, as his cash resources increased, purchased land from others in Ranotsara, until a back injury forced him to retire and leave business matters to his son, Philippe. Koto's youngest brother, Rivo, was similarly positioned with good land and many cattle. The brothers were both blessed with keen business sense, the willingness and energy to work hard, and the particularly useful skill of working well with outsiders.

Their sister, Baovita, had a son, Pascal, who, as the brothers soon recognised, shared their entrepreneurial vision; he even spoke a bit of French. While he did not have the lands or cattle of the two brothers, Pascal's outgoing personality, business sense and, best of all, his marriage to Rahasoa, a school teacher, provided him with the essential access to outside channels that the brothers needed to take advantage of outside resources and the ever in-coming *vazaha* (foreigners).

The 1970s were characterised as a postcolonial period in which the democratic-socialist President Didier Ratsiraka instituted an urban-based development programme that depressed the price of rice in the rural sector and led to several poorly conceived economic initiatives that culminated in World Bank structural adjustment programmes and devaluation of the currency and rapid inflation. By the mid- to late 1980s, as rising prices and severe cyclones led to rice and cash shortages, Rivo, Pascal and Philippe helped the villagers by loaning rice and cash, in exchange for repayment in double the following year. Thus, many people found themselves in debt to the three men, who quickly grew prosperous.

When the park project came to the village in 1990, the two brothers and their nephew were among the first to accept the new policies, rallying to receive the outsiders. Their seeming eagerness to embrace the new policies and embark on new farming techniques, along with

Ranotsara's close proximity to the forest and its relative proximity to the main town of Ranomafana, made the village appear particularly appealing to project officials and so it was subsequently selected as a pilot village for the project. The residents were assured that, by becoming a pilot village and giving assistance to the officials, they would receive development assistance in the form of fish for stocking fish ponds, beans for a woman's cooperative, cement and roofing for the school, and seeds for farming irrigated rice. With Rivo, Philippe, Pascal and his wife, Rahasoa, taking charge of distribution, these resources, often intended for the benefit of all the residents, seemingly disappeared and rumours as to where they ended up ensued.

As people could no longer keep up with the spiralling cost of living, and as their rice was being used to repay prior years' debts, most residents were no longer able to produce enough rice and other crops to survive. Consequently, according to a number of villagers who rented out their lands, Rivo, Pascal and Philippe offered landholders up to 50,000FMG (approximately $12.50 at the time of my fieldwork) to rent their fields for a period of three years.

This plan was most logical for those of the Zafindraraoto lineage because, not being directly related to the four men of the mixed lineage, they could receive, along with the cash advance, the opportunity to continue working the fields for daily wages of up to 30 cents a day, plus a daily meal. This strategy enabled the most impoverished residents to ensure their survival, while not entirely relinquishing their rights to their land, which would revert to them three years later, when times might be better or, if no better, renew the lease for additional cash. It further enabled Rivo, Pascal and Philippe, to manage the dirty business of securing fertilisers, chemical inputs, seeds, and other goods from the *vazaha*. By working for the four men, the villagers were assured that, rather than being subjected to the rule of outsiders, the outsiders would provide resources to the village, because Rivo, Pascal and Philippe knew exactly how to negotiate with them. And, no matter the unequal access to resources these men had, they remained family (intermarriage having cast everyone in some type of obligatory relationship); there are limits to the domination family members can exercise over each other, whereas history had shown that no such limits were respected by *vazaha*.

Thus, while so many of the Zafindraraoto lineage surrendered their lands, if only temporarily, those of the Zafinaraina lineage did not necessarily need to do the same, because by sending one or two sons or daughters to help out on their relatives' land, they were supporting their relatives' growing wealth, and in so doing, indirectly ensuring their own future protection. After all, in a village of 30 households, there weren't many fields held by the Zafinaraina lineage, who controlled most of the irrigated fields, that didn't already belong to one of these three men or their immediate family. But not all of the Zafinaraina lineage could afford the luxury of retaining their land. Some simultaneously rented out their lands, and provided unpaid child labour so that they could benefit from both the immediate cash provisions of renting out land, and the long-term protective welfare promised by the kin network.

As the Zafindraraoto rented out more and more of their fields, or worked as wage labourers for the Zafinaraina men, it came to be that in every Zafindraraoto household there were no longer enough people to work the fields that were not rented. It is in this way that the majority of the land and labour shifted from the Zafindraraoto to the Zafinaraina and, I believe, that the recasting of the Zafindraraoto from *hova* to *andevo* began to be whispered about the village.

Another significant change linked to the international economy contributed to land consolidation in Ranotsara. From 1993 to 1994, the national government promoted land titling in the Ranomafana region (Hanson 1997) – in accordance with World Bank efforts to privatise land holdings and thereby presumably encourage conservation (see Keck et al. 1994; Leisz et al. 1994). Hanson (1997) suggests that the land in the Ranomafana region that was registered with Madagascar's *Service de Domain* under this privatising campaign was almost all wet-rice fields.

That fewer *tavy* fields were registered might be explained by the registration requirements. In order to title land, the petitioner must have the land surveyed and mapped (Keck et al. 1994), a difficult process in a community where access to land surveyors and the money to pay them is short. In addition, it is not sufficient that one request title to property; it must also be shown that the land has been actively used for agricultural production for ten years, though in some cases this may be reduced to five years (Keck et al. 1994: 15). Hence, gaining title to one's *tavy* fields may prove problematic if the land has been left fallow. Finally, because in order to register land, one must pay an initial registration fee and annual taxes, only those with the most cash income are likely to participate.

Rivo, Philippe and Pascal, the three men whose control of community resources had expanded with the economic and social changes of the 1980s, were in the forefront of privatising land during the early 1990s. In fact, many people alleged that the lands they rented to the three were stolen, when the men, all literate, had the lands titled as their own. With the rapid rise in economic power of the three, there was concern that the local power of the *mpanjaka* (lineage chief) was diminishing.

Faly, *mpanjaka* of the Zafindraraoto, indicated that the role of the *mpanjaka* had changed in many ways in recent years. For example, he indicated that when he first became *mpanjaka*, if a person wanted to clear a new field, he could not do so until he first worked on the fields of the *mpanjaka*. Faly's son, Etienne, added that in past generations if a person wanted to clear a new field, they had to ask permission of the *mpanjaka*, but with the increasing land shortages of the last decade, they no longer asked permission, unless as a formality. 'Now the land belongs to all the people', he said, suggesting that ancestral land associated with a lineage was disappearing in favour of a new type of common property regime which a select few have been controlling.

Rather than challenging the local appropriation of land and power, Faly and many others chose instead to accept it, in order to reap direct and indirect benefits in this period of social change. Faly told me that he felt he had very little power to change the situation, yet he recognised that Rivo and the others could provide a relatively reliable conduit to the resources of outsiders. By resisting the temptation to invoke his authority as *mpanjaka* and accuse Rivo and his kin of enriching themselves by appropriating project resources, Faly chose to work with and for Rivo. By conferring unspoken approval upon the activities of the village's entrepreneurs, Faly was able to exercise continued and unchallenged authority over Rivo in non-economic matters of the village, avail himself of wage-work when needed, and not have to worry about dealing with *vazaha*.

In contrast, Liva, an elder of the Zafinaraina lineage, left the village rather than continue in a role he found to be ceremonial only. Tensions between himself and the three men continued, while he continued to invoke his authority as *mpanjaka-be* (great lineage chief) in order to position himself close to those in real power, and more importantly for Liva, contrast his own lineage to that of Faly, whom he regarded as *andevo*. Insisting that the Zafindraraoto were *andevo*, he maintained that his own position was the highest in the village and his own ancestry the most pure. Not only did he claim an historical right to his title as *mpanjaka-be*, but also, by excluding himself from the village, distinguishing his lineage from that of Faly and distancing himself from the three men who he pointed out were descended from a union with *andevo*, Liva claimed a moral right to his title because he was one of the few in the village who remained uncontaminated by the lineage of the inferior 'other'.

CONCLUSION

The question then remains, if, to the residents, 'Tanala' is a way of life, and 'Betsileo' an ancestry, what exactly is the 'Tanala' way of living? To the park project, it is the practice of *tavy*; agricultural strategy is the boundary, and tied to the way that one farms the land is a host of other social values, including cleanliness, intellect, modernisation, sexuality, superstition and willingness to work.

To the residents, the 'Tanala' way of living is the practice of *tavy*, as well as cash-crop production, irrigated rice farming, burial in caves, eating a diet of rice, greens, beans, manioc, and green bananas, giving birth at home, brewing and drinking *toaka gasy*, and recognising and giving homage to the ancestors of the forest region. *Tavy*, to the residents of this 'Tanala' village, is but one dimension of a complex economic and social system in which people attempt to support themselves and their families on a limited land-base constrained by the critical limitations of the forest environment; that is to say, heavy rains, cyclones, relatively infertile soils, steep terrain, and limited access to markets and roads. The economy is dismal; Peters (1999, fn), citing Samisoa (1992), indicates that:

In a random-sample survey of 100 village households in the Ranomafana National Park peripheral zone, 50 percent of all households (average size approximately 6 people/household) were found to have annual incomes from all sources of less than $50.00.

Contrary to the park project notion that to be 'Tanala' was to be a *tavy* farmer and to be 'Betsileo' was to be an irrigated farmer, in the village of Ranotsara, where the wealthier residents all owned both irrigated and *tavy* fields, and the poorer residents sold or rented their *tavy* and irrigated fields to the wealthier residents, there was no relationship between being 'Betsileo' and practising wet-rice agriculture, and being 'Tanala' and practising *tavy*. People practised agriculture based upon the type of land and labour available to them, which were determined by social histories, rather than based on 'the way of the ancestors' or one's ethnic identity.

Most importantly, there are not two different agricultural systems managed by two different types of people. There exists a single agricultural system which includes horticultural elements. That is to say, the people practise swidden and irrigated agriculture concurrently, along with cash-crop production. A common view of the persistence of *tavy* is that it is a form of resistance (e.g. Bryant and Bailey 1997; Hanson 1997; Jarosz 1993).

A comparable record of everyday resistance occurred in colonial Madagascar where, as Jarosz (1993) shows, French colonial officials sought to stamp out shifting cultivation, but in the process only incurred the implacable opposition of shifting cultivators in this colony. Shifting cultivation (or *tavy)* was a form of long-term land management used for centuries by the Malagasy, but concerns about the possible adverse effects of such cultivation on the island's commercially valuable forests prompted the French to ban this practice in those forests in 1913. As elsewhere in the colonial world (Bryant, 1994a; Jewitt, 1995), this policy was linked to a paternalistic quest to 'civilise' shifting cultivators through a sedentarisation programme that aimed to convert hill-dwelling cultivators into valley-dwelling commercial farmers. However, this 'colonial vision proved difficult to implement' as a result of the widespread resistance of the Malagasy to the restrictions placed on the *tavy* (Jarosz, 1993: 375). Everyday resistance here, as in Dutch-ruled Java, often involved nothing more than the perpetuation of practices that were now illegal, and shifting cultivators were arrested or forced to pay fines for burning and clearing state-protected forests. Indeed, the *tavy* represented a conscious quest to hold on to local culture and beliefs; the fact that such cultivation was undertaken in traditional dress and using traditional tools was a piquant rejection of French attempts to convert the Malagasy to a more 'civilised' European way of life (Jarosz, 1993). (Bryant and Bailey 1997: 171–2)

While sharing Bryant and Bailey's overall argument, I would also suggest that rather than conceptualising *tavy* as a form of cultural resistance, which it may well be, it may be equally useful to focus on how – and which – people do *not* resist intervention. While *tavy* may persist, many people do indeed embrace agricultural innovations (while not abandoning *tavy*) and economic change. Who is positioned to do so, and how they strategise such changes, illuminates the internal social differences that homogenised concepts of cultural belief systems fail to flesh out. Exploring one's memories of the land, and more importantly, the ways in which such memories contradict and collide, may better draw out social tensions shaping relations between people and land.

NOTES

1. This chapter is adapted from the author's *Endangered Species: Health, Illness and Death Among Madagascar's People of the Forest* (Durham, NC: Carolina Academic Press, 2002).
2. See Hanson (1997) and Peters (1997) on how participation has been represented and thwarted by project officials.
3. To this day, the long-term effects of this destruction are readily apparent from the eroded hillsides which flank the roads from the capital to the eastern coasts. The dry and fissured earth is commonly photographed to show the effects of deforestation from *tavy*, with no reference ever being made to the role the roadways (now paved highways) played in creating this damaged landscape.
4. All names are pseudonyms.

REFERENCES

Antananarivo Annual (1898) 'The Population of Imerina and Measures for Increasing It', *Antananarivo Annual* VI: 247–8.
Bloch, M. (1989) *Ritual, History and Power: Selected Papers in Anthropology*. London and Atlantic Highlands: The Athlone Press.
Boiteau, P. (1982) *Contribution à l'Histoire de la Nation Malgache*. Antananarivo: Éditions Sociales.
Bryant, R.L. and S. Bailey (1997) *Third World Political Ecology*. London and New York: Routledge.

Ferraro, P.J. (1994) 'Natural Resource Use in the Southeastern Rain Forests of Madagascar and the Local Impacts of Establishing the Ranomafana National Park', MSc Thesis, Durham, NC: Department of the Environment, Duke University.

Hanson, P. (1997) 'The Politics of Need Interpretation in Madagascar's Ranomafana National Park', PhD Dissertation, Philadelphia: Department of Folklore and Folklife, University of Pennsylvania.

Hardenbergh, S. (1992) 'Household Food Distribution of Subsistence Slash-and-burn Cultivators near Ranomafana National Park, Madagascar'. Presented at the Annual Meetings of the American Anthropological Association, San Francisco.

Harper, J. (2002) *Endangered Species: Health, Illness and Death Among Madagascar's People of the Forest*. Durham, NC: Carolina Academic Press.

Harrison, P. (1992) *The Third Revolution: Population, Environment and a Sustainable World*. London: Penguin Books.

Jarosz, L.A. (1993) 'Defining and Explaining Tropical Deforestation: Shifting Cultivation and Population Growth in Colonial Madagascar (1896–1940)', *Economic Geography* 69(4): 366–79.

Keck, A., N.P. Sharma and G. Feder (1994) 'Population Growth, Shifting Cultivation, and Unsustainable Agricultural Development: A Case Study in Madagascar', World Bank Discussion Papers no. 234, Africa Technical Department Series. Washington, DC: World Bank.

Kightlinger, L.K. (1993) 'Mechanisms of *Ascaris lumbricoides* Overdispersion in Human Communities in the Malagasy Rainforest', PhD Dissertation. Chapel Hill: University of North Carolina.

Knox, M.L. (1989) 'No Nation an Island', *Sierra* May/June: 78–84.

Larson, P.M. (2000) 'History and Memory in the Age of Enslavement: Becoming Merina in Highland Madagascar, 1770–1882', Portsmouth, NH: Heinemann Social History of Africa Series.

Leisz, S., A. Robles, and J. Gage (1994) *Land and Natural Resource Tenure and Security in Madagascar*. Report prepared for USAID/Madagascar. Madison: Land Tenure Center, University of Wisconsin.

Murphy, D. (1985) *Muddling Through in Madagascar*. Woodstock: The Overlook Press.

Peters, W.J., Jr (1997) 'Local Participation in Conservation of the Ranomafana National Park, Madagascar', *Journal of World Forest Resource Management* (8): 109–35.

—— (1999) 'Understanding Conflicts between People and Parks at Ranomafana, Madagascar', *Agriculture and Human Values* 16(1): 65–74.

Rabetaliana, H. (n.d.) 'Prospects for Natural Resource Management in Madagascar', unpublished manuscript, Worldwide Fund for Nature, Antananarivo, Madagascar.

RNPP (Ranomafana National Park Project) (1989) 'Survey of Ranomafana Park Pilot Villages', Document in RNPP administrative offices. Ranomafana, Madagascar.

—— (1994) *Ranomafana National Park: Integrated Conservation and Development Project 1994–1996*. Stoney Brook, NY: Ranomafana National Park Project.

Tacchi, A. (1892) 'King Andrianampoinimerina, and the Early History of Antananarivo and Ambohimanga', *Antananarivo Annual* 4: 474–96.

Vérin, P. (1986) *The History of Civilisation in North Madagascar*, trans. David Smith. Rotterdam and Boston: A.A. Balkema.

—— (1990) *Madagascar*. Paris: Karthala Press.

Zerner, C. (1996) 'Telling Stories about Biological Diversity', in S.B. Brush and D. Stabinsky (eds) *Valuing Local Knowledge: Indigenous People and Intellectual Property Rights*. Washington, DC: Island Press, pp. 68–101.

6 MOON SHADOWS: ABORIGINAL AND EUROPEAN HEROES IN AN AUSTRALIAN LANDSCAPE

Veronica Strang

TWO PLACES AND TWO GHOSTS

At the Rutland Plains homestead, on the western side of the Cape York Peninsula in Far North Queensland, is a small rectangular enclosure bounded by iron railings. Tucked behind the sheds and the horse yard, it contains the grave of Frank Bowman, who established the cattle station at the beginning of the twentieth century. To the pastoral community he was a 'brave pioneer'. To the local Aboriginal community, he was a murderer, 'a really dog'. (See Figures 6.1a and 6.1b, Jimmy Inkerman's memorial at Trubanamen.)[1]

Not far away, just on the other side of the cattle station boundary, at a place called Trubanamen, is a concrete plinth about 4 feet high. On its sloping top is a marble slab commemorating the life of a Kokobera man, Jimmy Inkerman (or to give him his Aboriginal name, Ngart-YapMalmanl),[2] who speared Bowman fatally in 1910, and was subsequently shot and killed. To the settlers and their descendants, Jimmy Inkerman was a 'treacherous spearman'. To the local Aboriginal community, he was and is a hero.

This chapter is about these two places, the memories and the meanings that they hold, and the two men whose identities are encoded in each place, and in a sense, at both places. It is also about two historical narratives: of the pastoralists who still live on the vast cattle stations in the area, and of the Aboriginal community which now inhabits the modern settlement of Kowanyama, on the Mitchell River. It considers how, over time, the voices telling these narratives have been muted or released to speak as the cultural landscapes around them have undergone changes in climate.

Figure 6.1a　　Distant view of Jimmy Inkerman's memorial at Trubanamen.

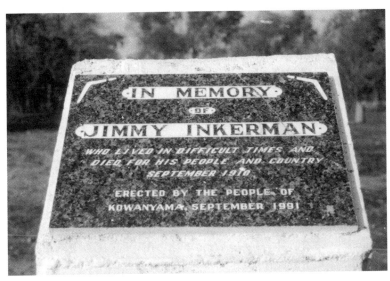

Figure 6.1b　　Close-up view of memorial.

Nearly 100 years ago, when Inkerman threw the spear that proved fatal for Bowman and himself, these two sites were situated within a very different cultural landscape. The peninsular savannah country, a particularly resource-rich environment, had supported a substantial population of Aboriginal hunter-gatherers for many thousands of years. At the time of the European invasion it was one of the most densely populated areas in Australia. The Kokobera-speaking community that lived around Trubanamen was neighboured by the Yir Yoront to the north, and the Kunjen language (Olkol and Oykangant) speakers to the east.[3]

Like other hunter-gatherers these groups maintained an intensely intimate relationship with this landscape: in small clan and family units, they moved around their clan land in accord with seasonal resource availability. Social identity was based on core themes: land, kin and knowledge which, as many ethnographers have described,[4] remain central to local concepts of Aboriginality today. Every individual was believed to come from an ancestral spiritual 'home' within the land, and to return to this place upon death. The spatial location of identity situated each person within a particular totemic clan and a system of kinship, upheld by a carefully balanced system of marriage and exchange.[5] The land mediated every aspect of life: social organisation, kin obligations, political power, economic rights and spiritual beliefs. It therefore acted as a comprehensive repository for identity and personal memory (see Morphy 1991; Munn 1984; Strang 1997; Harper this volume).

The European explorers who came to this area, first by ship, over several hundred years,[6] and then overland from the east coast, saw the landscape very differently, as a hostile wilderness defended by 'primitive savages'. Finding little in the way of technology or material culture, they failed to discern the complex relationship that the local inhabitants maintained with their environment. It was, in any case, more convenient to frame the place as 'virgin land' which would clearly benefit from the imposition of their 'civilising' culture.

As discussed by writers such as Ortner (1974), Schaffer (1989) and Rose (1992a), the Europeans brought with them a concept of Nature as feminine and 'wild' – something that had to be brought under the 'dominion' of rational, male Culture. They saw the indigenous population as being conflated with Nature, and therefore subject to the same battle for control. Writing about the exploits of Constable Willshire in the late 1800s – a 'pioneer' whose murderous and rapacious activities terrorised the indigenous population – Rose (1992a) suggests that this colonial enterprise was a fundamentally masculine endeavour. She portrays the male 'lone hero', with his phallic gun, as a patriarchal aggressor, pushing to achieve dominance over untamed 'Nature' and her 'denizens'.

By the time overland visits from the east became possible in the mid-1800s, the Aboriginal communities along the Gulf coast had already learned that the white 'ghosts'[7] arriving from the sea killed or kidnapped people. The local communities also had a keen sense of land ownership[8] and there were some unhappy confrontations. One of the first overlanders, Ludwig Leichhardt, travelled westwards along the river systems in 1845 to the area which is now Dunbar station. Here one of his team was speared, at a place which the European map memorialises as 'Gilbert's Rest'. In 1864, the Jardine brothers, droving cattle up the coast to Cape York, shot and massacred about 30 Aboriginal people near the junction of the Alice and Mitchell Rivers: this event – recorded with pride by one of the cattlemen – came to be known as the Battle of the Mitchell River (see Sharp 1952).

Further colonisation of the area followed the Palmer River gold rushes of the late 1800s, as people saw the opportunities to profit by supplying cattle to the miners. The graziers moved west to settle the Peninsula. Armed with rifles and revolvers, they pushed the indigenous population before them, forcing them either to flee their land, hide, or to provide unpaid labour in establishing the cattle stations intended to displace them. In some instances the indigenous inhabitants were given poisoned flour, and Aboriginal women were forced to become concubines. As one woman in Kowanyama reported:

Where their main camp used to be, people got poison [flour] from that old station.... And that's where my two auntie was taken away from there... they bin grab all them people there.... Some of them boys wanted them to be their wives. (Alma Wason, fieldnotes, Strang)

When Aboriginal groups speared cattle or horses, retribution was swift. Following the killing of a horse near Emu Lagoon, a number of Kunjen families were shot, leaving alive only a small baby still clinging to her mother's breast. In 1889 a mounted police contingent was formed at Highbury Station, and 'troublemakers' were deported in chains to a penal settlement in Palm Island.

The Aboriginal clans continued to fight back. A Scots coloniser, having taken a local man's wife and maltreated her husband, was speared in his tent.[9] As the story goes:

One day he – the Scotsman – threw a billy can of hot water – boiling water – over this husband. He went bush and got better, and came back with all his family. That old feller [the Scotsman] ... used to camp at night, under this big open fly [tent] and he used to have a carbide light inside. And they could watch him at night-time walking round in shadow behind this light. So they went there by night. That day they saw those women and they said 'don't you fellers stick there, you better take off'. They went there that night and they speared that feller through the [tent] fly. (Viv Sinnamon, fieldnotes, Strang)

However, though the Aboriginal landowners in Cape York tried to defend their land and their people, the superior firepower of the Europeans decimated the dense population of clans and created huge displacement and disruption.[10] By the beginning of the twentieth century the colonisers had moved right across the Peninsula. In 1903 the first cattle were brought to Rutland Plains, and the lease was taken up by Frank Bowman and his brother Archer. Their homestead was situated by a large lagoon which was, for the Kokobera landowners, an important catfish increase place, near an equally sacred increase site for sugarbag.[11]

As well as appropriating two important ancestral sites, Bowman soon became notorious for the raping and killing of local people. People still living in Kowanyama recall their grandparents telling them how he would go into camps and rape the women while the men were out hunting.[12] One elder described how Bowman murdered two men, and burned their bodies:

Up there, on the sand ridge there. [The whites] killed two men, then burnt them [their bodies] at that place.... People searched and searched [for them]. [A man] then saw footprints.... 'Those two [killers] burnt the men right here.' Then he returned as a messenger to the camp. 'Hey! Someone killed those fellows with a gun!' ... 'Then in that same place [they] buried them in the fire. They burnt them in the fire!'... They went back, a big mob of people. They went back up to that little sand ridge ... they came up and saw [the remains of the bodies]. They cried for those two at that place.... [They] buried their bones at that place. Then they gave a name to that place: 'Killed-Two-Men'.... Then, by and by, [Bowman] shot some others to the south, and again to the south, to the west, and again to the west, to the north and again to the north, and here too, and here in the east too, he was killing. This white man was killing them, long ago. (Minh-Worrpol, in Alpher 1966)

In this period of colonisation, the level of genocide in parts of Australia was such that humanitarians in Britain sent missionaries to try to intervene. In the same year that Rutland Plains was established, Bishop Gilbert White instructed the Reverend Earnest Gribble to set up an Anglican mission near the Gulf coast, to try to protect the Aboriginal people in the area. Though there is no public record that this was related to Bowman's activities, the site chosen for the mission at Trubanamen was beside a creek on the Rutland boundary. It was a practical choice in some ways, as the early missions and stations in the Gulf country were reliant upon supplies brought by boat rather than overland,[13] but it may also be interpreted as a social and moral challenge to the more brutal colonisers: a forerunner of the deep divide in attitudes to the indigenous population which has become so visible in recent Australian debates. As Bottoms comments:

A lot has been said against the missionaries, but it is a fact that they effectively put a brake on the genocide ... in the Gulf country. (1992: audiotape)

Though more benign, the missionaries' remit was not to prevent the colonial enterprise, but merely to reduce the violence and save souls: its protection represented a considerable loss of freedom and the acceptance of other religious, social and economic practices. However, the option of remaining 'out bush' had become increasingly untenable. The Europeans developed distinctive categories dividing those people who 'came in' and submitted to being infantilised as Station or Mission 'boys' and 'girls', from those who stayed 'out bush'. The latter were classified as 'wild blacks' or 'myalls', and prior to the arrival of the missions such recalcitrants could be shot with impunity. This was theoretically illegal, but few Aboriginal people spoke English, and they were, in any case, highly unlikely to initiate contact with the police. However, the missionaries provided an alternative form of white authority and a physical sanctuary. As one man said:

The mission wasn't standing; [we] were still chasing around [after game in the bush].... First the white man, this shooter here, now we are staying [here at the mission]. (Minh Worrpol, in Alpher 1966)

The missionaries tried to gather people in and dissuade them from attempting to defend their land. As he goes on to say:

When the mission came in, they set up tents. Then they built little houses. Then they called [people] in from out there ... from the south, in here from the north, in here from the west, in here from the east, [from] close to here as well, gathered in.... A minister came out to this place here: 'Aboriginal people: this place right here is a good one; peace! ... Do not kill'. (Minh-Worrpol, in Alpher 1966)

When the Trubanamen Mission was established the Superintendent, Mr Matthews, was warned by Frank Bowman to keep people away from the cattle station. As Bowman's stockman said later:

[Bowman] had notified Mr Matthews that in the event of any blacks been found on the run[14] [on the cattle station], their spears would be broken and their dogs shot. (McIntyre, in *Cairns Post* 7 Oct. 1910)

However, Matthews was unable to prevent Bowman's death, or that of Jimmy Inkerman, when the two met near the Rutland homestead in August 1910.

A STORY OF THE CRIME

The *Cairns Post* newspaper, reporting the events a month later, led with the headlines:

The Rutland Plains Tragedy

Spearing of Mr Bowman

———

Mission Black or Myall?

———

Story of the Crime

An Inquiry was held at Trubanamen Mission Station ... into the circumstances surrounding the spearing of Frank McArthur Bowman and the death of Jimmy, an aboriginal ... on August 28th last. (*Cairns Post* 7 Oct. 1910)

The major witness was Bowman's stockman, James McIntyre, who Aboriginal accounts insist was the 'real' killer of Jimmy Inkerman. McIntyre told a different story though. According to his report, he and Bowman had been riding about 9 miles from the homestead when they saw smoke rising from near a swamp:

... and rode there to ascertain what it was. There were nine or ten male blacks in the water.... When they rode into the swamp Mr Bowman shot at a dog on the bank across the swamp. (*Cairns Post* 7 Oct. 1910)

McIntyre dismounted and broke a number of spears that he found beside a tree, then, remounting his horse, he:

... rode after Mr Bowman and the blacks.... When he got within 20 yards he saw three of them in a fighting attitude, and others standing within a few paces. He noticed a womera [spear thrower] in Murdering Tommy's hand. He and Mr Bowman started to bring them to the mission, the blacks going in front of them. After going half a mile, Kangeroo wanted to fight. He had his spear slipped in his left hand and was yabbering. He was facing Mr Bowman. (*Cairns Post* 7 Oct. 1910)

McIntyre then took the womera from 'Murdering Tommy', and Kangeroo tried to hit him with his womera.

The womeras met in mid-air and both were broken. Just at that moment Mr Bowman was speared ... the next thing he noticed was Mr Bowman riding from his right ... with a spear sticking in his head. (*Cairns Post* 7 Oct. 1910)

McIntyre said he 'grabbed Mr Bowman's rifle, as he was in a falling attitude on his horse'. Another spear was thrown and went through McIntyre's hat (this punctured hat was exhibited in court). McIntyre says that:

The spear that struck Mr Bowman went in about an inch above the right temple, pinning his hat to his head. Mr Bowman pulled the spear out himself, remarking 'I'm done'. Witness [McIntyre] followed the blackfellow. He would not say whether he had done anything. (*Cairns Post* 7 Oct. 1910)

Apparently McIntyre suggested going to the Mission to report the incident, but Bowman said 'Don't bother, we might get a shower of spears any time.' According to McIntyre, 'the deceased was the only person with a rifle', and he describes Bowman as having said 'I put the rifle to my left shoulder and had a shot, on account of being completely blind in the right eye.' McIntyre insisted that he was about 70 yards from Bowman when he heard the shot. He helped his boss back to their camp, and the next day drove him to the homestead in a buggy. While at the camp, he took Bowman's revolver and went back and 'broke the blacks' spears' (*Cairns Post* 7 Oct. 1910).

Another stockman, Henry Slattery, had helped to bring Bowman home in the buggy. He told the Inquiry that:

Everyone in these parts carried firearms as a protection from blacks. He had been living here for the past ten or twelve years, and considered the blacks more treacherous now than before the mission was formed.... Before the mission started ... they would all put down their spears, but now when they were seen anywhere on the run, they kept their spears and looked at one with contempt. There were also rumours going around about their intention to kill whites. (*Cairns Post* 7 Oct. 1910)

Two police constables gave evidence that they had 'found the dead body of a blackfellow. There was only one wound caused by a bullet from a rifle.' Mrs Catherine Bowman described how her husband had sickened as the spear wound became infected, and died a few days after being brought home. When Mr Matthews had called to see him, the day after the incident, he said: 'No, I don't want to see him, as I consider him the cause of all this. You might bring him to see this wound, his pupil's handiwork.' On being told of Jimmy Inkerman's death, he added 'It is well to have had a little revenge. I put one in his back' (*Cairns Post* 7 Oct. 1910).[15]

Faced with the depositions of McIntyre and Mrs Bowman, and the accusation that the Mission was to blame in making 'the blacks' more defiant, Mr Matthews must have had an uncomfortable time. He insisted to the Inquiry that: 'He did not know the deceased blackfellow.... He was not a mission boy but a myall' (Mr Matthews, in *Cairns Post* 7 Oct. 1910). His concern to deny responsibility is understandable. It is clear from the tribunal records that the land at the time was far from 'settled', and from the graziers' point of view the homestead – probably just a few shacks and a yard at that time – was a symbolic fortress in a hostile and violent environment in which 'wild' blacks were becoming more and more dangerous, thanks to the protection provided by the Mission. Bowman and McIntyre are presented as merely trying to protect themselves and their property from the depredations of 'myall' blackfellows. This viewpoint rested on some basic assumptions: that the land now belonged to the cattlemen, and that the indigenous populace was not entitled to challenge this appropriation, make use of the resources (i.e. the cattle) placed upon their land, or even fish or hunt 'on the [cattle] run'.[16] They must remain on the Mission. Should they stray back onto their own country, it was apparently acceptable to shoot their dogs, to disarm them, and to round them up like cattle and force them to go to the Mission.

Although there is some ambiguity in the public reportage of Bowman and McIntyre's behaviour – the care taken to justify their actions is telling – on the whole they emerge as brave men in a dangerous situation, who became victims of 'treachery'. The evidence of the pastoralists and police is recounted in detail, while Matthews's evidence gets short shrift, and the spite directed towards the missionaries suggests that these 'do-gooders' were seen as complicit in that 'treachery', and deemed to be obstructing the settlers' cause.

'THAT HOSTILE AND DANGEROUS MAN'

No Aboriginal version of the situation was recorded in 1910, and Aboriginal voices are absent from the tribunal records, but it is plain from later accounts that this was a terribly traumatic period, in which their whole way of life was savagely besieged. The story of what happened to Jimmy Inkerman has been passed down orally from one generation to the next in Kowanyama. There are many versions,[17] but all share a portrayal of the Bowmans and their employees as frightening adversaries. As Sommer notes:

Neither McIntyre nor the Bowmans had reputations for anything but gross cruelty, murder, and sexual abuse of Aboriginal women. (1998: 313)

For example, one elder described Mrs Bowman's response when he and another boy working at the homestead let some goats loose.

She was beating us with a thick stick. Then another white man came to us and said 'you two go back down to the Mission.... She says she's going to kill you two'.... We went inside, tied up our swags and cleared out.... Yes she was evil too. She never did any work. She used to carry a ti-tree waddy and hit you, whack! Just as she went along. (Bully Mitchell, in Sommer 1998: 313, 316)

One account of the incident in which Jimmy Inkerman was shot suggests that this came about because Bowman and McIntyre caught a number of people looking for turtle at a swamp not far from Rutland Plains homestead.

Those people there went in the water for turtle. The Aboriginal fellow [Jimmy Inkerman], that grandfather [of] this old man Harry Daphne.... His name was Ngart-YapMalmanl ... his Aboriginal name ... Bowman [coming towards them] ... caught sight of them. 'Yes, they're climbing up the bank'. He shot them with a gun. He shot them. First he shot the dogs: Chuuw! He took a shot at them.... He shot and shot. Then and there that old man got his spears. He speared that white

man Bowman right here [in the temple], chup! The butt of that spear broke off;
only the shaft lodged [in his head]. His mate, another man, another white man,
took another shot, and another.... He [McIntyre] shot him [Jimmy Inkerman] in
the back, here, down in the creek ... just to the west here, Topsy. Then he went
[down] and sat down[18] by the water just so, thut! He was dead. (Koch Yawrronl,
in Alpher 1988)

When this was reported at the Mission, Matthews went looking for the
body:

The white man, our boss, Mr Matthews, he went looking.... 'This one man, where
is he?' Saw him. 'Here – shot him dead'. Then the white man [Mr Matthews] went
upriver, up there to Rutland Plains homestead. There they talked. Then he, that
other white man [McIntyre], he named Bowman [as the killer]. The real one
[was] that other white man ... McIntyre. He's the one who killed him. (Koch
Yawrronl, in Alpher 1988)

When Bowman died a few days later the Aboriginal elders described this
as a 'return' for his behaviour:

In return ... [Jimmy Inkerman] speared the white man ... and today [he is] in the
cemetery at Rutland homestead. They buried [him] there.... [They said] 'Today,
[Jimmy Inkerman] has speared that white man, that hostile and dangerous man.'
(Minh-Worrpol, in Alpher 1988: 133)

All Matthews could do was to conduct the burial service and try to
prevent further retribution, stressing the advantages of adopting Christian
ways. It appears that other missionaries came to help calm the situation:

The missionary who went up there, went and buried him. [He] spoke for him in
church; there [they] prayed for him. Then [we stayed at Trubanamen] for a long
time.... People gathered together from out there, whites as well, to that Mission....
Then that man [the minister] spoke in church.... 'This place has come to be a
good one. Let us all desist from spearing one another. It is a job well done for us
all. Come on, the boat, the boat is coming from there, with food. Just look at this
tobacco here, this tucker here! Great abundance this here.' (Minh-Worrpol in
Alpher 1988: 133)

Some semblance of calm was therefore restored, and as Koch Yawrronl
commented: 'Then, nowadays, it's finished; [they] speared Bowman
dead. Nowadays [they] don't kill' (in Alpher 1988: 133)

THE 'GOLDEN AGE'

Conflicts in this contested landscape rumbled on over the next two or
three decades, but under tightening colonial control, the eruptions of
opposition subsided. Even so, it is said that right into the 1930s
Aboriginal troublemakers were quietly taken out bush and shot, and the

pastoralists remained insecure. A manager at Koolatah station recalled
that in the 1930s his grandfather still lived in fear of being speared:

When he came here in 1930 there was still wild, you know, wild Aborigines here:
they used to come in and spear the horses! When they [the stock team] were
mustering, camping out, they had to have someone on watch in the night, every
night. They rigged a mosquito net up and put a blanket and a hat in it and
[would] go and camp somewhere else. He [his grandfather] actually had a hat,
with a spear went through the hat – [they] snuck up at night-time and put a
spear through the net. Yeah that wasn't too long ago was it – it's only sixty years
ago. (David Hughes, in fieldnotes, Strang)

Afraid of the consuming 'wilderness', the pastoralists set out to enclose
it: stringing fences; cutting roads to enable freedom of movement;
building more solid homesteads, ringed with defensive barriers. At
Rutland an old hotel was carefully transplanted from further south and
reconstructed in an oasis of carefully tended greenery. Elbowing aside
the two sacred sites, its sturdy pillars appeared to stand for 'civilisation'
in the dusty, untrammelled bush; an imposition of culture, and
ascendance over nature. More Europeans came into the area, and the
Mission moved to Kowanyama, a better watered place beside the main
Mitchell River. As one elder put it:

Another white man came to stay, and another white man came to stay. Another
priest came to stay, and another priest came to stay. And also another time...
they came here to stay. (Minh Worrpol, in Alpher 1966)

The settlers – missionaries and graziers alike – were keen to place the
earlier period of conflict as being 'in the past' and over with. Under the
repressive Mission and pastoral regimes the Aboriginal community led
covert double lives, attending church on Sundays but taking care of their
sacred sites and conducting rituals while ostensibly working as
stockmen. They kept silent about colonial events: when Lauriston Sharp
went to Kowanyama in the 1930s he found that people were unwilling
to discuss these traumas, professing 'not to remember' events such as
the Battle of the Mitchell River (see Sharp 1952).

By the 1940s, relations between the indigenous population and the
pastoralists, though hugely unequal, had achieved some stability. There
was a period of peaceable coexistence, and this 'Golden Age' brought the
full flowering of a marvellous myth: the glorious Australian narrative
about the pioneering 'battlers' who had settled this 'untamed' country;
and the 'childlike' Aboriginal people who came to depend upon them.
The popular literature of this period abounds with uncritical stories of
life in 'the bush' (e.g. Durack 1959; Gunn 1910; Lane 1928) which
simply assume the racial and cultural superiority of the white settlers

and the rightness of their endeavour to make the land and the indigenous population productive in European terms. The violence of the earlier settlers is airbrushed from the picture. In an account of Rutland Plains written in the 1940s, Blanche Maynard describes Bowman's grave site as a shrine to the colonial enterprise:

Frank Bowman was speared by a native and died a week later on the 2nd of September 1910 from an infection in the wound in the temple made by a three inch nail on the spear. He shot the treacherous spearman who came from the nearby Trubanamen mission. This intrepid pioneer was only 45 years old at his death and sleeps beneath a headstone beside the squarecut horseyards that complement the station buildings. (Maynard 1949, Kowanyama archives)

Thus, in this written memorial, he is redefined as a classic 'lone hero', an iconic frontier figure (as defined by Rose 1992a; Slotkin 1992; Sunderland 1989). Brave and self-sufficient; able to deal with the hostile environment, he embodies the supposed virtues of the colonial enterprise: the imperial imposition of righteous capitalism in which 'might is right'. His grave site is presented as a stubborn symbol of pride and accomplishment, of a triumph not only against 'savage' people and Nature herself, but also against the alternative moral perspective offered by the missionaries, in which indigenous people were seen as souls to be saved rather than as adversaries. By the 1940s the cattle stations and mines in Cape York had prospered, providing the land-holding 'squattocracy' with some security and considerable political influence. The memorialisation of Bowman as a hero reflects this dominant voice and its particular values. In Maynard's account Inkerman appears – again – as the 'treacherous spearman', only able to bring Bowman down through covert and immoral means. The Mission is condemned in the same breath, suggesting that almost 40 years after the incident the Mission was still perceived as a subversive influence, a betrayal of the colonial endeavour.

While Bowman's grave was being valorised in the popular European media, the old Mission site at Trubanamen remained – at least to the naked eye – just a dusty abandoned place near the creek where Jimmy Inkerman 'sat down'. However, for the Aboriginal community the memories of his death were held there, invisibly, alongside the ancestral forces in the land. Relatives visiting the site would have not only called out to the ancestral beings, they would almost certainly have referred to the events which took place there, and – reflecting a practice which is still common – they may well have spoken to his ghost directly.[19] Thus although the voices telling Inkerman's story were subdued, the landscape provided an implicit memorial, articulated through ephemeral performances which served to carry his narrative forward from one generation to the next.

WINDS OF CHANGE

The 'Golden Age' of stability was short lived. In the latter half of the twentieth century Hurricane Dora swept away the palm-roofed houses in Kowanyama (in 1964), and the Anglican Church handed the community over into state care. New laws, demanding that all stock workers should be paid proper wages (Award Wages Act 1965), resulted in many cattle stations expelling the large communities of Aboriginal people who had managed to remain on their clan land by providing labour in exchange for flour, tobacco and tea. Kowanyama therefore experienced a sudden influx of people who had not been so thoroughly controlled by the Mission life, and whose traditional knowledge and practices had been less disrupted.

Further afield, the broader cultural landscape was also experiencing winds of change. In the 1960s and 1970s the Australian population enlarged, urbanised, and became more diverse. Several related movements began to gain ground: feminism, environmentalism, civil rights, land rights – movements which shared a vision of greater equality between human beings, and between humankind and its environment. Aboriginal voices began to be heard, offering less glorious memories of the colonial encounter. Dragons' teeth of doubt were sown, challenging comfortable assumptions, raising doubts about the colonial enterprise and 'revisioning' the 'official' history of Australia.

This liberalisation did not go unchallenged. Just as the missionaries had earlier discouraged Aboriginal communities from dwelling upon colonial conflicts, and dominant colonial voices had denigrated the values of the missionaries, conservative politicians and their con-stituencies (primarily the pastoral and mining groups) attempted to suppress these new threats to the status quo, denying their veracity, suggesting that they were unpatriotic, and labelling them – later – as 'black armband history'. Representational countermoves produced a rash of 'heritage sites' celebrating colonial history.[20] A prime example of these efforts is Queensland's famous 'Australian Stockman's Hall of Fame' in Longreach, conceived in 1974 and opened by the Queen in 1988.[21] (See Figure 6.2.)

This museum is a passionate homage to the 'pioneer battlers', as evidenced by the introduction on its web site:

The outback – remote, remorseless and magnificent in its magnitude – the heart of Australia. It was conquered by pioneers who gave up the comfort of coastal

Figure 6.2   The Australian Stockman's Hall of Fame in Longreach, North Queensland.

settlement to carve a new life in the unknown interior of this vast continent. The Australian Stockman's Hall of Fame is dedicated to the story of these unsung heroes, the men and women who opened up outback Australia. (Home Page)

At a local level in Cape York the representational contest also gathered force. Since the early 1980s Rutland Plains had been owned by Don MacDonald, a key figure in the conservative National Party. His managers at the station took pride in their 'battler' heritage. Julia Cannon, the manager's wife, described how her mother had written a book, *Dear Descendants*, recording her early experiences of outback life and lauding their ancestor, a well-known cattleman called Jack Makim, as a great pioneer.[22] Visitors to the station were shown Bowman's grave.[23] It was a historic site, a place worthy of mention, though with few written records the details of the events that it marked seemed to be lost in the transitions between different managers and owners.

These details were not forgotten though, in the Aboriginal oral history which had been carefully – but quietly – preserved on the other side of the station boundary. With rapidly improving transport and communication links with other communities, and access to wider media, Kowanyama was no longer so isolated. People could observe that all over Australia other Aboriginal communities were bringing their own history to the surface in stories, in songs, in art and in written work. Memories held in the land rose like an army of ancestral beings to assist Aboriginal communities in their battle for equal rights and land rights, and to assert a version of history which did not exclude their experience. Once manifested within the political landscape, this alternative history could not be readily subsumed.

By the 1980s the Aboriginal groups in Kowanyama had gained considerable self-determination,[24] and in 1987 the former Mission Reserve area was handed to the community under a Deed of Grant in Trust (DOGIT) agreement. With the help of various anthropologists, linguists and archaeologists the various language groups began to compile evidence to try to reclaim their traditional land. Places were visited systematically, and the memories held in them were opened up, spoken about and recorded. Out at Trubanamen, Jimmy Inkerman's ghost stirred and sat up.

THE SKELETON IN THE CUPBOARD

The wider political changes had a profound effect upon the position held by the pastoralists in the surrounding area. By the 1990s the cattle industry was in trouble: the crucial Mabo decision in 1992,[25] finally admitting the existence of Native Title, had placed a question mark over its tenure. It was, in any case, emasculated by increasing financial problems which threatened its survival.[26] As the political climate grew cooler towards its version of events, it became marginalised, retreating defensively towards the far right One Nation and National parties. Alternative narratives of colonisation (e.g. Layton 1989; Merlan 1978; Morphy 1993; Reynolds 1987), which considered events from an Aboriginal perspective, had tarnished the lone heroes' armour, and the huge public debate about land rights finally removed it, revealing the uglier side of conquest.

Emboldened by these events, and always cognisant of the power of narrative, people in Kowanyama began to give voice to their own history. Elders, who in the 1930s had refused to talk about traumatic events, began to speak about them more critically. Long-held feelings about the colonial process surfaced, and Bowman's and Inkerman's names began to appear with regularity in the community's self-representations as a focus for these feelings. Asked by her niece to sing a story about their country, an elderly Kunjen woman chose to sing not about her home country, or in her own language, but to offer a Kokobera song about the places where Bowman had shot Aboriginal people. Her niece translated:

Bowman used to go round killing people here, and 'nother lot from that way.... Bowman used to shoot the people down before, early days, that's what she singing, you know. Lot of people bin get shot down there. (Alma Wason, translating for Jessie Burrie, fieldnotes, Strang 1992)

Another elder, Colin Lawrence, suggested that Bowman was acting in the interests of the government, and drew a direct parallel between his depredations and the earlier massacre carried out by the Jardine brothers:

I've been told by my grandfather too. He tell me a lot.... Now a man like Bowman, you know, bin going round shooting people.... What he bin do it for, for fun?... But probably he bin sent by the Government. The Government might have sent him.... That feller he was wicked, he was a really dog. My dad, he used to tell us, he was only a boy himself, [at the] old Mission there.... Mission was already established there [at Trubanamen]. Them people too frightened to go a long way. They bin going out for that Dead Log Lagoon or whatever they call it: just out from Mission there. And this dog come riding in there and shooting them all. Some old lady – like Reggie['s] mother there – she used to tell us how that bin happening.... But not only him there, that other feller ... that Jardine feller. (Colin Lawrence, in fieldnotes, Strang)

Another elder recalled how the need to flee to the Mission forced people off the land.

Nobody living round this country now. Years back, when people used to live out in this bush.... All round there, camping round there, all out along the Alice here. People used to be all along here, camping about in the bush. But once they bin take them all back to the Mission, nobody out here now. (Victor Highbury, in fieldnotes, Strang)

His account also draws attention to the frustration people felt in being confined to the Mission, unable to move about and take care of the land. He implies that the literal killing resulted in other cultural deaths – the loss of songs and stories (*patens*) about the ancestral landscape:

Everything was dying away, paten, as soon as they put this Mission [at Trubanamen].... They pick all the young people belong to us; all us fellers too, policemen brought them down to that Mission there, that's why we stayed there now. (Victor Highbury, in fieldnotes, Strang)

In these contemporary Aboriginal discourses Bowman has therefore come to represent colonial dispossession, embodying the hegemonic appropriation of the land. He appears as a demon figure, and his description as a 'really dog' is revealing, coming from an elder whose totemic cosmology includes a story in which the ancestral Moon (Ort), assisted by a giant dog (Udh),[27] made horrific forays into the area to capture and eat its Aboriginal inhabitants. As Lefty Yam tells the story:

[Moon] he went with that dog bilong him, a big old dog, go hunting ... eating a person like you and me.... Big dog too, biiiig dog ... big as a lion, or more bigger. When he gallop, he gallop like a horse.... Find 'em [people], you know ... that dog bin find 'em.... That dog would come right here, smell them. 'Oh! Over here!' he go, and old Moon, he had to follow. (Lefty Yam, in fieldnotes, Strang)

This dog and the cannibal Moon were killed by ancestral heroes, the Two Brothers, Antujil. As Lefty put it:

Brother ... he hide there, under that tree ... that old dog won't see him now....
[Moon] keep coming this way.... They meet him with a spear too.... Killed him dead with spear. Worry about him eating all them people there. (Lefty Yam, in fieldnotes, Strang)

Thus Bowman, riding into history on his horse, is aligned with the ravening ancestral Moon and his giant dog. His narrative, which once haunted only the dispossessed local populace, has now come to haunt his successors and is used to silence them. Having kept the memories alive, members of the local Aboriginal community now throw them like symbolic spears at other groups who seek to control their land and their activities. For example, at a recent meeting between traditional landowners and the National Parks department, after listening in frustration to a long and unresolved argument about restrictions on hunting in national parks, Kunjen elder Colin Lawrence rose to his feet and pointed out succinctly that, having sent Bowman to shoot Aboriginal people previously 'like dogs', the government was now seeking to prevent the survivors from shooting so much as a wallaby for food. A stunned silence followed.

This new bluntness is indicative of some equalisation in relations between the Aboriginal community and other groups, including the local pastoralists. Always one of the most conservative stations, Rutland has found this difficult to accept. Since the early 1990s it has ceased to employ Aboriginal stockworkers from Kowanyama, preferring to bring in non-Aboriginal jackeroos and, more recently, contract musterers from further afield. Still, the pastoralists have become less sure of their totemic sites. The grave site of Frank Bowman, the man who was said to hunt Aboriginal people 'for sport', is no longer shown or visited. It has become a dusty, neglected space, overgrown with weeds. A large pigsty has been built alongside it: a foul-smelling pen, filled with ferocious squealing pigs and the stench of rotting meat and bones from the weekly 'killer'.[28] The voices which used to speak about Bowman's memorial with pride have trailed away into silence, conscious of the more critical gaze from the Aboriginal community nearby, and of the waning sympathy elsewhere.

In this way, sites such as Bowman's grave have become a much less certain identity marker for modern Australians. For the increasingly beleaguered pastoralists they now symbolise a difficult ambivalence: on the one hand a growing unease about their grandparents' role in a formerly unquestioned past; on the other a deep resistance to change, and a defiant refusal to wear the sackcloth and ashes thrust upon them by Aboriginal revelations and new interpretations of colonial history. Many still see an adversarial pioneering spirit as a laudable quality, framing the bush as a place where 'real men' can express themselves away from the strictures of civilisation, and where they can find redemption. As a former manager at Koolatah station put it:

Most fellers who work in the bush are physical, they like a challenge, the feeling of challenge, that's why they're here.... They like that adrenaline flow, and I've found some of the better blokes I've had working here ... in the cities they've had a pretty bad name, but they get out here ... and they do all right. (David Hughes, in fieldnotes, Strang)

Understandably, this confusion has produced real anger and resentment. Having been respected and admired as pioneers and battlers for much of the twentieth century, the pastoralists now feel betrayed by the defection of the mainstream towards a more liberal position, in which colonial violence is seen as shameful, and the role of the rural community commensurately reduced in status. As one put it: 'they think *we're* all myalls [rednecks]' (David Hughes, in fieldnotes, Strang).[29] Though in private the Rutland jackeroos still mutter macho jokes about 'shooting the Abos', no-one mentions Bowman, the skeleton in the family cupboard.

ANCESTRAL RE-CONNECTIONS[30]

Across the boundary, on Aboriginal land, Jimmy Inkerman's story has taken a very different trajectory. All along, of course, he has been both tragic victim and local hero, symbolic of the crushing of Aboriginal life, and its dogged regeneration. Passed down like a well-polished family heirloom, his memory has always contained these obverse aspects of Aboriginal experience: victimhood and survival; pain and pride. Until relatively recently though, this heirloom was passed quietly from hand to hand within the community, shared only with the few Europeans trusted and adopted as 'kin'. Latterly, though, Jimmy Inkerman's name has achieved iconic status. In local mythology his story now sits alongside that of the Two Brothers, Antujil, and his exploits are recounted in the same style. His grandson, Harry Daphne, tells how Inkerman fought back as the white men embarked on their shooting spree:

A few got away from Bowman and McIntyre, and my grandfather stood behind a tree and he said 'I got one special spear for Bowman. He [will] run past me here and I'll put a spear through him.' So he did, he did put a spear through him. And McIntyre looked back and he saw him [Bowman] with a spear through his brain box.... McIntyre stood behind a tree and ... shot my grandfather straight through the back of the head. (Harry Daphne in Bottoms 1992: audiotape)

In 1991 the leaders in Kowanyama decided to create a more concrete memorial to mark this event and celebrate Jimmy Inkerman's life. A plan emerged to build this at the Old Mission site, near where he was killed. Little remains of the former settlement: a small scattering of bricks, a few mature mango trees, but in an open clearing within this space, a concrete plinth was erected, and a marble plaque placed on top of it, which reads:

In memory of Jimmy Inkerman, who lived in difficult times and died for his people and country. September 1910. Erected by the people of Kowanyama, September 1991.

In 1993 the community held a formal 'opening ceremony' for the monument. This was conceived as a large public event, and was delayed several times to enable key people to attend. There was some uncertainty about it at the time, partly because it touched upon a long-held trauma, but also because it was a much more public and unequivocal statement of identity than the community had embarked upon previously. This shift towards a more European-style of representation created some ambivalence, although the creation of a memorial object resonated with customary ritual practices and material culture in which the dead were commemorated by their kin with art works (such as painted sculptures and mourning strings), body painting and songs and dances. The form of the occasion also drew upon the 'tombstone opening' ceremonies which are modern adaptations (created under missionary pressure) of these earlier mortuary rituals.

The choice of this particular form of ritual was important. Tombstone openings generally take place about a year after someone has died. They allow that person's home country, which may have been closed for some time after their death, to be properly reopened, and their name to be spoken again, and passed on to a junior relative. They mark a recapitulation of that person's life, through stories, song, music and dance depicting their ancestral connections. Crucially, they also mark an end to the most intense period of mourning: people 'cry for the body' but also find some release from their grief. So in some respects, the creation of a memorial to Jimmy Inkerman, and an 'opening ceremony' was an internal matter for the community, assisting it in coming to terms with a deeply traumatic series of historical events.

In Aboriginal terms, though, a place referring to death is not merely a site at which to mourn. After all, this is a cosmology in which identity and place are inseparable: human spiritual being emerges from a home place, onto the visible plane of life, and upon death is brought back to that place to be reunited with the ancestral forces. Sites imbued with memories of death are therefore also powerful sources of life and spiritual regeneration. Jimmy Inkerman's memorial at Trubanamen affirms the permanence of his descendants' links with that land and the collective and individual forms of identity encoded in it. In doing so, it refutes the dispossession and displacement that led to his death. Perhaps most importantly it underlines their connection with the powerful ancestral forces in the land, which embody Aboriginal cultural knowledge that defines indigenous identity. In this sense the memorial manifests and upholds customary beliefs and values in defiance of the colonial context in which they were subdued.

Thus Jimmy Inkerman's memorial is a well-honed political weapon in support of local aspirations: to gain respect for Aboriginal experience and to forward the community's aims. It is worth noting several details about this new piece of material culture. Unsurprisingly, in a society for which place is everything, its location is vital. It is not only close to where Jimmy Inkerman died, it is – though still on Reserve land – right on the Rutland boundary, almost pushing up against the fence. Second, it is on the site of the Old Mission where, according to Victor Highbury, Aboriginal culture first began to 'die away'. Third, it is beside Topsy Creek, which memorialises the baby girl who was the sole survivor of the Emu Lagoon massacre.

The form of the monument is also worth considering: a concrete pillar with a sloping top, it is somewhat phallic in shape, suggesting a homologue of the ancestral generative potency held in the land, and thus referring to the regeneration of indigenous life and culture (see Morton 1987; Strang 1999). In this contested space it stands erect, on millennia of history, a direct challenge to the colonisers who appropriated the land. The inscription is also challenging: in English, rather than Kokobera, its message is clearly directed outwards.

In effect, this is a sacred site which, like conventional totemic sites, situates the indigenous inhabitants of the landscape 'in place', spiritually, socially, economically and politically. Traditionally, the meaning of sacred sites is directed inwards, towards ever more restricted knowledge held only by Aboriginal elders: in this way these sites maintained the elders' gerontocratic powers. In the contemporary cultural landscape though, this is changing, and ancestral sites are also being used, like Jimmy Inkerman's memorial, to direct meanings outwards towards a larger political arena, thus empowering the community as a whole. Inkerman's memorial, though focused upon local history and social identity, also encapsulates a non-local, wider concept of Aboriginality linking the members of the community to an 'indigenous' identity which stretches not only across Australia, but around the world. Similarly, by commenting upon Bowman implicitly, as the cause of 'difficult times', the memorial shifts his identity from a local to a national level, so that, as well as being a local demon, he stands for the Goliath – the cannibal Moon – of colonial violence and hegemony.

In this way Jimmy Inkerman's memorial spearheaded Kowanyama's input into national discourses about colonial history, land rights and morality (see O'Hanlon and Frankland, this volume). The creation of the memorial site signalled a change which has become common in a number of the representational forms now constructed by the community (see Strang 2000). On the one hand it refers to an entire system of local knowledge and history, much of which is implicit (see Smith, this volume). In this sense its meanings are local and intimate, the deeper messages only accessible to the Aboriginal community. At the same time, however, by objectifying and reifying historical and personal experience it articulates a much more explicit message for a wider, non-local audience. Thus, in the terms of Sider and Smith (1997), it demonstrates a shift away from subversive silence and voicelessness, and offers a dissonant voice in opposition to the previously dominant ballads about European heroes and pioneers, and colonial 'heritage'. The construction of a physical memorial, like many such endeavours, manifests a particular cultural and political statement of identity.[31]

Thus the memories and meanings encoded at Trubanamen, and expressed in the material culture of the memorial, are both internal and external. The memorial upholds some of the most central continuities of Aboriginal culture – beliefs in the power of land, the ancestral forces, the embedding of personal and collective identity in place – and it also makes an explicit statement in support of these beliefs and values, setting 'traditional' and 'authentic' relations to land against 'modern' and 'imposed' settlement. It therefore asserts an indigenous prior claim to the land.

With Bowman's grave site always in metaphorical opposition, it also enters a broader discourse about environmental values. Bowman's actions were impelled by a set of ideas about land in which the goal was to mould it for economic purposes and make it 'productive and profitable' (see Strang 1997, 1998). It is an alienating, commodifying view that, like his grave site, encloses land from the outside. Today, although longer association with place has brought a much more complex array of attachments to the land, the pastoralists' economic mode still frames land as a commodity and they still talk about simply 'selling up and moving on' if the production of cattle should become non-viable for environmental, political or economic reasons.[32]

For the local Aboriginal population, under Ancestral Law, land and people are indivisible and are seen as having coexisted 'since the Story

Time'. A hunter-gatherer economic mode, though now part of a more diverse set of economic activities, still carries with it an intimacy of involvement that is reliant upon close-grained local knowledge and a long-term relationship with place. The indigenous community points to thousands of years of continuity as the foundation – and authority – for its relationship with land. This kind of permanent and intimate tie necessarily incorporates a commitment to sustainability, although Aboriginal environmental relations have only recently been articulated in these terms. The Aboriginal community, like many indigenous groups around the world,[33] now presents its land management as containing this moral superiority, and thus as having greater validity. Inkerman's memorial, by encapsulating and promulgating this environmental relationship (and implicitly critiquing the converse) therefore furthers Aboriginal interests in local, national and international debates between indigenous groups and others, about environmental values, sustainability, and the morality of commodifying land and resources.

IN MEMORIAM

To conclude: both of the memorials described here concretise the different beliefs and values of the opposing groups. Each stands for a particular interpretation of a shared history, and for the cultural identities which are emergent from this history. They represent two very different environmental relationships, and an ongoing contest about the ownership and control of the land. Their emanations of power have waxed and waned over time. For many years Bowman's grave upheld imperial assumptions. Now, though Jimmy Inkerman was unable to prevent the appropriation of his country, his descendants have called him back to take the moral high ground, empowering them to speak. Just as he stood his ground against the invaders, his memorial stands in the political landscape as a challenge to the continuing dominance of the European population and the memory and history which validates its claim to the land. Clearly his descendants hope that such symbolic spears will cause them to hesitate, to reconsider, and perhaps to offer compromise and reconciliation.

However, although the memory of Frank Bowman and his fellow colonists may be a source of shame to some Australians, a reconciliation of these two narratives is still a distant hope. There are many people, particularly in the rural community, who go to considerable lengths to preserve an unsullied vision of the 'pioneers'. To admit that the actions of people like Bowman were more than an occasional, aberrant exception would topple a central pillar in their collective identity and undermine the foundations of their own claim to the land. The High Court ruling on Native Title created a savage backlash: in the subsequent elections extremist right-wingers like Pauline Hanson were elected in Queensland, and the Howard government was elected in 1993 specifically to dismantle the Native Title Act. It has since won two subsequent re-elections.[34] One of the first moves of this Conservative-led coalition government was to make swingeing cuts in funding to Aboriginal organisations, and to the intellectual institutions which had dared to offer a revisionist history. Despite considerable public pressure from the large section of the population that is willing to reconsider Australian history, Howard has consistently refused to apologise to the Aboriginal population for any wrongdoing in the past, and, like the early missionaries, people who become involved in helping Aboriginal communities – such as anthropologists – are regularly attacked as 'bleeding-heart liberals' and 'interfering do-gooders'. Powerful interest groups have turned to the law in an attempt to silence Aboriginal voices and those of their sympathisers: for example, in the notorious Hindmarsh Bridge land claim, where a group of Aboriginal women opposed the development, the company concerned attempted to sue the anthropologist who compiled the evidence for millions of dollars. At Rutland Plains, the new manager – the son of the owner and former National Party leader – has refused to let any anthropologists onto the station to assist the local community in collating evidence for its land claim.

In the first dozen years of its life, the Stockman's Hall of Fame was visited by over 840,000 visitors, 97.5 per cent of whom were Australian. That's more than the entire indigenous population of Australia.[35] Its web site trumpets that:

Considering its remoteness from the major population centres, the popularity of the museum is a testament to the strength with which visitors relate to the Hall of Fame's theme, philosophy and aims.

In real life, the odds on Jimmy Inkerman's ghost are poor: the colonial giant may be momentarily blinded in the right eye by his spear; it may even be 'in a falling position', but it is still very much alive. For Inkerman's descendants these are still 'difficult times'.

ACKNOWLEDGEMENTS

As ever, I must begin by expressing my gratitude to all of my friends and colleagues in Kowanyama and the surrounding cattle stations for their kindness is sharing knowledge with me. In particular, I would like to thank Viv Sinnamon, who has greatly supported my research in the community, and the Rangers and other staff – Johnny Clarke, Vol Norris and Gary Drewien – in the Land Office. I would like to thank the other researchers: Bruce Sommer, Philip Hamilton, and most particularly Barry Alpher, who have kindly permitted me to draw on their records and their vastly superior linguistic skills. I also remain indebted to the late Lauriston Sharp for his generous gift of much unpublished material from his own studies of the Yir Yoront. This particular research was made possible through the support of the Royal Anthropological Institute and Goldsmiths College London, who provided funding as well as a welcoming academic community. As always, the journey through Australia has been greatly assisted by the practical help of John Trude, and the enduring friendship and support of Howard and Frances Morphy.

NOTES

1. Political tensions in the area have heightened considerably in the last decade. The present incumbents at Rutland Plains (the current manager is the son of the owner) are now intensely sensitive about their public image and their relations with the local Aboriginal community. With the additional tension produced by a land rights claim over the property, the station manager has now refused to allow access to any anthropologists or to Europeans working with the local community. It was therefore not feasible to gain permission to photograph Bowman's grave site.
2. This is a 'bush name', that is, a proper Aboriginal name, which associates its holder with a particular ancestral story. According to Alpher (1988) Ngart-YapMalmanl means 'covering up fish, hiding it in bushes'.
3. Alpher (pers. comm. 2000) divides the language groups slightly differently, into Kokoper, and then to the north, Yirrk-Mel and Yir-Yoront, and inland, Pakanh and Uw-oykangand. However, I have kept to the broader terms more commonly used in Kowanyama.
4. See Alpher (1991), Berndt (1985), Chase (1984), Durkheim (1961), Charlesworth *et al.* (1984), Morphy (1984, 1990), Myers (1986), Rose (1992b), Sharp (1937), Strang (1997).
5. Detailed accounts of local kinship and totemic organisation are provided in Sharp (1937), Thomson (1972) and Sutton (1978), although the latter deals more directly with a neighbouring community. A history and contemporary ethnography of the community in Kowanyama may be found in Strang (1997).
6. Christovão de Mendonça in 1522, Willem Jansz in 1606, Jan Carstenz in 1623, Abel Tasman in 1644, Matthew Flinders in 1802.
7. Roth (1984) notes various instances in which Aboriginal groups used terms meaning ghosts, bogeymen or corpses to describe Europeans.
8. There are various ancestral stories describing the killing of trespassers onto the land, and although there was plenty of travel and exchange between groups, this required the use of message sticks which acted as 'passports' for people travelling beyond their own country.
9. Such spearings were seen as appropriate revenge for extreme wrong-doing under the Ancestral Law which was applied equally within the Aboriginal community: for example Jack Bruno tells how when his father was speared, there was a punitive expedition: 'they avenged my father. Avenged him. They carried his grievance' (in Alpher 1966).

10. The work of linguists such as Alpher (1991), Sommer (1998) and others suggests that many inland clans were pushed westward by the colonial movement from the east.

11. An increase site may be defined as a place where the ancestral power held in the land is particularly potent. Stimulation of the site – by hitting a tree, throwing bark or dirt in a particular direction, rubbing a rock, or similar rituals – is believed to encourage the land to produce more of a particular resource. The Aboriginal name for the actual homestead at Rutland – Kan-ngar-manl – means catfish, and refers to another nearby increase place. According to the elders:

> All that fish there, you like fish ... you take the dirt around here, throw it everywhere, [you will get] all the fishes. [And] this sugarbag country, this here. They want to come here get sugarbag, they come hit this tree here ... (Banjo Patterson and Jerry Mission, fieldnotes, Strang 1993)

As Morphy (1993) points out, Europeans often took over important sites of this kind, because they tend to be particularly rich in resources – usually water, or feed – which are equally essential for humans, game and cattle.

12. This information was confided to Johnny Clarke, the Senior Ranger, but such matters are rarely discussed openly and the informant prefers to remain anonymous.

13. The use of the sea in preference to overland travel continued for some time, with the cattle stations sending oxen and drays to pick up supplies from boats, and sending cattle out on these vessels as well.

14. Although this phrase refers to the cattle 'run' its more common usage as a way of describing fugitives is interesting.

15. It seems unlikely that Bowman, with a 3-inch nail in his right temple, and 'in a falling attitude' could have fired the shot (and McIntyre himself says he took up the rifle) but, perhaps knowing that he was dying, he appears to have shouldered the responsibility to protect his stockman.

16. The 'run' is a word used for the area on which cattle have been placed. It arises from a period in which grazing land was not fenced into definable paddocks and yards.

17. A number of versions of this story have now been recorded (Alpher 1966, 1991; Sommer 1986, 1998; Strang 1997). The various historical and contemporary accounts were painstakingly archived by Viv Sinnamon, who worked in the community for many years.

18. This phrase is commonly used to describe the moment at which an ancestral being, having travelled and formed aspects of the landscape, goes back into the land to remain there as a spiritual force. It is also used to describe the death of a person, and the moment at which they too return to their home in the land, to be reunited with their ancestral totem.

19. This is common practice at important Aboriginal sites. The elders will often call out to their 'grandfathers' to let them know they are there. In several instances, when we were compiling a cultural mapping report, they also asked permission from the ancestral beings for me to take photographs for them (see Strang 1997). Visiting the mass grave at Emu Lagoon recently (2000), the Kunjen elders spoke to the dead at the site, explaining the purpose of the visit.

20. 'Heritage' is now a key buzz word, but it is a term which some writers have suggested is indicative of a population that has become insecure about its identity.

21. Conceived by an ex-stockman Hugh Sawrey in 1974, this project entailed the raising of Au$12.5 million. In 1977, 40 sites were submitted for consideration, but Longreach, an old teamster stop on a major stock route, was chosen. The Hall of Fame took ten years to complete. It received significant funding support from both state and federal governments as part of the Bicentennial Programme, and was opened by Queen Elizabeth II in 1988. Since then it has had over 840,000 visitors.

22. There are many such documents. For example, at the neighbouring station, Koolatah, the Hughes family compiled an 'album' of diaries, letters and other documents detailing their own family history on the station since 1912 (see Hughes 1989).

23. I can recall the manager of the station showing me the site with pleasure in 1982.

24. For example, some degree of local governance in the form of an elected Community Council.

25. This legal decision by the High Court ruled that Native Title to land – an indigenous system of land ownership – had, in fact, existed prior to the colonisation of Australia. In doing so, it refuted 200 years of denial. Although it also ruled that some subsequent forms of tenure extinguished Native Title, it was ambiguous about leasehold, thus raising a question over the 'ownership' rights of cattle stations and similar forms of tenure. This led to a massive political upheaval.

26. Since the first boom offered by the nineteenth-century gold rushes, the financial viability of the industry has always been tenuous, except in wartime. The land is not well suited to cattle grazing and the distance to markets is considerable.

27. The name of this giant dog actually means 'horse'.

28. The 'killer' is a beast which provides the beef ration for the station. An animal is usually shot every week during the mustering season. The pigs are fed all the unusable parts, and leftovers. It is said that 'they will eat anything, even a human being', and stockmen tell newcomers fearsome stories about how, if they are knocked unconscious from their horse, they will be eaten alive by feral pigs.

29. This has come to mean 'rednecks' in modern parlance but – as will be clear from the Inquiry reported in the 1910 *Cairns Post* – it used to refer to 'wild blacks', that is, those uncontained by mission or station life. This suggests that for some urban Australians, the intensely conservative rural groups have replaced Aboriginal people as a focus of disapproval.

30. See Morphy (1991).

31. The concretisation of identity in this kind of way is of course ubiquitous. For example, in its form, Inkerman's memorial is visually similar to Scottish, Irish and Welsh commemorative stones discussed by Strathern and Stewart (2001).

32. There are some significant problems with cattle farming in Cape York. The local ecology is in many ways quite unsuited to cattle rearing: the soils are delicate and friable, and degrade easily, the water sources are sometimes unreliable, and there are growing problems with introduced weeds such as rubber vine, feral animals (pigs) and salination due to overuse of artesian wells. Distances to markets are considerable, and many stations have 'gone under' financially in recent years.

33. This discourse about Aboriginal relations to land and sustainability has become one of the most powerful tropes for the environmental movement in many countries, and is clearly an important element in the achievement of indigenous rights (see Berglund 1998; Milton 1998, 2002; Strang 1997).

34. John Howard is only the fourth Australian Prime Minister to win three successive terms.

35. The Aboriginal population makes up roughly 2.5 per cent of the whole population of 18.5 million. Of course some of the visitors to the Hall of Fame may have been Aboriginal people, but visiting the Hall of Fame is expensive ($18) and in any case, many of its exhibits – three-dimensional 'light up' maps of explorers' routes and suchlike – may lack appeal for the local Aboriginal community.

REFERENCES

Alpher, B. (1966) 'The Bowman Story, with a Capsule History of Mitchell River Mission', by Minh-Worrpol, trans. B. Alpher. Unpublished ms.

—— (1988) 'The Bowman Story', by Koch Yawrronl, trans. B. Alpher, unpublished ms. Kowanyama Archives.

—— (1991) *Yir-Yoront Lexicon: Sketch and Dictionary of an Australian Language.* Trends in Linguistics Documentation 6. Berlin, New York: Mouton de Gruyter.

Australian Stockman's Hall of Fame, Web Site, <http://www.outbackheritage.com.au/>

Berglund, E. (1998) *Knowing Nature, Knowing Science: An Ethnography of Environmental Activism.* Knapwell, Cambridge: The White Horse Press.

Berndt, R.M. (1985) 'Identification of Deity through Land: An Australian Aboriginal Visible Religion', in *Annual for Religious Iconography*, IV–V. Leiden: E.J. Brill.

Bottoms, T. (1992) 'Introduction to Kowanyama', radio script. Kowanyama: Kowanyama Land and Natural Resources Management Office.

Cairns Post (1910) 'The Rutland Plains Tragedy', in *The Cairns Post* [newspaper] 7 October.

Charlesworth, M., H. Morphy, D. Bell and K. Maddock (1984) *Religion in Aboriginal Australia.* Queensland: University of Queensland Press.

Chase, A. (1984) 'Belonging to Country: Territory, Identity and Environment in Cape York Peninsula, Northern Australia', in L.R. Hiatt (ed.) *Aboriginal Landowners*, Oceania Monograph No. 27. Sydney: University of Sydney.

Durack, M. (1989 [1959]) *Kings in Grass Castles.* Australia: Corgi Books, Transworld Publishers.

Durkheim, E. (1961) *The Elementary Forms of Religious Life.* New York: Collier Books.

Gunn, A. (1910) *We of the Never Never.* London: Hutchinson and Co.

Hughes, R. (1989) 'Family Album of Herbert Maddock and Laura Hughes: Their Forebears, Descendants and Relations', unpublished ms. Southport, Queensland.

Lane, C.G. (1928) *Adventures in the Big Bush.* London: Hutchinson and Co.

Layton, R. (1989) *Uluru: An Aboriginal History of Ayers Rock.* Canberra: Aboriginal Studies Press.

Maynard, B. (1949) 'Rutland Plains', *Cummings and Campbells Monthly Magazine* February.

Merlan, F. (1978) '"Making People Quiet" in the Pastoral North: Reminiscences of Elsey Station', *Aboriginal History* 2: 70–106.

Milton, K. (1998) 'Nature and the Environment in Traditional Cultures', in D. Cooper and J. Palmer (eds) *Spirit of the Environment: Religion, Value and Environmental Concern.* London and New York: Routledge.

—— (2002) *Loving Nature: Towards an Ecology of the Emotions.* London, New York: Routledge.

Morphy, H. (1984) *Journey to the Crocodile's Nest.* Canberra: Australian Institute of Aboriginal Studies.

—— (1990) 'Myth, Totemism and the Creation of Clans', *Oceania* 60: 312–28.

—— (1991) *Ancestral Connections: Art and an Aboriginal System of Knowledge.* Chicago: University of Chicago Press.

—— (1993) 'Colonialism, History and the Construction of Place: The Politics of Landscape in Northern Australia', in B. Bender (ed.) *Landscape, Politics and Perspectives.* Oxford: Berg.

Morton, J. (1987) 'The Effectiveness of Totemism: Increase Rituals and Resource Control in Central Australia', *Man* 22: 453–74.

Munn, N. (1984) 'The Transformation of Subjects into Objects in Walbiri and Pitjantjat-jara Myth', in R.M. Berndt (ed.) *Australian Aboriginal Anthropology.* Nedlands: University of Western Australia Press.

Myers, F.R. (1986) *Pintupi Country, Pintupi Self.* Canberra, Washington, London: Smithsonian Institute and Australian Institute of Aboriginal Studies.

Ortner, S. (1974) 'Is Female to Male as Nature is to Culture?', in M. Rosaldson and L. Lamphere (eds) *Woman, Culture and Society.* Stanford: Stanford University Press, pp. 67–87.

Reynolds, H. (1987) *The Law of the Land*. Victoria, London, New York: Penguin.

Rose, D. (1992a) 'Nature and Gender in Outback Australia', *History and Anthropology*, 5(3–4): 403–25.

—— (1992b) *Dingo Makes Us Human: Land and Life in an Aboriginal Australian Culture*. Cambridge: Cambridge University Press.

Roth, W.E. (1984) *The Queensland Aborigines*. Sydney: Australian Museum/Hesperian Press.

Schaffer, K. (1989) *Women and the Bush: Australian National Identity and Representations of the Feminine*, Working Paper No 46, C. Bridge (series ed.). London: Sir Robert Menzies Centre for Australian Studies, Institute of Commonwealth Studies.

Sharp, L. (1937) 'The Social Anthropology of a Totemic System of North Queensland', Unpublished PhD thesis, Harvard University.

—— (1952) 'Steel Axes for Stone Age Australians', in E.H. Spicer (ed.) *Human Problems in Technological Change: a Casebook*. New York: The Russell Sage Foundation.

Sider, G. and G. Smith (eds) (1997) *Between History and Histories: The Making of Silences and Commemorations*. Toronto, Buffalo, London: University of Toronto Press.

Slotkin, R. (1992) *Gunfighter Nation: The Myth of the Frontier in Twentieth-century America*. New York, Oxford, Singapore, Sydney: Atheneum, Macmillan.

Sommer, B. (1986) 'The Bowman Incident', in L. Hercus and P. Sutton (eds) *This is What Happened: Historical Narratives by Aborigines*. Canberra: Australian Institute of Aboriginal Studies.

—— (1998) 'Kunjen: Kinship and Communication', unpublished MA thesis, Northern Territory University.

Strang, V. (1997) *Uncommon Ground: Cultural Landscapes and Environmental Values*. Oxford, New York: Berg.

—— (1998) 'Competing Perceptions of Landscape in Kowanyama, North Queensland', in P. Ucko and R. Layton (eds) *The Archaeology and Anthropology of Landscape: Shaping Your Landscape*. London: Routledge, pp. 206–18.

—— (1999) 'Familiar Forms: Homologues, Culture and Gender in Northern Australia', *Journal of the Royal Anthropological Society* March: 75–95.

—— (2000) 'Showing and Telling: Australian Land Rights and Material Moralities', *Journal of Material Culture* 5(3): 275–99.

Strathern, A. and P.J. Stewart (2001) *Minorities and Memories: Survivals and Extinctions in Scotland and Western Europe*. Durham, NC: Carolina Academic Press.

Sunderland, L. (1989) *The Fantastic Invasion: Kipling, Conrad and Lawson*. Melbourne: Melbourne University Press.

Sutton, P. (1978) 'Aboriginal Society, Territory and Language at Cape Keerweer, Cape York Peninsula, Australia', unpublished PhD Thesis, University of Queensland.

Thomson, D.F. (1972) *Kinship and Behaviour in North Queensland*. Canberra: Australian Institute of Aboriginal Studies.

7 HISTORY, MOBILITY AND LAND-USE INTERESTS OF ABORIGINES AND FARMERS IN THE EAST KIMBERLEY IN NORTH-WEST AUSTRALIA

Ruth Lane

In the East Kimberley, in north-west Australia, the development of irrigated agriculture since the 1960s has brought new groups of people with new sets of interests to the region. The recent nature of this land use forms a marked contrast with the continuity of Aboriginal land use in the region. So far, the expansion of irrigated farmlands has excluded Aborigines from country of historical and cultural significance to them. However, recent legal developments that give formal recognition to Aboriginal interests in land have the potential to impact on planning processes affecting future land use, either in maintaining separate interests for Aborigines and farmers or in promoting greater interaction between the two groups. Similar issues are likely to arise in development proposals in other parts of Australia where Aboriginal land interests have also been recognised in law.

The contrast between the development of Stage 1 of the Ord Irrigation Area in the 1960s and a proposal put forward in the late 1990s for greatly expanding the area of irrigated agriculture as Stage 2 of the scheme, highlights changes to legislation and policy that affect both farmers and Aborigines. In the government-driven planning for Ord Stage 1, Aborigines were not consulted and no assessment was made of potential environmental or ecological impacts of the scheme.[1] In 1996, the Western Australian government engaged the Wesfarmers-Marubeni Consortium to develop a proposal that would use water from the gargantuan storage dam, Lake Argyle, to transform a further 32,000 hectares of land, currently leased by pastoral companies, into intensive irrigated agriculture focused on corporate farming of sugarcane (see Figure 7.1). Both government policy and legislative frameworks of the 1990s obliged the developers to conduct an environmental impact assessment for the project. Further, a 1998 ruling by the Federal Court of Australia that Miriuwung and Gajerrong people hold native title to part of the country being proposed as the 'project area' for the Ord Stage 2 development (Federal Court of Australia 1998), required developers to negotiate with native title holders who are described as 'stakeholders' in their proposals. Two other native title claims yet to be heard, and a further claim made under the Aboriginal Land Rights Act, Northern Territory (1976), cover the remainder of the project area (see Figure 7.2).[2]

Figure 7.1   Ord River Valley looking north from Kununurra

Two different propositions were put forward for the relationship between native title holders and the project area, one by the developers in their document assessing environmental and social impacts for Ord Stage 2, and the other by the Kimberley and Northern Land Councils representing the interests of Miriuwung and Gajerrong people. The developers emphasise their desire to negotiate an Indigenous Land Use Agreement (ILUA) in which native title rights and interests over land would be surrendered in return for a benefits package. The developers consider that Aboriginal land use is incompatible with the proposed agricultural land use, and that the project area must be controlled by a single management structure representing the interests of the developers and relevant government agencies. 'Miriuwung and Gajerrong people',

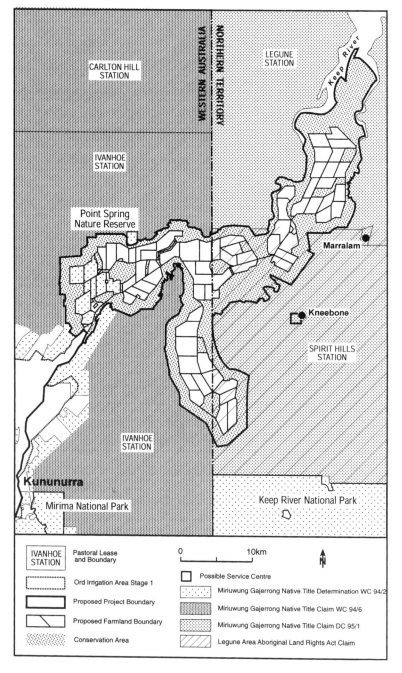

Figure 7.2   Proposed Ord Stage 2 Project Area showing Conservation Area and Aboriginal land claims

defined legally through the native title process, could continue to access areas designated as reserves for either cultural or environmental reasons. These areas would be excluded from the project area (see Figure 7.2) and would be important 'buffer zones' mediating impacts. The proposed benefits package could include:

compensation for the loss or temporary impairment of native title rights; management and protection of cultural heritage and environmental values; training and employment; establishment of business opportunities; and improving the social and economic development of Miriuwung and Gajerrong people. (Kinhill 2000: 12–18)

In their joint response to the impact assessment for Ord Stage 2, the Northern Land Council (NLC) and the Kimberley Land Council (KLC) contest the assumption of incompatibility between native title and the management of the project area and suggest an alternative approach in which Aboriginal interests are maintained throughout the project area (Table 1). Further criticism is made of plans for the role of environmental management to be vested in an authority representing only the developers and the Western Australian government. The NLC and KLC express concern that the concept of environmental management will be framed entirely in terms relating to the physical environment (NLC/KLC 2000: 10). Instead they assert the need for a more socially oriented understanding of the 'environment' of the project area, in which impacts on 'bush tucker habitats could be assessed along with the use and management of terrestrial vegetation by Aboriginal people' (NLC/KLC 2000: 31).

The developers' proposal posits different relationships with the project area for Miriuwung and Gajerrong people and for farmers that discursively frame land use interests for each. While these interests are presented as static, they nevertheless entail a particular interpretation of land use history in the region and carry implications for relations between Aborigines and farmers in the future. The developers stress the continuity of farming practices in the Ord Valley and assert that current farming practices have benefited from the experience of cotton farmers involved in the first stage of the Ord River Irrigation Area (ORIA):

ORIA Stage 1 has been operated continuously for the purpose of irrigated agriculture since 1963. Over that period, a wide range of commercial crops has been grown and farm management practice has evolved in response to the new crops, improved knowledge of local conditions, and improvements in agricultural practices generally. (Kinhill 2000: v)

However the continuity portrayed here does not entail social continuity, but rather a continuity of certain land use practices. The first farmers

Table 1   Contrast between the Wesfarmers-Marubeni proposal and an alternative model for Aboriginal involvement and land use in the Ord Stage 2 project

ERMP* perspective	Alternative approach
Native title and 'development' regarded as *incompatible* – necessitating 'voluntary surrender of native title rights and interests in the land, THEREBY enabling development to occur' ...	Native title and 'development' regarded as *compatible and coexisting* – and realized in new tenures, joint ventures or joint management arrangements
Unitary interests in land in the Project area – with the interests of the developer being paramount. Application of a Security Management Plan to prohibit unauthorized access to the project area	Recognition of a *plurality of interests* in land in the Project area and overlapping, coexisting land uses
Other interests, including indigenous and conservation interests legally *neutralized, partitioned, excised or extinguished* (via 'voluntary surrender') – in favor of *exclusive* use by developer – justified by 'need for certainty' and 'risk minimization'	Overlapping, coexisting tenures reflecting multiple rights and interests in land in the Project area
Broad-acre sugar *mono-culture* alongside partitioned or excised conservation areas linked by corridors or 'green access paths'	'Mosaic' land use maintaining *ecological diversity and connectiveness*
Local people and local ecology regarded as *potential objects or 'impactees'* of externally sourced development. A 'community consultative plan' implemented by EME to 'consult' with local people to mitigate these impacts	Local people and ecology *central* to project design, implementation, evaluation and as *major beneficiaries* of development

*   ERMP = Environmental Review and Management Programme

Source: Reproduced from the NLC and KLC report with permission.

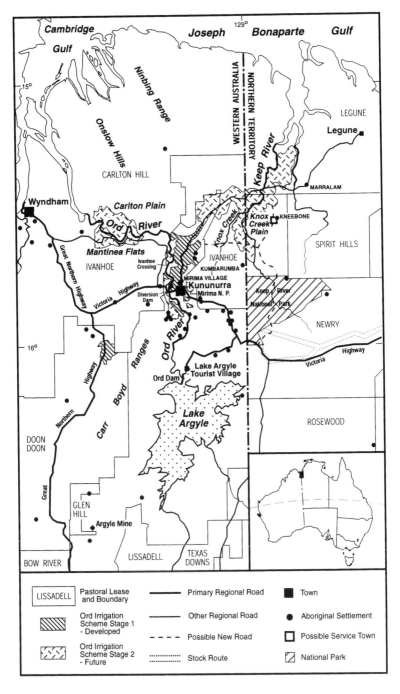

Figure 7.3   The East Kimberley region

who came to the Ord Valley in the 1960s grew cotton but, after initial optimism, were beset by a range of problems including insect and bird damage.[3] Most had deserted their farms by 1972 due to financial difficulties. The horticulturalists who arrived later to grow crops such as bananas, mangoes and melons had no prior experience with farming in the Ord Valley.

The category of 'farmer' is used in a generic sense, referring to agricultural practice rather than to specific groups of people at specific times. This allows the success of 1990s horticulturalists to be presented as evidence of the potential of the area for large-scale sugarcane farming. In the project plan, 3,000 hectares of the total of 32,000 is designated for sale to independent farmers to grow crops of their own choice. In time, the project planners anticipate that other land, initially established as corporate sugarcane plantation, will eventually be 'sold-down' to independent farmers as smaller farms (Kinhill 2000: ii). Horticulturalists currently established on lands developed in Stage 1 of the Ord scheme, are thus envisaged to have a potential future role in the Ord 2 project area.

I challenge the static representations in the developers' impact assessment by tracing changes in land use interests of Aborigines and farmers since the 1960s. My historical approach is influenced by developments in human geography which foreground place as a relational concept (Massey 'with the collective' 1999; Whatmore 1997), constructed through interactions between people and their material environment that change over time and connect the specific situation of the East Kimberley with a broader social and political environment. Since the 1960s, land use interests have changed for both Aborigines and farmers as they have engaged, in very different ways, with changes in legislation, government policy and the material environment. I concentrate specifically on mobility as an aspect of the material engagement of people with place, which visibly changes over time, and show how mobility is both an influence and an outcome of interests in land (Cresswell 2001). I then explore the responses of contemporary Aborigines and horticulturalists to the Ord Stage 2 proposal and relate these to the historical experiences of each to demonstrate the role of history and memory in contemporary land use politics.

The interplay of history, memory and land use has unfolded very differently for Aborigines and farmers since the 1960s. Whereas the mobility practised by Aboriginal people highlights continuity with past spatial practices and social identifications, mobility for farmers has ensured social discontinuity.

ABORIGINAL LAND USE INTERESTS IN THE EAST KIMBERLEY

Aboriginal Mobility During 'Station Times'

Aboriginal experiences of pastoralism, until recently the dominant land use in the East Kimberley, provide an important context for their contemporary interests in land. From 1886 a legislative framework that regulated mobility, employment and other forms of interactions with Europeans underpinned the relationship between Aborigines and pastoralists (Bolton 1981). Police collaborated with station managers to coerce Aborigines to work on stations (Rose 1991; Shaw 1981). Mobility, while constrained, endured as part of the seasonal cycles of the monsoonal climate. By the time of the Second World War, a pattern had developed of living in ration camps on pastoral stations throughout the dry part of the year and moving to bush camps during the wet season, referred to as 'holiday time'. Work on stations ceased during 'the wet' and Aborigines were required to fend for themselves in a more traditional manner.

Wet season journeys usually involved following watercourses and camping at specific waterholes, and land surrounding these paths and campsites was used intensively for bush foods. While station ration camps could include people from different language groups who may not have resided together prior to European contact (Kolig 1981: 25; Sullivan 1996: 14), the wet season became characterised by a different pattern of social relations, as family groups travelled in different directions and joined with other groups independently of those they resided with in the ration camps (FCA 1997: 4792). Because of the emphasis in native title legislation on the maintenance of traditional links with land, activities during 'holiday time' became important evidence supporting the claim.[4] Witnesses provided extensive details of the routes taken for wet season journeys and of places where different groups met up, camped for a period and performed ceremonies.[5]

In the East Kimberley, the term 'Ngarranggarni' is used to refer to dreaming stories associated with different parts of the country, which bind people in kin relationships with specific places. One man made this connection in evidence to the court when he explained that the 'skin name' that each person carries, comes 'From the mother and from the land' (FCA 1997: 1762). One ceremony associated with Argyle Station was described in more detail in the court transcripts and segments were performed for the court. It was called 'Ngalwirriwirri' and was described as a 'Joonba' ceremony. A senior Miriuwung man explained that it was 'found' by Boxer and Daylight, two Aboriginal stockmen who travelled from Queensland with the Durack family in 1885 and subsequently held key roles in supervising stock work at Argyle Station (FCA 1997: 954). The ceremony refers to the waterhole on the Behn River called Ngal-wirriwirri, upstream from the old Argyle Station homestead at a site now flooded by the Argyle Dam. Marjorie Brown described some of its content, which included references to Aboriginal people in chains at the courthouse in Wyndham and other events and places associated with intercultural experiences. It was presented to the court as an Aboriginal record of East Kimberley history. Although the ceremony is clearly owned by Miriuwung and Gajerrong people and concerns places in their traditional country, neither Boxer nor Daylight who were referred to as having 'found' it, were Miriuwung or Gajerrong people themselves. The cultural ties between place and people contain the flexibility to accommodate new people and new experiences.

The country in the immediate vicinity of Kununurra contains a number of significant sites for Miriuwung people. The stretch of the Ord River between Carlton Hill Station, Ivanhoe Station and Argyle Station was well traversed every wet season during the station times, and the river and its tributaries provided fishing and hunting grounds as well as a wide range of plant foods. People working at Ivanhoe Station lived in the ration camp at Ivanhoe billabong and made extensive use of the resources of this stretch of the Ord River. During the wet season, groups of people travelled to Ivanhoe from surrounding stations for ceremonies and camped at Ivanhoe Crossing.

Coming in to Kununurra

In the 1960s, changes occurred in pastoral practices: The introduction of helicopter mustering reduced the need for stockmen, and compulsory award wages meant that station managers were required to pay Aborigines the same wages as white stockmen. As a consequence, they dismissed the extended family groups residing in ration camps and retained only a few skilled stockmen.[6] In the early 1960s Aborigines began leaving the stations and moving into Kununurra, lured in part by access to work on cotton farms and construction work in the new town. Employment on cotton farms was seasonal, with most of the weeding required at the end of the wet season in February and coinciding with the station lay-off (Willis 1980: 19).[7] The extension of social security benefits to Aborigines in 1960 also influenced residence and mobility (Sullivan 1996: 8; Williams and Kirkby 1989: 16–17). Many of those who had worked for rations on stations became unemployed and dependent on social security payments administered by government officers in Kununurra.[8] While men found employment on farms or in the new town, employment of Aboriginal women during this period diminished.[9] Bill Lawrie, an Aboriginal man interviewed by Shaw in the 1970s, compared the work on cotton farms unfavourably with the cattle work with which he was more familiar: 'I used to follow up this cattle game all my life and enjoy it for everything. That was our life' (Shaw 1992: 95). While some men maintained a degree of mobility between Kununurra and the stations through continued casual employment, women's access to pastoral lands was greatly reduced.

Witnesses to the 1997 native title hearings described how they first lived in canvas shelters beside Lily Creek near the town centre, but moved to the reserve area when it was designated in 1963.[10] One woman recalled that during the early years in Kununurra they hunted and fished at the Junction and Lily Creek (FCA 1997: 3387). Another woman described hunting around Ivanhoe Crossing and at Mirima. She explained that they used to fish in the river before there were farms at Packsaddle but stopped that after the creation of farms prevented access to this section of the river (FCA 1997: 2559–69). Prior to the construction of the Diversion Dam, a stretch of the Ord River known as Jalinem, which had sand banks and a billabong, was a favoured fishing spot (FCA 1997: 3887). It is clear that throughout the 1960s, as Aboriginal people moved into Kununurra, bush foods and other resources were obtained in the surrounding land. However these activities were increasingly curtailed by expanding farmlands, and favoured fishing sites were flooded by the construction of the Diversion Dam in 1963.

The 1990s – Outstations, Land Rights and Self-Determination

Mobility of Aboriginal people in the 1990s displayed different patterns to that of the 1960s. I concentrate here on two different forms of mobility, one associated with family groups living on outstations and another associated with large groups attending ceremonies and meetings. Together, they help to illustrate some significant changes since the 1960s.

Exclusions from pastoral leasehold lands, the sites of places important for traditional cultural connections and for recent social memory, were and are greatly resented by Aboriginal people. In the 1970s and early 1980s, a strong movement developed to obtain living areas on traditional country for 'outstations', also known as 'community living areas'.[11] With the passage of the Aboriginal Land Rights Act, Northern Territory (1976) there was also political value in demonstrating ownership and continuing interest in land (House of Representatives Standing Committee on Aboriginal Affairs 1987: 16–17). Groups began camping on traditional land from around 1980 and, after often lengthy negotiations with government authorities and pastoral leaseholders, came to hold leasehold tenure to small living areas, forming excisions within existing pastoral leases. Prior to native title, a range of options was available to Aboriginal people in the Northern Territory to obtain access to traditional lands (Head and Fullagar 1991).[12] However access to land was much more difficult for those residing on the Western Australian side of the border. Many of the claimants to land in Western Australia who gave evidence in the 1997 native title hearings spoke of their aspirations for obtaining living areas and clearly hoped that native title would assist them. To the south of Kununurra, Aboriginal communities have acquired leases to several large pastoral stations on traditional land.

Outstations in the 1990s were frequently located at the site of old station ration camps, stock camps or wet season camps (see Figure 7.1), on land that held many memories for older residents. Marralam Outstation, for example, was formed by families who lived on Legune Station and worked there for rations between the 1950s and the 1970s (Head 1994: 179). A social identity embedded in land, kin relations, memory and cultural knowledge, linked outstation groups with the ration camps from the station times (Sullivan 1996: 13–14).[13] Although usually encompassing no more than a few hectares, the presence of outstations introduces new forms of mobility. In a detailed analysis of the significance of bush foods in the economy of the Marralam Outstation in the Northern Territory in 1990, Head and Fullagar (1991) recorded extensive mobility in hunting and gathering activities on the neighbouring pastoral leasehold lands, noting the influence of access to vehicles, the location of roads and fences, and the attitudes of station managers. However, Sullivan (1996: 29) comments on the severe restrictions on Aboriginal access to pastoral leasehold lands in Western Australia, which lacks a legislated basis for land rights. The extent of mobility between outstations and Kununurra is influenced by a range of factors, including access to vehicles, medical needs associated with poor health status, and requirements that children attend school (Head and Fullagar 1991; Sullivan 1996: 28). Shop foods remained important. At Marralam Outstation, a commercial-sized freezer room allowed storage of both shop foods and animal carcasses, reducing the need for frequent trips to town.

When asked in the native title hearings about their reasons for wanting to live on outstations, most witnesses framed these in terms of protecting children from troubles associated with alcohol consumption in the town, the desire to pass on traditional knowledge to younger generations, and to provide children with a sense of purpose and economic self-sufficiency. One woman outlined the connections between visiting traditional lands, eating traditional foods and spiritual well-being. Her work for the Gawooleng Yawoodeng women's cooperative involved driving elderly women, confined to living in town for health reasons, around their traditional country to get bush foods:

A lot of these old people are getting really old now and they need to see a lot of their country before they die, and plus they go back to country and eat bush tucker; it gives them strength; it's like medicine to them. (FCA 1997: 2782)

The language of nurturing, preservation and protection was used to describe the connections between older generations, younger generations, Ngarranggarni stories and the country that both the people and the cultural traditions relate to. The older generation was keen that their children learn how to sustain themselves in the bush, indicating a strong scepticism about reliance on a cash-based economy.[14]

Unlike the 1960s, when many Aboriginal men worked on cotton farms, few have sought employment in the horticultural ventures of the 1980s and 1990s. The policy shift to self-determination allowed alternatives for economic survival outside mainstream employment, although often at odds with other policies aimed at promoting the absorption of Aboriginal people into paid employment (Altman and Taylor 1987). My own observations from fieldwork at the Marralam Outstation in 1998 confirmed the importance of outstations for health, alcohol rehabilitation and access to bush foods.[15] Biddy Simon, a diabetic herself, constantly asserted the healthy qualities of bush foods as opposed to town foods and drinking water. The educational requirements of children played a critical role in determining who could stay living at Marralam. There was a constant quest for qualified teachers prepared to live at Marralam to conduct a school there.[16] Without a teacher, families with school-age children were obliged to move back into town. The establishment of the Marralam Alcohol Education Centre in 1995 brought additional resources in the form of accommodation and professional assistance for clients and their relatives. Sales of arts and crafts provided further income, and researchers too contributed by paying rent for accommodation and fees for assistance with work in the surrounding country.

Another form of mobility of Aboriginal people that changed between the 1960s and 1990s was that of ceremonies and meetings. During the 1970s more expansive social networks developed among Aboriginal communities throughout northern and central Australia, facilitated in part by access to vehicles (Akerman 1980). Kolig (1981: 49–50) describes increasing geographic and social inclusiveness of religious activity in the Kimberley, with people travelling much greater distances by road to attend major events. Sullivan describes the development of the 'bush meeting' from the early 1970s as a new form of cultural practice promoted by the newly formed Kimberley Land Council that combines Aboriginal and European elements (Sullivan 1996: 106–7). Kimberley Land Council meetings are usually held on the traditional land of a host community and those attending from distant places may travel for up to three days to get there. Sullivan comments on the social and cultural significance of the 'sudden and regional mobilisation', in which the journey itself may take longer than the meeting. In explaining the expansion of the catchment of initiation ceremonies in Central Australia at the same time, Peterson (2000) makes an additional point that government-inspired regional meetings for policy issues and for major sporting events also played a role in expanding the social networks that could be drawn on for ceremonies.[17]

In the Miriuwung and Gajerrong native title hearings, senior Miriuwung women described how, for a period after they were forced off the stations and moved into Kununurra, no women's ceremonies were held locally. During this time they travelled to Turkey Creek, Christmas Creek and Mulan for ceremonies. Later, they began holding ceremonies at Migeme near Kununurra, a place where people from Carlton and Ivanhoe Stations used to camp during holiday time (FCA 1997: 4037–8). In the native title hearings a video was presented showing a large women's ceremony held there recently, for which women had travelled from Ringer Soak, Malan, Balgo, Turkey Creek, Kununurra, Timber Creek, Fitzroy Crossing, Kildurk and Yuendumu (FCA 1997: 4027). Young and Doohan (1989) describe the development of large women's ceremonies such as this across northern and central Australia during the 1980s.[18]

Ceremony places near Kununurra have gained in importance because of increased use. Other places, which were important during the station times, are no longer used. Change is also occurring in the social dynamics associated with ceremonial practice, reflecting changes to residential patterns and mobility since the station times. Road networks and access to vehicles clearly contribute to this story, as does the removal of legal constraints on Aboriginal movement along with increased access to cash.[19] Consultative processes such as the 1997 native title hearings and those associated with the Ord Stage 2 proposal also involved travel, contributing yet another form of mobility focused on traditional country.

Summary

Aboriginal people's mobility has increased significantly since the 1960s, both within the East Kimberley region, as demonstrated by the movement of people from towns to outstations, and between the East Kimberley and other regions, as indicated by the size of social groupings that come together for ceremony and in the distances that people travel. They have been facilitated by access to vehicles and cash. However the pattern of this mobility is primarily one of travel between Aboriginal settlements and Kununurra. In Western Australia, traditional lands are largely closed to Aboriginal people, whereas Aboriginal people with traditional lands in the Northern Territory stand a better chance of negotiating access due to stronger legal recognition of land rights.

ORD VALLEY FARMERS

The 1960s – the First Farmers

A documentary film made by the Australian Broadcasting Commission in 1962 projected a new rhetoric for the East Kimberley in which the Ord Valley formed a discrete region where modernisation and scientific progress would support a new generation of pioneers, distinguishing it from the 'old north' associated with the pioneers of the pastoral industry. In this rhetoric, a new history was to begin for the region along with the first farmers to arrive in the Ord Valley.

Only a handful of the farmers who came to the Ord to farm in the 1960s remained in the area in the late 1990s. In 1998 and 1999 I recorded interviews with three women who came to the Ord in the early 1960s with their farmer husbands from wheat-growing and sheep-rearing areas of south-eastern Australia.[20] Unlike the majority of 1960s farmers, they continued to identify the region as their home despite sometimes lengthy periods away in the cities of the south. For Di Oliver, Barbara Dickey and Rosalie Hamilton, the Ord Irrigation Scheme offered a unique opportunity to carve out new lives for themselves and their families. They identified themselves as 'pioneers', related memories of their first epic journey to Kununurra in the early 1960s, and described the hardships of the early years with a sense of pride and humour.

A film produced by the Western Australian Department of Industrial Development to promote the Ord Scheme conveys the instrumental approach taken by government planners to social and economic objectives for the region:

Kununurra is a new concept of living in the north, planned as a key feature of the Ord Project. The basic idea is simple – instead of living on their properties the farmers will live in town. Thus a community is formed. A community that can be served economically with electric power, with water, with good roads and public services. Secondary industry can also begin, construction materials can be made, and farm products processed. Already a cotton ginnery is being established. (WADID 1963)

It is clear that the design and layout of the residences within the town and their relationship to the farmlands enshrined social divisions. A common theme among the farming community was frustration with a planning decision that prevented the construction of residences on the farms. Rosalie Hamilton explained that one of the main reasons for this was official concern about the possible health effects of chemical sprays used on the farms. The policy, however, served to exaggerate the division between the domestic lives of women in the town and the working lives of men on the farms. The women wanted more involvement with the farm and their husbands' working lives but felt they had no capacity to influence decisions made by government planners. It introduced a pattern of daily mobility as farmers drove from their houses in town to their farms every morning and returned every evening. The instrumental approach to planning extended to the agricultural areas too. The Western Australian government advised new farmers to grow cotton, with financial incentives provided by a Commonwealth government bounty (Graham-Taylor 1982).

The women I interviewed described a strong social division between the farmers and the government officials, especially those employed by the Public Works Department. Farmers resented the subsidies that government employees received and commented on the high turnover among this sector of Kununurra's population. The farmers from this period identified themselves as the ones who added value to the community in contrast with short-term government employees who they considered exploited it. As Di Oliver put it:

And I think we were farming the place, we were just doing it. Whereas the other people who were here, the Public Servants came and went. They came in, schools had to be filled or hospital ... came and went, came and went. Whereas we were here forever and I don't think there was the assistance given in those early days, to the farmers, that we needed. (interview Kununurra, June 1999)

The 'assistance' she referred to took the form of special allowances such as those for air conditioning and travel.[21] Similar tensions were revealed in criticisms made of the research agenda pursued by government agricultural scientists at the Kimberley Research Station. Farmers interviewed by Bruce Shaw in 1970 felt that the scientists were no more knowledgeable about what crops were viable than they were themselves. Instead of scientific research, they stressed the need for continuity of farming over time and an accumulation of knowledge among farmers in the Ord (interview with Pat Ryan, Kununurra 1970).

Interactions with Aboriginal people took place around the school, and on the farms, but the town precinct seems to have been experienced as a predominantly white environment. Barbara Dickey reflected on this:

Um, one of ... the things ... thinking back, that I notice now, is that within the town area, I can't remember seeing Aboriginal people very often. And as over the years they've come into town, that's quite a change now, to have them, to see lots of Aboriginal people in the town. (interview Kununurra, November 1998)

With the creation of Mirima Reserve in 1963 Aboriginal people living at Lily Creek, near the town centre, relocated to the outskirts of town where they were less visible. Di Oliver recalled that her husband employed Aboriginal men who resided at the reserve to pick weeds on their farm:

And so Ian would go out very early in the morning and go to the reserve. There was a reserve here in those days. Collect them, put them in the back of the truck. Go out, make a big fire, cook them a great, big mess of baked beans and hot tea and fresh bread. He'd collect fresh bread from the bakery. Give them breakfast then they would go and chip at the farm. Old Alfie Deakin – oh lots of – George Brumby. Lots of these old, Aboriginals worked out there. All men used to work out there.... And then when cotton finished, well we didn't use them any more. (interview Kununurra, June 1999)

By the early 1970s, the long-term pattern of mobility among farmers was that of leaving the region altogether as their cotton farms failed. Di Oliver recalled that she and her family experienced this period as a social trauma and discontinuity as their closest friends left the region. New arrivals at that time were more likely to be government employees on two-year contracts. Some of the cotton farmers who did stay, such as Barbara and Carold Dickey, left farming for other businesses in the town.

The 1990s Horticulturalists – Social Identity and Mobility

Most of the horticulturalists, who were the majority of farmers in the Ord Valley in the 1990s, arrived after 1980. They had some experience of farming in very different environments in southern Australia. Like the cotton farmers of the 1960s, they tended to be nuclear families whose relatives lived thousands of kilometres away in the south of the continent. However, unlike the cotton farmers, they resided in houses on their farms and husbands and wives frequently operated as business partners. In the 1990s women were prominent in horticultural growers' associations in the Ord Valley. While the Ord River District Co-operative played a significant role in marketing produce from the region, many individual growers had identified niche markets and transport methods for their own produce (Agriculture Western Australian 1997). This task involved travel both within Australia and to south-east Asia, networks among growers and marketing organisations and extensive use of communications technology.

In November 1998 I interviewed Spike Dessert, a seed grower associated with a large agribusiness based in the United States, and in March 1999 I interviewed three horticulturalists who were active in growers associations in the Ord Valley, Elaine Gardiner, Jill Parker and John Mack. The prime attraction of the East Kimberley for these people was the availability of water suitable for irrigation. Jill Parker explained that it was the aesthetic qualities of the vast expanses of water in an otherwise arid landscape, and what that symbolised in terms of irrigation potential, that motivated her and her husband to move to the region:

The water. It was just – you come over that diversion dam after driving from Broome, or from Port Hedland even and the water's stunning. You just realise that huge scope of being able to irrigate land with that much water. So that was the main issue. Um ... anyhow it was nice. We enjoyed ourselves, we had a good holiday here and it was an environment that we thought we could live in. I don't think we anticipated how hot it was going to get. But yes, mostly you'd just say the water. (interview Kununurra, March 1999)

Social identifications and values were articulated most clearly when farmers contrasted their own approach to farming with that of past land use. Elaine Gardiner and Spike Dessert emphasised the poverty of the grazing lands as they existed prior to irrigation farming. They regarded their cropping activities as more sustainable than grazing, and a more productive use of the land based on a much greater investment in labour and infrastructure. Elaine Gardiner expressed a pragmatic view of the history of land use and management:

Realistically, I think a lot of this country probably shouldn't have ever been settled because it's very delicate, very fragile country. But having said that, the change has already occurred so now, in our time, in our life-time, I think the best thing that we can do now, is to manage the change as well as we can. And make sure that it doesn't either get worse if that's the way you perceive the change or – and try and – or sort of keep the status quo. (interview Kununurra, March 1999)

Spike Dessert, who came to the Ord Valley in 1973 described changes along the river since he first arrived in the area, noting that there was very little vegetation along the river bank in 1973 whereas in the late 1990s there were more trees and Cumbungi and the river was much more narrow. He thought that the Ord River was beginning to resemble the lower Colorado River in southern California:

They look very, very, similar – except the trees are bigger here. But similarities is – like, the Colorado River has been turned – there is no longer big floods that wash out the trees and the channels and stuff, and the Cumbungi, to flush the river out. (interview Kununurra, November 1998)

However farmers generally viewed the damming of the rivers and associated changes as improvements, making the country of the Ord Valley more aesthetic, useable and accessible.

The 1990s farmers distanced themselves from the cotton farmers of the 1960s. Spike Dessert and John Mack both felt strongly that government subsidies for cotton in the 1960s had worked against farmers making long-term investments in the Ord Valley and taking their own initiatives in experimenting with different crops. They considered that the policy of encouraging a single crop, or monoculture, was the key reason for failure. John Mack (see Figure 7.4) attributed the difference between 1990s farmers and those of the 1960s to the removal of government subsidies:

One, the West Australian Government said: 'No more white elephants, no more subsidies.' And a lot of the smart but albeit lazy farmers that were up here playing around but making a good living out of collecting government subsidies, pissed off. And smart farmers came in who saw good soils, excellent access to very high quality water, potential to grow out-of-season crops. (interview Kununurra, March 1999)

While the arguments different farmers made about the failure of cotton varied in the way they ascribed blame to government authorities, they all featured a narrative critical of those who only planned to stay in the region for a short time and asserted the importance of longer-term commitments. Jill Parker described the need for longer-term experience in farming in the region:

And I think probably one of the biggest things is experience. No one up here has long-term experience, so you're all newcomers. I mean even the oldest farmers have only been doing it for 20 years. And then it varies from different soil types because you've got the clays, the levee soils, the black soils, the sand, and everything is a different story. (interview Kununurra, March 1999)

Farmers highlighted the different time scales needed for the establishment of different crops and for the development of markets. John Mack outlined a ten-year time frame for trialling new root stocks for citrus trees (interview Kununurra, March 1999). Elaine Gardiner contrasted the time frame for farming bananas, which are a perennial crop, with that of melons:

Rockmelons, if you have a problem with the crop you can plough it in. You lose money but you can plough it in. You can plough bananas in but your whole

Figure 7.4   John Mack, horticulturalist

irrigation infrastructure and things like that – and it takes 12 months for [a] banana plant to produce, whereas a rockmelon takes 9 to 12 weeks. So, realistically a lot of us in bananas are keen to stay in bananas. Those in melons, they think we're all mad, so you know [laughter]. And you can't jump in and out of bananas because of the infrastructure that we have to have in place, for the irrigation. Whereas you can jump in and out of other crops. (interview Kununurra, March 1999)

Her comments indicate how specific land use interests could develop in association with the cultivation of particular crops.

Whereas farmers in the 1960s had relied on Aboriginal men for seasonal labour, the horticulturalists of the 1990s relied on backpacking tourists. Elaine Gardiner explained that the itinerant nature of this labour force worked against the development of skills and productivity:

To get a good banana packer, it'll take you maybe two or three weeks to get them packing – bring some speed and then they leave within some six weeks after that. So, it's really not a good system. (interview Kununurra, March 1999)

However Jill Parker explained that she had advertised for fruit packers in the local paper and had no response from local people. Neither Aborigines nor resident whites appeared interested in undertaking physically demanding work in often-extreme climatic conditions for low pay. Some of the backpacking tourists I encountered in Kununurra explained that they were prepared to undertake hard work for low pay because they had no legal work permit.

Horticulturalists saw themselves as having a capacity to learn about and adapt to both the land and fluctuating markets, due to the small scale of their farming enterprises. Because of their personal investment they had strong motivations for making their farms profitable. If one crop or variety failed they could cut their losses and try something else. They attributed the success of the Ord Valley farming in the 1990s to crop diversity. Their self-identification as innovators and the values they placed on crop diversity were reinforced in a 1997 promotional brochure produced by the Western Australian Department of Agriculture to encourage more farmers to move to the Ord. It stated that 'The success of the ORIA relies on the production of high-value niche markets, on diversity rather than monoculture' (Agriculture Western Australia 1997: 17).

Summary

Farmers who arrived in the Ord Valley in the 1960s saw themselves as establishing a new frontier, with all its implications of restarting history from 'Year Zero' (Rose 1997). Mobility took the form of travelling to Kununurra from southern Australia, and later leaving to return to the south. The spatial practice of daily life was dominated by journeys between the town and the farms. Despite asserting the need for social continuity, they failed to achieve it. Those who did stay identified as battlers and criticised decisions of government planners that imposed social divisions that were unwelcome, and promoted crops that failed.

The most striking aspect of social identifications among 1990s horti-culturalists was the extent to which they distanced themselves and their farming practices from cotton farmers of the 1960s. By contrast, they presented themselves as smart, efficient, flexible, entrepreneurial and environmentally responsible. Horticulturalists arrived with land use interests they had developed in other farming areas and adapted these to the new circumstances they experienced in the Ord Valley. While their relationship to land was founded primarily on the requirements of commercial productivity, they linked this productivity to a concept of good environmental management. Their aesthetic appreciation of the East Kimberley environment was vested in the presence of water and its potential for future productivity. While horticulturalists stressed the importance of social continuity for the development of both crops and markets, the continuity they envisaged began and ended with their own working lives, as they expected their children would leave the region and find work elsewhere.

RESPONSES TO ORD STAGE 2

Aborigines

Aboriginal sentiments about the Ord Stage 2 proposal were clearly influenced by their experience of the first stage of the Ord Irrigation Scheme.[22] Older people still grieved for the loss of land associated with the flooding of Lake Argyle.[23] Witnesses in the native title hearings expressed concern about the impacts of the existing irrigation area on fish and vegetation along the Ord River.[24] One senior Miriuwung woman was particularly concerned about recent fish kills resulting from farm runoff carrying endosulphin pesticide. She explained that she now only fishes in the Ord River upstream of the channels that drain the farmlands. In a 1999 documentary film, Ben Ward described damaging ecological consequences of the damming of the Ord River:

Before, this river used to flood right over on top of all these banks and by [the time] the dry season come, all this'd be lush and green and new topsoils and everything you know, and a lawn'd grow here. Look at it now. It's all dying. There's no space. Look at the weeds behind you. They're all dying because everything's cramped up. See this bloke [his young son], when he grows a bit bigger, might come down here to do fishing. Where the hell he's gonna go? (Hughes 1999)

People referred to the growth along the water's edge as 'rubbish', explaining that it hindered fishing and made the risk of crocodile attack much greater. The same changes that were critical in attracting horti-culturalists to the East Kimberley were perceived by Aboriginal people to be detrimental to the resources of the river and restricting of their access to it.

Some responses to the Ord Stage 2 proposal suggested a scepticism that decisions would be made regardless of Aboriginal interests, in line with

Figure 7.5   Bush meeting of Miriuwung women convened by the Northern Land Council to discuss the Ord Stage 2 proposal

past experience. Biddy Simon intimated that if the development did take place, she would claim significant compensation for loss of bush foods near Marralam Outstation. Some younger women expressed interest in proposals for new roads to service the new irrigation areas, as these could assist their own access to land. However, one senior woman was concerned that new farms would exclude Aboriginal people from their country. Another Miriuwung woman with traditional responsibility for land proposed for the Ord 2 development, voiced a particular concern that the proposed farms could disturb the habitat for a particular frog, which in Ngaranggarrni stories is responsible for making it rain. Ben Ward was concerned about the potential for silting of watercourses and salinity caused by rising water tables. However, he also flagged the possibility that his children might one day work on farms.[25]

Aboriginal people contrast their continuing land use interests with the transient history of farmers in the East Kimberley, and of non-Aborigines generally. As Ben Ward expressed it:

We live here. I don't go to England. I don't go to any other country. We live right here. This is where we belong, here. And this is where my kids are gonna be. (Hughes 1999)

Terms such as 'sustainability', central to the rhetoric of contemporary environmental impact assessments, have a very different meaning for

Aboriginal people. For them, environmental issues and social issues cannot be addressed separately.

Horticulturalists

While some horticulturalists I spoke with expressed concern about the prospect of Ord Stage 2 developing as a large corporate sugar plantation, all were interested in the potential of the proposed new farming areas to increase economies of scale for horticultural produce. Jill Parker and Elaine Gardiner both expressed concerns about a sugarcane monoculture in the context of Ord Stage 2, referring to the disastrous history of cotton monoculture in the 1960s and 1970s. Jill Parker articulated her concerns primarily in terms of vulnerability to market fluctuations (interview Kununurra, March 1999). Apart from the issue of a monoculture, they worried about their capacity to purchase land in the new irrigation areas. These concerns were voiced at a public meeting addressed by the Wesfarmers project manager in August 1998 (*Kimberley Echo*, 3 September 1998: 3). The project manager explained that this strategy was considered necessary to establish the project economics but stressed that some blocks would be available for independent farmers and that the farm design would allow for future subdivision and sell-off.

John Mack was generally positive about the Ord 2 development and confident that land would be released for horticultural blocks. However he was closely scrutinising proposals relating to use of irrigation water and remained wary of the concept of large-scale corporate farming in the region:

Unlike here on a lot of the M-2 [the proposed new channel to service a new irrigation area on the flood plain of the lower Keep River to the east], they've got salt. So rising ground water would be a really significant problem out there, because it will bring up salt. So they're looking at alternative types of irrigation, that minimise that impact. And I – I can't say that I'm ecstatically happy about the idea of a super mill. Um, or any large corporate farm on that sort of a scale, taking up 80 or 85 per cent of the land, albeit – maybe for five or ten years, until they've recouped their capital. I just have some concerns. (interview Kununurra, March 1999)

Elaine Gardiner took a pragmatic view of land use planning issues in the Valley, asserting the need to keep a focus on the existing farms rather than directing all planning efforts to Ord Stage 2. She was mainly concerned that care was exercised in allocating water to the irrigation areas and environmental changes were monitored.

While many local businesses in the Ord Valley, including orchards, registered formal opposition to the native title claim (FCA 1997), the farmers I interviewed seemed most concerned about the impasse on buying and selling land that was attributed to the legal deliberations. John Mack did not think native title was likely to be a major influence on land development in the future, although he thought it could slow down the development of Ord Stage 2.

CONCLUSION

A subtext to any comparison between people traditionally associated with a hunter-gatherer subsistence and agriculturists is inevitably an engagement with an intellectual history which has portrayed one as static and primitive and the other as dynamic and modern (Attwood 1996; Beckett 1988; Head 2000). This legacy is evident in planning processes for Ord Stage 2 and is to some extent reinforced by the legal concept of native title.[26] It is only by asserting continuities with traditional land use practices through the native title process that Miriuwung and Gajerrong people have acquired a legal and political interest in land. This interest brings with it the right to be consulted about land use change and a platform from which to express ongoing interests in land. It offers a 'power to define' (Anderson 1986; Mitchell 1993) interests in land, provided that these interests fit with social identifications acknowledged in the native title process. For farmers, on the other hand, social discontinuity has prevented an accumulation of memory and experience. New land use interests are constructed for successive generations of farmers that are more closely aligned with generic farming practices than with specific engagements with the East Kimberley environment.

The history of relations between Aborigines and farmers in the East Kimberley has largely been characterised by exclusions, and the developers' preferred model for negotiating a surrender of native title rights in the project area would continue this tradition. In legislation and policy frameworks for environmental impact assessment in the 1990s, 'environment' is discursively framed as external to human subjectivity. Given the nature/culture binary thus engaged (Proctor and Pincetl 1996), it is hardly surprising to find a lack of fit between the framework for environmental impact assessment and the approaches suggested by the NLC and KLC for incorporating social and cultural values of the land for Miriuwung and Gajerrong people.[27]

There are some parallels between the Ord Stage 2 proposal and instrumentalist approaches to agricultural planning in the 1960s, although the 1960s rhetoric of modernisation has been replaced by one of economic and environmental sustainability. A new geographical entity 'the Project Area' would be excised from the surrounding country and managed according to scientifically informed guidelines for sustainability. Unlike Miriuwung and Gajerrong people, horticulturalists are envisaged as owning land within the project area in the future, bringing with them a diversification of land use and ownership and potentially a new set of social relations. Their self-identification as entrepreneurial, efficient and environmentally conscious, and the commercial basis of their relationship to land clearly fit more closely with the concept of the project area than does the land use interest of Miriuwung and Gajerrong people validated by native title. The link they make between aesthetics and commercial productivity strengthens their position in a political economy that links economic with environmental sustainability. For Aborigines, whose lives, and those of their children, are bound up with the longer-term future of land use in the East Kimberley, sustainability must be also be socially grounded. The extent to which native title and contemporary land use planning processes allow 'a progressive sense of place' (Massey 1993) to develop that allows engagements between Aborigines and farmers in land use practices in the future remains to be seen.

ACKNOWLEDGEMENTS

I would like to thank the following people for their comments on drafts of this chapter: the volume editors – Pamela Stewart and Andrew Strathern, and also Lesley Head, Gordon Waitt, Tim Rowse, Yasmine Musharbash, Patrick Sullivan and Ingereth Macfarlane. Further thanks must be extended to those people in the East Kimberley who gave their time to speak with me during the course of my fieldwork. The Northern Land Council and the Kimberley Land Council gave permission to cite from their unpublished report. Bruce Shaw generously made available his notes from interviews recorded with farmers in 1970 as part of his PhD dissertation (Shaw 1974). My research was supported by the School of Geosciences at the University of Wollongong as part of a PhD candidature.

NOTES

1. Attention was drawn to both these issues in a 1979 *Joint Commonwealth and Western Australian Review* of the Ord River Irrigation Area (Young 1979).
2. In December 2001, the Wesfarmers-Marubeni Consortium announced that it was abandoning plans for the Ord Stage 2 development due to low sugar prices in inter-

national markets. However, the issues raised by their planning and impact assessment process are likely to affect any future proposals for agricultural expansion in the region.

3. The Ord River Irrigation Scheme was conceived in the context of defence concerns about the vulnerability of Australia's 'empty North' during the Second World War (Butlin and Shedvin 1977: 712–13). Water was identified as a key national resource and irrigation seen as important to regional development (Northern Australian Development Committee 1947). Davidson (1972) and Graham-Taylor (1982) document the political wrangling between the Western Australian and Commonwealth governments over funding for the Ord scheme from its conception in the 1940s to the construction of the two dams on the Ord River in 1963 and 1972 respectively. They argue that decisions were made expediently for political rather than economic reasons.

4. Approximately 60 people from Miriuwung and Gajerrong and neighbouring language groups gave evidence to the 1997 native title hearings, and the substantial part of the hearings took place on lands under claim in and around Kununurra. I draw on the transcripts of these proceedings for evidence of patterns of social identifications and mobility associated with the pastoral era, and subsequent changes since the formation of Kununurra in 1962.

5. Rumsey (1996) identifies accounts of journeys as a distinct narrative form among Aboriginal people who lived and worked on northern Australian pastoral stations. Similar narratives framed by a detailed orientation to place can be found in historical accounts of Aboriginal people from the East Kimberley recorded by Shaw (1981, 1983, 1986) and Bohemia and McGreggor (1995). Merlan (1998) describes this orientation among older Aboriginal people around Katherine in the Northern Territory as a characteristic cultural form which she refers to as a 'travelling mode of experience and knowledge', and notes that it shows 'the same sort of sequencing typically found in some accounts of the travels of Dreamings over country' (Merlan 1998: 106).

6. Willis (1980: 33) notes that by 1968/9 the number of women employed on stations as domestics dropped from over 100 to nil and argues that this played a critical role in the desire of family groups to move into Kununurra.

7. Peter Willis, a Catholic priest based in Kununurra in the 1960s and early 1970s, described the transition between station life and Kununurra as a gradual one, with Aborigines moving between stations and the Kununurra Reserve, working on one and holidaying on the other (Willis 1980: 42).

8. Impacts of the introduction of compulsory award wages on Aboriginal employment have been described across Australia (e.g. Altman and Nieuwenhuysen 1979; Peterson 1991; Rowse 1998).

9. Rowse (1998: 164) highlights the gendered dimension of waged labour at that time in Central Australia, noting that the 'award' wage was intended as 'family' wage.

10. Willis (1980: 20) cites evidence from records of the Native Welfare Department indicating a shortage of seasonal labour in 1965/6 and that farmers and station owners competed for Aboriginal workers. He asserts that the migration to Kununurra was different from 'the brutal banishment' that occurred in other places, such as Fitzroy Crossing, because of the availability of employment and of the richness of the local environment for bush foods (Willis 1980: 35).

11. While Shaw recorded aspirations to obtain land in the early 1970s (Shaw 1986: 11–12), it was not until the 1980s that the movement gathered momentum, assisted by changes in government policy and legislation, particularly at the Commonwealth level.

12. Access to land in the Northern Territory was facilitated by the enactment of the Aboriginal Land Rights Act (NT) in 1976 and some pastoral excisions have been

converted to freehold title. However, in Western Australia, applications for excisions from pastoral leases were more readily thwarted by objections from lease-holders and other interested parties (Head and Fullagar 1991). Sullivan (pers. comm. 2002) notes that there is no Aboriginal freehold worth noting in the Kimberley in Western Australia.

13. Sometimes men resident at Marralam Outstation were hired for casual assistance with stock work on Legune Station.

14. Since the 1980s, various studies have addressed the movement of Aboriginal people from towns to outstations and homelands throughout Australia, but particularly in northern and central Australia (Altman and Taylor 1987; Baker 1999; Cane and Stanley 1985; Young and Doohan 1989). This literature shows that Aboriginal people elsewhere share the motivations presented above.

15. In a recent review of the resourcing of indigenous communities, Altman et al. (1998) highlight the many social and economic values of outstations, including alcohol rehabilitation, art production and an alternative means of economic support based on subsistence (Altman et al. 1998: 6).

16. In their assessment of mobility of Aboriginal people in Central Australia, Young and Doohan (1989) made similar observations about the role of school education as a constraint on living at outstations.

17. These meetings were associated with the shifts in government policy that followed the election of the federal Labor government in 1972.

18. A meeting held at Malan in 1985 'attracted at least 300 women, representing well over thirty different communities and Aboriginal organizations in the Kimberley's Northern Territory, and Pitjantjatjara lands in South Australia and Western Australia' (Young and Doohan 1989: 96–7).

19. There are many common patterns between the patterns of mobility in the East Kimberley and those described in more detail by Young and Doohan (1989) for Central Australia.

20. Interviews conducted by Bruce Shaw in 1970 with nine farmers provided a useful supplement to my own interviews and allowed some correlation between the views of male farmers and women married to farmers.

21. Bruce Shaw's interviews in 1970 also record tensions between farmers and Public Works Department employees.

22. In March 1999 I attended a consultative meeting convened by the Wesfarmers project manager, Andrew Hopkins, with Miriuwung and Gajerrong people as part of ongoing consultations about the Ord Stage 2 proposal. In June 1999 I participated in two preliminary meetings of mainly senior Miriuwung women to discuss the social impacts of proposals to expand the irrigation area and construct new roads and, potentially, a new service town. These meetings were convened by the Northern Lands Council in anticipation of an Aboriginal social impact assessment for the Ord Stage 2 development proposal.

23. In an interview with Bruce Shaw in the 1970s, Bulla Bilinggiin described his grief at the loss of sacred objects for which he was personally responsible, under the rising waters of Lake Argyle (Shaw 1986: 171–2).

24. During the cotton growing period in the 1960s and early 1970s, large quantities of DDT were used to deter insect pests and herbicides such as 245T were used in the harvesting process. Both these chemicals have since been banned due to harmful environmental impacts of residues.

25. Although preliminary meetings were held to discuss the proposals, the detailed social impact assessment required as part of the broader environmental impact assessment for the proposal did not eventuate. That process, like most other consultative processes involving the Miriuwung and Gajerrong community, was affected by the appeal and

counter-appeals to the 1998 Federal Court ruling, and the requirement under The Native Title Act (1993) to form a Prescribed Body Corporate to represent the interests of native title holders. It became clear that the creation of such a consequential legal entity would be a protracted process that could take some years of negotiation.

26. Head (1999) elaborates further on similarities between Stages 1 and 2 of the Ord Irrigation Scheme highlighting the persistence of three colonial themes in the rhetoric of Ord Stage 2. These are 'the empty landscape, the invisible Aborigine, and the idealisation of agricultural land use'.

27. Similar issues concerning policy and legislative frameworks have been raised in the context of cultural heritage assessments made by the New South Wales National Parks and Wildlife Service (Byrne et al. 2001).

REFERENCES

Agriculture Western Australia (1997) *Ord River Irrigation Area: Kununurra Western Australia*, Bulletin 4225: Perth: Agriculture Western Australia.

Akerman, K. (1980) 'The Renascence of Aboriginal Law in the Kimberleys', in R.M. Berndt and C.H. Berndt (eds) *Aborigines of the West: Their Past and Their Present*. Perth: University of Western Australia Press, pp. 234–42.

Altman, J.C. and J.P. Nieuwenhuysen (1979) *The Economic Status of Australian Aborigines*. Cambridge: Cambridge University Press.

Altman, J.C. and L. Taylor (1987) *The Economic Viability of Aboriginal Outstations and Homelands: A report to the Australia Council for Employment and Training*. Department of Political and Social Change, Research School of Pacific Studies, Australian National University, Canberra: Australian Government Publishing Service.

Altman, J.C., D. Gillespie and K. Palmer (1998) *National Review of Resource Agencies Servicing Indigenous Communities, 1998*. Canberra: Aboriginal and Torres Strait Islander Commission, Commonwealth of Australia.

Anderson, K. (1986) 'The Idea of Chinatown: The Power of Place and Institutional Practice in the Making of a Racial Category', *Annals of the Association of American Geographers* 77(4): 580–98.

Attwood, B. (1996) 'The Past as Future: Aborigines, Australia and the (Dis)Course of History', in B. Attwood (ed.) *In the Age of Mabo: History, Aborigines and Australia*. Sydney: Allen and Unwin, pp. vii–xxxviii.

Baker, R. (1999) *Land is Life, From Bush to Town: The Story of the Yanyuwa People*. Sydney: Allen and Unwin.

Beckett, J. (1988) 'The Past in the Present, the Present in the Past: Constructing a National Aboriginality', in J. Beckett (ed.) *Past and Present: The Construction of Aboriginality*. Canberra: Aboriginal Studies Press, pp. 1–10.

Bohemia, J. and W. McGregor (1995) *Nyibayarri: Kimberley Tracker*. Canberra: Aboriginal Studies Press.

Bolton, G.C. (1981) 'Black and White after 1897', in C.T. Stannage (ed.) *A New History of Western Australia*. Perth: University of Western Australia Press, pp. 124–78.

Butlin, S.J. and C.B. Shedvin (1977) *War Economy, 1942–1945*. Canberra: Australia War Memorial.

Byrne, D., H. Brayshaw and T. Ireland (2001) *Social Significance: A Discussion Paper*. Sydney: New South Wales National Parks and Wildlife Service.

Cane, S. and O. Stanley (1985) *Land Use and Resources in Desert Homelands*. North Australia Research Unit Monograph. Darwin: Australian National University.

Cresswell, T. (2001) 'The Production of Mobilities', *New Formations* 43: 9–25.

Davidson, B.R. (1972) *The Northern Myth: A Study of the Physical and Economic Limits to Agricultural and Pastoral Development in Tropical Australia*, 3rd edn. Melbourne: Melbourne University Press.

Federal Court of Australia (1997) *Transcripts for Ben Ward and Others on Behalf of the Miriuwung Gajerrong Peoples* v. *The State of Western Australia and Others*; Justice Lee. File Number: WAG 6001 of 1995. Perth: Western Australia District Registry.

—— (1998) *Ben Ward and Others* v. *State of WA and Others* [1998]. FCA 1478 (24 November). Perth: Western Australia District Registry.

Graham-Taylor, S. (1982) 'A Critical History of the Ord River Project', in B.R. Davidson (ed.) *Lessons from the Ord*, Policy Monograph No. 2. St Leonards, NSW: Centre for Independent Studies.

Head, L. (1994) 'Aborigines and Pastoralism in North-western Australia: Historical and Contemporary Perspectives on Multiple Use of the Rangelands', *Rangelands Journal* 16(2): 167–83.

—— (1999) 'The Northern Myth Revisited? Aborigines, Environment and Agriculture in the Ord River Irrigation Scheme, Stages One and Two', *Australian Geographer* 30(2): 141–58.

—— (2000) *Second Nature: The History and Implications of Australia as an Aboriginal Landscape.* New York: Syracuse University Press.

Head, L. and R. Fullagar (1991) '"We All La One Land": Pastoral Excisions and Aboriginal Resource Use', *Australian Aboriginal Studies* 1: 37–52.

House of Representatives Standing Committee on Aboriginal Affairs (1987) *Return to Country: The Aboriginal Homelands Movement in Australia.* Canberra: Australian Government Publishing Service.

Hughes, J. (1999) *River of Dreams*, produced by Donna Cameron and John Hughes. Canberra: Ronin films.

Kinhill Pty. Ltd. (2000) Environmental Review and Management Program Draft Environmental Impact Statement – Ord River Irrigation Area Stage 2: Proposed Development of the M2 Area. Prepared for Wesfarmers Sugar Company Pty Ltd, Marubeni Corporation and the Water Corporation of Western Australia. Perth.

Kolig, E. (1981) *The Silent Revolution: The Effects of Modernization on Australian Aboriginal Religion.* Philadelphia, PA: Institute for the Study of Human Issues.

Massey, D. (1993) 'Power-geometry and a Progressive Sense of Place', in J. Bird, B. Curtis, T. Putnam, G. Robertson and L. Tickner (eds) *Mapping the Futures: Local Cultures and Global Change.* London: Routledge, pp. 59–69.

Massey, D., 'with the collective' (1999) 'Issues and Debates', in D. Massey, J. Allen and P. Sarre (eds) *Human Geography Today.* Cambridge: Polity Press, pp. 3–21.

Merlan, F. (1998) *Caging the Rainbow: Places, Politics, and Aborigines in a North Australian Town.* Honolulu: University of Hawai'i Press.

Mitchell, D. (1993) 'State Intervention in Landscape Production: the Wheatland Riot and the California Commission of Immigration and Housing', *Antipode* 25(2): 91–113.

Northern Australia Development Committee (1947) *Development of Northern Australia.* Canberra: Northern Australia Development Committee.

NLC/KLC (Northern Land Council and the Kimberley Land Council) (2000) *Ord River Irrigation Area Stage 2, Proposed Development of the M2 Area: Comments on the Environmental Review and Management Programme and Draft Environmental Impact Statement.* Submission by the Northern Land Council and the Kimberley Land Council.

Peterson, N. (1991) 'Cash, Commoditisation and Authenticity: When do Aboriginal People Stop Being Hunter-Gatherers?', in N. Peterson and T. Matsuyama (eds) *Cash, Commoditisation and Changing Foragers.* Osaka: National Museum of Ethnology, pp. 67–90.

—— (2000) 'An Expanding Aboriginal Domain: Mobility and the Initiation Journey', *Oceania* 70(3): 205–18.

Proctor, J.D. and S. Pincetl (1996) 'Nature and the Reproduction of Endangered Space: The Spotted Owl in the Pacific Northwest and Southern California', *Environment and Planning D: Society and Space* 14: 683–708.

Rose, D.B. (1991) *Hidden Histories: Black Stories from Victoria River Downs, Humbert River and Wave Hill Stations*. Canberra: Aboriginal Studies Press.

—— (1997) 'The Year Zero and the North Australian Frontier', in D.B. Rose and A. Clarke (eds) *Tracking Knowledge in North Australian Landscapes: Studies in Indigenous and Settler Ecological Knowledge Systems*, Canberra and Darwin: North Australia Research Unit, School of Pacific and Asian Studies, The Australian National University.

Rowse, T. (1998) *White Flour, White Power: From Rations to Citizenship in Central Australia*. Cambridge: Cambridge University Press.

Rumsey, A. (1996) 'Aspects of Native Title and Social Identity in the Kimberleys and Beyond', *Australian Aboriginal Studies* 1: 1–10.

Shaw, B. (1974) 'Social relations and commitments in a planned new town in Western Australia', unpublished PhD thesis, University of Western Australia.

—— (1981) *My Country of the Pelican Dreaming*. Canberra: Australian Institute of Aboriginal Studies.

—— (1983) *Banggaiyerri: The Story of Jack Sullivan, as Told to Bruce Shaw*. Canberra: Australian Institute of Aboriginal Studies.

—— (1986) *Countrymen: The Life Histories of Four Aboriginal Men as Told to Bruce Shaw*. Canberra: Australian Institute of Aboriginal Studies.

—— (1992) *When the Dust Come in Between: Aboriginal Viewpoints in the East Kimberley Prior to 1982*. Canberra: Aboriginal Studies Press.

Sullivan, P. (1996) *All Free Man Now: Culture, Community and Politics in the Kimberley Region, North-Western Australia*. Canberra: Australian Institute of Aboriginal and Torres Strait Islander Studies.

Whatmore, S. (1997) 'Dissecting the Autonomous Self: Hybrid Cartographies for a Relational Ethics', *Environment and Planning D: Society and Space* 15: 37–53.

Williams, N. and I. Kirkby (1989) *Summary of Findings and Recommendations, Ethnography of the East Kimberley Work in Progress: Location and Status of Aboriginal Communities*. East Kimberley Impact Assessment Project, Working Paper No. 33. Canberra: Centre for Resource and Environmental Studies, Australian National University.

WADID (Western Australian Department of Industrial Development) (1963) *Ord River Project*. Perth: Ken Lobascher.

Willis, P. (1980) *Patrons and Riders: Conflicting Roles and Hidden Objectives in an Aboriginal Development Programme*, Occasional Papers in Community Development No. 2. Canberra: Institute for Aboriginal Development Inc.

Young, E. and K. Doohan (1989) *Mobility for Survival: A Process Analysis of Aboriginal Population Movement in Central Australia*, Northern Australian Research Unit Monograph. Darwin: Australian National University.

Young, N. (1979) *Ord River Irrigation Area Review, 1978: A Joint Commonwealth and Western Australian Review*. Canberra: Australian Government Publishing Service.

8 CO-PRESENT LANDSCAPES: ROUTES AND ROOTEDNESS AS SOURCES OF IDENTITY IN HIGHLANDS NEW GUINEA

Michael O'Hanlon and Linda Frankland

A point sometimes made in popular accounts is that 'first contact' in the Highlands of Papua New Guinea in the 1930s was so late, and the terrain there so rugged, that Highlanders often encountered aircraft before they became acquainted with roads or with vehicles. It is quite true that early patrols were often supplied by air drops, and that the expansion of colonially controlled territory was marked by a proliferation of small landing grounds, since brief hops by plane obviated punishing weeks of walking precipitous Highlands trails. But it was the Australian Administration's road-making which, from the 1940s, more permanently and overtly imprinted itself on the Highland landscape.

Highlanders were recruited to construct these roads which are often considerable engineering achievements, whether they are switchbacking up lofty passes always prone to landslips, or bridging the many Highlands rivers which, while generally no more than purling streams, are capable of giving a passable impression of the Yangtze in flood after heavy rain. In at least one early case, road-making appears to have become the focus for short-lived resistance to the imposition of colonial authority. Simpson (1962: 190ff.) records a struggle for Highlands hearts and minds between Ian Downs, the District Commissioner determined that 'the road must get through', and a local leader, Kamindo, who is painted as a mini-Hitler and who commits suicide when his opposition to the road is publicly seen to fail.[1] In some places, competitive road construction also became a new idiom in terms of which interclan rivalries could be played out (Strathern and Strathern 1971: 44).

Roads additionally became the ambivalent focus for ideas about 'landscape' in the more extended senses defined by Hirsch (1995: 4ff.). For peripherally located peoples in the Highlands, anticipation of the arrival of a connecting road became a metaphor in terms of which a whole set of issues to do with centrality and modernity were thought about and acted through (Hayano 1990; Hirsch 1994: 698). In some cases, local people in remote areas set about making roads of their own volition, as testament to their perception of themselves as newly modern and hence meriting a connection to 'government' (Sinclair 1966: 216).

Elsewhere in the Highlands, and more recently, roads have acquired a darker image.[2] In parts of Simbu Province, for example, the road in the form of the Highlands Highway has indeed come but most of the goods borne on it are in transit only, bound for the richer Western Highlands Province and beyond. Local people have responded by regularly erecting road blocks and raiding the contents of the trucks in question (see here Strathern and Stewart [2003] for an analysis of contemporary Papua New Guinea in terms of political flows and blockages). Roads can also be a source of death, both directly through traffic accidents and indirectly through 'payback' killings resulting from unsatisfied claims for compensation. Roads are feared, too, as a conduit for crime and disorder: some of this – along with the exhilaration of connectedness and movement which roads equally embody – is captured in the film *Tinpis Run* (Nengo 1991), to our knowledge Papua New Guinea's only 'road movie'. It is also no secret that many inhabitants of the capital, Port Moresby, have long opposed the construction of a connecting road to the Highlands since they fear that down it would come swarms of disorderly Highlanders.

The mid-Wahgi people, inhabitants of the Western Highlands Province, readily evince such ambivalent feelings towards the roads which criss-cross the lush and dramatic landscape of the Wahgi Valley. At one level, roads are welcomed as a source of connectedness: to the small local towns of Banz and Minj with their provisioning stores, to the Nazarene hospital at Kudjip, and beyond that to the major centre of Mt Hagen to the west, with its airport, and – via the Highlands Highway – to the port of Lae far away to the east. In this mode, Wahgi people press to have dirt roads sealed, so that the minibuses in which they travel no longer envelop each other in clouds of gritty white dust as they pass; and they campaign to have the log bridges which span small streams upgraded to metal ones, to allow easier passage for the pick-ups which ply the backroads buying the cash crop of coffee. Children push round the ingenious wheeled wire toys they make, which they call 'Highways' after the big trucks which transport goods up the Highlands Highway from Lae. At the same time, the Wahgi also have a lively appreciation of the drawbacks of roads. There have been regular deaths from road accidents, each of which is capable of rekindling any tensions between the clans of driver and victim, and causing clanspeople on either side to rush to phone relatives in faraway towns to alert them in case they become the object of payback killings. There is also a lively apprehension of the corridor of disorder which a road going through a clan area potentially brings. The bandits known locally as *raskol* come and go on such roads, particularly after dark. Especially since the late 1980s, as they have armed themselves with guns, such bandits have passed beyond the control of local clan-leaders. In the 20 years since our own first fieldwork in 1979–81, we have watched the corridor of threat represented by one quite minor road on the north wall of the Wahgi progressively widen, so that even in daylight women were being urged not to walk down to the road unaccompanied.

But the argument of this chapter is that the ambivalence with which the Wahgi regard roads is not new, even though vehicular roads themselves may be. For there is a highly developed indigenous notion of 'roads' or 'paths' – specifically of marriage roads – which are valued for their connecting properties but are equally seen (from a particular male perspective) to pose a threat to clan-based communities. We will argue that Wahgi people have, in fact, two competing identities – analytically separate, if deeply intertwined – each of which is implicated in a different way in the landscape. One identity is as clanspeople, rooted to a particular place, and viewed in certain respects as the outcome of that place; the other is as the product of marriage roads which ramify outwards to other places elsewhere in the Wahgi Valley and beyond it. Anthropologists have recently been urged to abandon their characteristic 'dwelling' metaphors, as privileging cultural holism, in favour of 'travelling' metaphors, seen as more in keeping with contingent times of movement, permeable boundaries and indeterminacy (Clifford 1997; Gupta and Ferguson 1997). In the Wahgi case, we will argue, both metaphors are locally in play, and we interpret the great Wahgi Pig Festival as ritually establishing the primacy of a 'vertical' rooted identity over the distributed identity of ramifying 'roads'. We then go on to look at how each of these identities has fared over the colonial and post-colonial period, concluding by suggesting one particular way in which they are brought together and sedimented into the contemporary landscape.

THE ROOTS OF CLANSHIP

Today there are some 80,000 mid-Wahgi people living in dispersed settlements scattered over the valley walls both in the central section of the Wahgi Valley, and also extending over the Sepik–Wahgi divide to the north. Our own fieldwork has largely been in the north-west corner of the mid-Wahgi area, with Komblo and Sekaka tribes who live either side of the Kar River (O'Hanlon 1989, 1993). Like their Highlands neighbours, the Wahgi are traditionally farmers of sweet potato, the staple food both for people and for the pigs they also raise. Since the late 1950s, the Wahgi have also taken to cash-cropping coffee, which (depending on its price on the world market) generates an often substantial income, though also appropriating some of the best sweet potato-growing land. The income from coffee is used right across the scale: from the tinned fish and rice with which the Wahgi complement their sweet potato staple, to school fees and church contributions (most Wahgi being members of one of the plethora of denominations which have established themselves in the area since the 1940s), to pick-ups and petrol and beer, and finally to a substantial economy of ceremonial exchange.

Most ceremonial exchanges are organised in the name of one of the levels of agnatically oriented, localised, segmentary groups into which the Wahgi divide themselves. Politically, the most important level tends to be that of the exogamous clan, though clans are often grouped into larger tribes (such as Komblo and Sekaka) and sometimes into dispersed phratries. Bridewealth payments, along with the life-cycle payments that are owed to maternal kin, are generally organised at the subclan level, but even here such payments may publicly be identified with the higher clan level. The compensation payments made to the kin of road accident victims, or to allies who have helped assemble such payments, are almost invariably associated with the clan or tribal level. It is also the clan and tribal level of grouping that is principally involved both in the inter-group warfare which has re-convulsed parts of the mid-Wahgi area since the early 1980s, and in the peace-making and compensation payments which bring warfare to an end. Finally, it is the clan level that is most associated with the greatest Wahgi ritual, the once-generational Pig Festival or *konggar* (Luzbetak 1954; Reay 1959).

The Pig Festival is an elaborate and extended ritual cycle whose overt purpose is to promote the growth and numbers of a clan's pigs and of clanspeople themselves. Early Pig Festival rites entail a clan dedicating its pigs to the Festival and ritually cutting itself off in certain ways from other groups. A ceremonial ground is cleared, on which will take place the dancing which is one of the principal expressions of Pig Festivals. There, for many months, clansmen and unmarried girls arrayed in headdresses built up from valuable Bird of Paradise plumes, will parade in front of allies, rivals and enemies. The local term for a ceremonial ground is *penem*, meaning 'open' or 'public space' and there is a strong sense that, in mounting a Festival, a clan is publicly putting itself on the line, revealing to its own members – and to critical spectators – whether it has the resources, the internal unity and the ancestral support necessary to bring such a project to a successful conclusion. At the end of the Pig Festival, marked by months of more regular dancing and competitive visits by troupes of dancers from other clans, a ritual structure is erected on the ceremonial ground. In the western part of the Wahgi area the structure has until recently been a pig-fat-smeared post known as *ond mond* (lit. *mond* tree); this is being displaced by the small *bolyim* house (*bolyim gar*), the use of which is moving westward from the rest of the Wahgi where it has already been adopted. Differences in appearance not withstanding, the two are symbolically very similar. Both are erected at night by men who, ideally, are the sons of those who built the structures at the clan's previous Pig Festival, a generation or so before. Both structurally model the clan, with radiating twists of vine (in the case of *ond mond*) or house posts (in the case of *bolyim gar*) each said to stand for one of the clan's constituent subclans. Both are supposedly secret from women, who greet the sight of them on the ceremonial ground the morning following their erection with ritual cries of astonishment, and in both cases the men who erect the structures are burdened with taboos (*dop mapil*) on eating, drinking and consorting with outsiders, especially from enemy clans. The next day, men and girls of the performing clan plus their guests climb onto specially erected platforms and there, in front of dense crowds of spectators, gorge themselves on pork fat (*kopong, taming*), occasionally throwing fragments or items of decoration to the crowd below. Finally, the clan's pigs are clubbed around the *mond* post or *bolyim* house, butchered, and then cooked in pits dug in the ceremonial ground.[3] The pork is distributed to affines and allies who originally provided the plumes for Pig Festival dancing, and everyone goes home, bringing the public part of the Festival to a close.

In an earlier account of the Pig Festival (O'Hanlon 1989: 71–9), one of us has interpreted it as an assertion of the autonomy of the clan which momentarily realises itself as self-sufficient, capable of reproducing itself ritually through the *bolyim* house or *mond* post, overwriting the contributions both of in-married wives, and of the external clans from which they came. Perhaps most dramatically, this is expressed in the autogenic image of men publicly re-internalising the fat from the pigs they claim to have raised. In terms of the symbolism of substances, the Pig Festival represents the clan's fertility as maintained by a closed, vertical 'grease cycle', in which grease or fat circulates as a male, clan product. The *bolyim* house and *mond* post are both buried on top of masses of fat; the structures themselves are heavily greased; and at the climax of the festival, men publicly re-absorb masses of fat which Wahgi regard as something of a wonder substance, with formal similarities to semen

Figure 8.1 Standing atop the *bolyim* house, men of Komblo Kulka clan consume pork fat at the climax to their Pig Festival

(O'Hanlon 1992: 597), capable of inducing miraculous growth. Fat is also regarded as prone to 'leak' from the ideally closed male cycle through intercourse: people may say of a man when they learn that his wife is pregnant 'Ah! I thought his skin looked dull.'

This general interpretation of the Pig Festival as momentarily erasing external contributions to clan fertility and prosperity does seem to hold, and to make sense of many of the ritual restrictions and actions which comprise the Festival. At the same time, it does not sufficiently disentangle the extent to which the Festival is not simply an assertion of the self-sufficiency of clansmen but of clansmen rooted in the particular territory they inhabit, especially in the ceremonial ground itself. It is this aspect of the Pig Festival that we wish to foreground here. It is, of course, not unexpected that, at a general level, there should be an association between a major ritual like the Pig Festival, and the 'placedness' of the clan that performs it, especially in the turbulent Highlands social landscape in which inter-group warfare, dispossession and refugeeship were common and have again become a threat. But there are also three more specific ways in which the Pig Festival represents its performers not simply as 'clanspeople' but identifies them as people of a specific place and ceremonial ground.

The first resides in the songs which accompany the Pig Festival dancing. The dancing itself is a compelling spectacle, enhanced by the often airy beauty of the ceremonial grounds on which it takes place. The phalanx of decorated clansmen moves slowly up and down the length of the ground, the black sprays of the dancers' headdresses of Stephanie and Sicklebill Bird of Paradise plumes finding a visual echo in the green fountains of bamboo, clumps of which often shade ceremonial grounds. Though Pig Festival songs are short and repetitive, the words are passed from the front of the phalanx to the back and then forward again, lending the songs a memorable swelling and fading quality, rising over the sharp jingling of the shells on men's belts. The songs frequently deal allusively with intergroup competitiveness, but what is important for the present argument is that in them clans are never referred to by their ordinary names which are used in other contexts. Instead, groups are denoted either by the names of birds singing in particular places, or by the direction in which a group's ceremonial ground lies, or by the names of the ceremonial grounds themselves. Pig Festival songs turn clanspeople into people of a particular place.

The same is true in relation to the *mond* post or *bolyim* house erected by a clan towards the climax of a Pig Festival. As we have seen, these certainly embody clanship in their own physical structure, but it is clanship rooted in the ground. Both the *mond* post itself and the posts of the *bolyim* house are substantial pieces of timber, whose bases are deeply buried. Immediately the Pig Festival is over, the ceremonial ground – already ravaged by the construction of earth ovens on it – is ditched and turned into sweet potato gardens, each section belonging to one of the constituent subclans – the ground where the blood of the pigs was spilled is said to be especially fertile. Then, some time after the close of the public parts of the Pig Festival, the *mond* post or *bolyim* house will be secretly dismantled and their wooden parts now completely buried in a moist spot elsewhere on clan land, to await the clan's next Pig Festival when they will be re-erected – it always being emphasised that they never rot. Water from the spot where the ritual items are buried will be used in cures for sick pigs, while in the place of the *mond* post/*bolyim* house will be planted a *bekrap*, whose white fleshy leaves we have heard people liken to pork fat. Throughout this ritual sequence we see an interdigitation of clan and place. If, in ideological terms, the Pig Festival reproduces the clan and its pigs, it does so in ways which construct the clan as emplaced in a particular spot, especially in its ceremonial ground which might be seen as providing an idealised vision of clan land held as a homogeneous block. In practice, clan land is not so constituted: in part due to the historical movement of clans down from the valley walls onto flatter land more suitable for coffee-growing, in part due to the gifting of land to non-agnatic kin. What the ceremonial ground and associated Pig Festival rituals do is ideologically to de-fragment clan land, reconstituting it as a solidary block which is then ditched and shared between the constituent subclans.

Over the years that follow, the ceremonial ground will grow over, becoming a cool shadowy grove, whose deserted quiet is yet capable of evoking by contrast the riot of colour, song and clamour of the Festival's now long-past climax. And this is the final way in which the Pig Festival turns clanspeople into places, through the trees that grow up there. There is anyway in Wahgi life a pervasive identification between trees and men, and between trees and clansmen. Men (but not women) are named after trees; a parallel is drawn between killing men and cutting down trees; and an equation made between men growing tall, trees growing tall and intra-clan solidarity. But more specifically, the *mond* post and *bolyim* house are not just made from wood but from one perspective *are* trees, as well as being 'the clan'. When we asked why the *mond* post is sometimes referred to as 'the old tree' or 'left-over tree', we were told 'Trees are men's brothers. ... Trees are men, don't you see?' While the *bolyim* house and *mond* post are dismantled some time after the end of the Pig Festival, they leave their structural equivalents in the trees that grow up on the ceremonial ground.

To suggest in this way that clans have a strong 'place' dimension is not new in the context of New Guinea Highlands ethnography. In fact, Feil (1987: 118ff.) – drawing on much earlier work by Gitlow (1947) – argues that, in parts of the Highlands, kinship relations were giving way to more hierarchical relationships predicated upon place, a process that he contends was arrested and reversed by the arrival of Australian colonialists. Our own concern here is a more limited one, and has been to argue that the Pig Festival construes clanspeople's identities as strongly rooted in place. We should note here that in arguing this we are not suggesting that ceremonial grounds, or clan land, are immutably fixed in place. Nor are we suggesting that Pig Festivals are the only thing that symbolically tie clans to places. Garden land does so too, as do burial grounds. In fact, burial grounds are often adjacent to ceremonial grounds, and there is a strong idea of reciprocity between the dead, who enjoy watching their descendants dance, and the living, who benefit from their ghostly support. The relationship with the dead may also be alluded to in Pig Festival songs, which on occasion capture in a single evocative nexus all these ideas of clanship expressed in the form of trees on a ceremonial ground watched over by ancestral ghosts:

> My brothers have gone inside Koskal [Koskal is a fig tree]
> My brothers have vanished into *owol* [leaves]
> They have departed altogether
> In the afternoon *kulung* headdresses are completed
> *Kokn* headdresses are made ...

Here, the reference to Koskal is to the trees on Ngunzka clan's former ceremonial ground at Koskalmel, but also to the adjacent graveyard there. The brothers who have 'departed' are in fact dead, and buried in that cemetery. Meanwhile, their surviving clansmen have finished making the elaborate headdresses (which mark a particular stage of the Pig Festival) but still sorrow for their dead fellows who they thought would be dancing alongside them but now lie in the graveyard.

In highlighting the way in which Pig Festival ritual places clans on – and in – the land we have also noted in passing certain details which suggest that this identity is constructed in opposition to another identity reaching out along 'roads' to other clans, from whom girls come in marriage. It is to this alternative identity that we now turn.

'ROADS' AS COMPETING SOURCES OF IDENTITY

Marriage relationships among mid-Wahgi people are explicitly thought of in terms of 'roads' or 'paths' (*kol, wusingal*), radiating laterally and linking groups together. Like vehicular roads, marriage roads have first to be blazed and then must be kept clear through the passage of brides along them, if they are not to become overgrown. And just as Wahgi pay taxes to the local council, one of whose tasks is to construct and maintain vehicular roads, so people consider that those who control marriage roads must be paid if brides are to continue flowing along them, and if those brides' marriages are to be fertile. In many respects, such marriage roads – and the clans elsewhere in the Wahgi Valley and beyond to which those roads lead – constitute a rival, externally located form of identity for Wahgi people.

The primary form of this external identity lies in the relationship with maternal kin. If a man is asked where his 'main road' (*wusingal mam*) lies, he is likely to give the name of his maternal kin group (whether subclan, clan or tribe are named in this regard will depend on the enquirer's knowledge of the local context). The relationship with maternal kin is a highly important and ritually charged one in Wahgi society. Wahgi maternal kin are credited with the power to heal and cure their sisters' children if well disposed, but also to curse them (*kipe si* – literally, ancestral-ghost taking) with death and infertility if angered and not assuaged. A man's indebtedness to his maternal kin is also expressed in the life-cycle payments he owes them, including the duty (if asked) of finding a bride for his mother's brother's son's son. This latter practice is explicitly seen as returning a girl to his mother's natal clan: indeed, if a man proposes to deploy his own daughter to satisfy the obligation he may name her after his mother to mark the fact that she is intended to take her grandmother's place.[4] The powers credited to maternal kin are also felt to be possessed in more diffuse form by ego's mother's mother's people, father's mother's and – insofar as they are known – MMM's and FFM's. Ego does not owe these more extended connections the life-cycle payments due to maternal kin but does refer to all of them as 'root people' or 'source' (*pul alamb, mambnem*). In one sense, it is this kind of laterally rooted identity, ramifying out to groups all over the Wahgi Valley, that the clan-focused ritual of the Pig Festival momentarily eclipses, with its own emphasis on the vertically rooted qualities of the *bolyim* house and *mond* post, as they are successively buried and re-excavated.

While Wahgi think of marriage roads as multiply connecting clans all over the valley, marriage itself is regarded as difficult, partly because Wahgi men traditionally tend to treat women as valuables in short supply. In these circumstances, there are particular categories of people who can 'warm the road' (*kol gale*) because they own it; if the marriage is to endure and be fruitful, these people must be located and paid. Thus when bridewealth and its counter-payment are handed over, two additional payments will also be made, one from the groom's group to that of the bride and one from the bride's to that of the groom. The gift made by the groom's side ideally goes to a woman from that group who has earlier married into the bride's, or to the descendant in the bride's group of such a woman. This payment is likely to be phrased as one for having persuaded the new bride to leave her kin and come in marriage to the groom. The second gift, made by the bride's side to that of the groom, goes to the woman identified as most closely preceding the bride in marriage from the bride's group to the groom's, or to the descendants in the groom's group of such an earlier marriage.

These two sets of people are regarded as standing at either end of – and as controlling – the 'road' or 'path' which links the two groups in marriage. Such individuals are termed *kol kep alamb* ('road link people'); they may also be described as 'holding [the bride] by the hand' (*angel amble*), referring to the fact that the woman (or descendant of such a woman) in the groom's group who has been identified as most closely preceding the present bride down the marriage road may literally hold the new bride's hand as she walks across the cleared space from her natal kin to join her husband's group when her bridewealth is handed over. The payment made to *kol kep* people takes the form of a modest gift of money together with some pork: in particular they should receive the belly fat, stomach or head from one of the bridewealth pigs. 'Road link people' should also either club the first of the bridewealth pigs or – if the *kol kep* is a woman or a child, neither of whom customarily club pigs – they should physically hand the club to the man who will do so.

Those 'road link people' within a clan into which a bride marries have a duty to care for her – she may actually live with them rather than with her husband to begin with. They are expected to help her in any problems she has with her husband or his kin – indeed, a new bride may be instructed to go only to them for support, and not to call on her own parents. In return, a newly married couple are expected to assist their *kol kep* within the clan with garden work and house construction – especially since 'road link people' are also thought to exercise certain powers over the marriage and its progeny. These powers are in fact precisely those of maternal kin, for 'road link people' are nothing less than surrogate maternal kin within the clan – an 'internal externality', to borrow a term coined to describe a different situation among the Duna people of Papua New Guinea's Southern Highlands Province (Stewart and Strathern 2002: 10). This equation is explicit and thoroughgoing. Like maternal kin, 'road link people' are credited with the power to cure sick children of the marriages they enable; equally, if displeased, they can curse a marriage with infertility, or with producing only daughters. One circumstance in which this may be thought to arise is if the wrong *kol kep* is chosen. There is often potential for argument about who the true *kol kep* should be – should for example, a close clan sister of the bride married into a more distant subclan take precedence over a more distant classificatory sister married into the very subclan into which the bride is now marrying? The woman not selected as the 'road' (or her descendants within the clan) may then say 'Very well then! The road is my road. Now someone else has been made "road link". Will the marriage bear children? Certainly not!' Finally, the identification between *kol kep* and maternal kin extends to kinship terminology, with the children of a marriage calling the 'road links' who enabled it '*apam*', the term reciprocally used of MB/Zch.

The origins of the institution of 'road link' people is obscure: it may well lie in the disconnections caused by warfare and other population movements which separate people from their maternal kin and create the need for internal surrogates (see Meigs 1984: 13ff. for a parallel case).

But what is undoubtedly the case is that such instances of the recognition of non-agnatic relationships among agnates have not received the attention they merit in the otherwise exhaustive Highlands literature on group structure and composition, where the focus has tended to be on the reverse process: the conversion of non-agnates into clansmen. As Daryl Feil (1978: 399) noted many years ago 'an aura of agnation' hangs over the relationship between clansmen, with the clan treated as 'an inviolate conceptual unit'. Feil himself went on to analyse how Tombema Engan fellow clansmen trace out their non-agnatic connections, the better to enter into *tee* exchange relationships with each other. But where the Wahgi 'road link' system is unusually intricate in its situational creation of non-agnatic relationships between clansmen lies in what happens when a number of brides from the same external clan successively act as 'road link' to each other. This results in a cascading series of *kol kep* relationships within the clan, in effect stacking up vertically a series of surrogate MB/Zch relationships which would otherwise be found distributed laterally in space.

This nesting may at any moment intervene in the relationship between clansmen. For example, at a marriage ceremony for Paiye's daughter Bup we noticed Tolmbanz and Nosa, two of Paiye's Karukanem subclansmen, in emphatic conversation with each other over a leg of pork which had been given in payment. Tolmbanz was insisting that it was perfectly alright for Nosa to accept it: '*Na kros na-pam*' ('I'm not angry'), he maintained. Nosa, Bup's own father's brother, kept demurring but was eventually persuaded to bear the pork away. The following day, when we were able to ask about the incident in more detail, it was explained that Tolmbanz's mother had been the 'road link' bringing Nosa's mother in marriage, and she had in turn brought Bup's mother, all three women being natally, or maternally, from the same external subclan of Kulka Aluakup. Because Tolmbanz's mother was at the source of this cascading set of internal *kol kep* relationships within Karukanem of which Bup was the fruit, Tolmbanz's permission was required before Nosa, further down the chain, could accept the pork. Had Nosa borne it off without that authorisation, Bup herself would have become sick. When there is an internal hierarchy of *kol kep* in this way, the club used to kill the first bridewealth pig may itself be handed down the chain from one to another before the pig is finally despatched.

Nor is it just among clans*men* that the relationship set up by marriages on the same 'road' may intervene. Women married in on the same 'road' from a common clan feel a cohesiveness with each other, and may support each other in disputes and lobby to bring in further brides from their natal clan. Women who are *kol kep* also exercise circumscribed powers over men in the clan into which they have married. For instance, one of the 'road links' for the marriage of Kinden, our sponsor in Kekanem clan, is Akpe, married to Kinden's clansman Bumbye.[5] On one occasion, Kinden received a gift of fruit pandanus from his outmarried daughter. Instead of sharing the pandanus with Akpe (who, as the *kol kep* for Kinden's marriage, is the 'source' of Kinden's daughter), Kinden gave the pandanus elsewhere. Angered at being neglected, Akpe threatened to use her powers as 'source' to extract Kinden's daughter from her marriage; equally, once assuaged, Akpe declared that Kinden's other children would not get sick. So if a 'clan' landscape, with its ideology of vertical rootedness, is fairly unambiguously and exclusively gendered as 'male', 'roads' have strong 'female' aspects. These roads are sometimes given names, either after the place from which the women come, or from the goods obtained in bridewealth for them. Within Komblo, for example, Kekanem clan refer to marriages with the Kekup section of Kulka clan as '*Taman Ku wusingal*' ('Taman Ku road' – Taman Ku being Kulka territory). Again, marriages to Kurup Maiamka, a tribe on the south wall of the valley living close to the famous stone axe mines at Aviamb, were described as '*Nze kunzin wusingal*' ('*kunzin* stone axe road'), after the most prized variety of stone axe received as bridewealth for daughters marrying into Kurup Maiamka.

Our argument so far is that 'roads' potentially constitute a second, alternative source of identity to that of emplaced clanship, with individuals indebted for their existence to their immediate and extended matrilateral kin scattered in clans across the valley, and also to their surrogate maternal kin stacked up within the clan itself. These two sources of identity are not necessarily at odds with each other – frequent brides coming down a marriage road swell the strength of the recipient clan through their offspring: indeed marrying 'on your road' (*kola*) is specifically said to produce many children, the girls among whom will in turn be candidates to be sent back to the original donor clan in due course.[6] But it is precisely this density of Wahgi marriage patterns which lends the alternative identities grave political consequences when they are precipitated in opposition to each other. As we have noted, a man is enjoined to return a girl in marriage to his mother's clan; the Wahgi also practise direct sister exchange; these, together with the favouring of marriage roads, mean that a clan is often substantially composed of segments, each of which has an orientation outwards to a particular external clan. The individuals making up these segments, or 'shadow communities' (to borrow a term coined by Meigs [1984: 13]), feel a cohesiveness, in addition to the internal connections they are likely to have as 'road link' people to each other. One 'shadow community' within a clan may conspire against another to bring in new brides from their respective source clans.[7] Equally, a shadow community may ritually block the passage of further brides from their source clan if they consider that a bride has been badly treated by one of their clansmen, planting a cordyline (*go tom*) to block the marriage road. Until the cordyline is uprooted, it is said that no further girls will come down that road.

However, it is in warfare that the intra-clan 'shadow communities', to which restricted Wahgi marriage patterns and the system of 'marriage roads' give rise, emerge most sharply as a threat to the clan. The effect of two clans fighting may be to split (*bou nim*) a third clan heavily married into the antagonists, as the 'shadow communities' in the third clan each rush off to support their respective source clan in battle, finding themselves on the opposite side of the battlefield. Equally, while inter-married clans should not fight, they occasionally do fall out, giving rise to profound internal tensions for those people whose maternal kin or other 'roads' are in the opposing clan, tensions that are felt to give rise to patterns of infertility and death down the decades if maternal kin are killed (O'Hanlon and Frankland 1986).

In her article on conceptions of landscape among the Mongol people, Humphrey (1995) suggests that two quite different conceptions of landscape are in play, one 'vertical', favouring patriliny, statehood and hierarchy, the other 'lateral', the landscape of shamans. The 'vertical' or 'punctual' landscape, Humphrey suggests, is not fixed but constitutes a centre that moves with the nomads from whose cosmology and practices Humphrey has extrapolated it. In certain respects, this image of identities organised along contrasting axes applies well to the Wahgi case. What we have argued so far is that the Pig Festival energises a 'vertical' identity of place, manifested in the uprights of the *bolyim* house and *mond* posts as they are successively erected, dismantled, reburied and re-excavated, represented in the trees which are their structural equivalents, and centred in ceremonial grounds which yet may move over time. If there are any 'roads' open in this mode, they are to buried ancestors – indeed, it was because the 'door' to the ancestors was said to be open that certain knowledge relating to the Pig Festival was initially withheld from us while the Festival was in progress. What this 'vertical' identity momentarily overlays is a lateral one, represented by marriage roads ramifying out in different directions to other clans, as well as being stacked up internally in the form of 'road link' people. What we now do is to sketch how these two identities have fared over the past half century as each has been suppressed, diluted or augmented by a multiplicity of colonial and post-colonial effects.

IDENTITIES OVER TIME

One of the implications of the foregoing would be that each of the identities has its own kind of history. From this perspective, 'clan' history would be 'punctual', like clan identity, and consist of an endless and unchanging 'vertical' cycling of ritual items, which never rot, into and then out of the ground. 'Roads' history, in contrast, would be developmental, with new women going back and forth along marriage roads, keeping them open, and stacking up new 'road link' relations within the clans in question. However, the history in which we are interested here is a more complex colonial and post-colonial one than this. Of course, in the nature of things we must be selective: this cannot be a complete conspectus of the last half century as it bears on the two modes in which we have suggested that Wahgi identity is sedimented into the landscape. For all that, it can still be suggestive, in the same way that Humphrey's own selective exercise succeeds in being.

Taking the Pig Festival first, one immediate point is that in the last 20 years Pig Festivals have become truncated, where they have happened at all. In fact, the Pig Festivals performed by Komblo and Sekaka climaxing in 1979–80 were the last full ones we know of. A number of reasons for their decline are advanced by the Wahgi. Some say that Pig Festivals simply take too long, and that the years of ritual activity and dancing which they entail interfere with the production of coffee as a cash crop. A second point is that the orientation of Pig Festivals towards ancestral ghosts is at odds with the more fundamentalist of the forms of Christianity practised in the Wahgi; indeed, adherents of the Swiss Mission and some Nazarenes reject decoration and dancing altogether. A final reason advanced by older men is that younger people, roaming around and eating with enemy clans, lack the strength of purpose to uphold the taboos associated with Pig Festivals, in particular taboos relating to the *mond* post and *bolyim* house. Older men emphasise that these two ritual structures are potentially lethal: of great benefit if the relevant taboos (which mainly focus on separation from enemies and from rival Pig Festivals) are adhered to, but extremely dangerous if transgressed.

If, then, Pig Festivals are no longer 'rooting' clans in the way that they once did, can we ask, without sounding too functionalist, what it is that is fulfilling that role now? One point to make is that the relative regularity of Pig Festivals in the decades before 1980 was not a 'traditional' feature that latterly succumbed to intrusive 'modernity' but was itself partly an artefact of colonialism. Older Wahgi in the north-west part of the valley, which we know best, say that it was the colonially imposed peace that provided the stability necessary for the regular performance of Pig Festivals (O'Hanlon 1989: 71). While Pig Festivals assertively lay claim to place in the way that we have suggested, they actually require relative peace for their performance – indeed the upsurge in warfare in parts of the Wahgi since the 1980s may be an additional reason why few have been performed recently there. What Wahgi people often say they now have instead of Pig Festivals are *pati* (Pidgin: parties): speeded-up cycles of dancing and gift-giving, at the close of which one clan (or cluster of clans) will present another with many dozen pigs or with cattle, the prestation being phrased either as repayment from an earlier such *pati*, or as a return to allies for help in warfare or for assistance in assembling a compensation payment following warfare or a road accident. It seems likely that such *pati* fulfil, at least partly, the 'rooting' role of Pig Festivals, even though they do not involve the 'vertical' cycling of *mond* post or *bolyim* house. A point to make in this context is that even when clans do perform Pig Festivals, the upright *mond* post and *bolyim* house may now be accompanied (at least in Catholic-dominated areas) by an upright Christian Cross, and there is a sense in which Christianity, a distinctly 'vertical' religion, has merely been slotted in, with 'Papa God' above in heaven caring for the ancestral ghosts (cf. LiPuma 1988: 53), which are nevertheless wont to 'slip away' to trouble their descendants.

The converse to the question as to what, following the decline of Pig Festivals, 'places' the clan in the landscape, is the issue of the extent to which clans themselves are quite so prominent organisationally as once they were (see also Reay 1981: 1). At one level clans remain formidably important, in particular in respect of defining marriage restrictions. But, at another level, much politics has now moved beyond the clan, and talented young people, anxious to make their name, think of regional and national arenas, rather than of achieving renown as the leaders and spokespeople of their clans.

The overall picture in respect of how clan identities are 'emplaced' today is, then, slightly cloudy. To some extent, it is accomplished through *pati*, the successor to the Pig Festivals; to some extent, the Pig Festivals which fulfilled that role in the past were themselves regularised by colonial contact; to some degree, clans are not the sole political force they once were. What is the position so far as what we have argued to be the rival identity: that constituted through marriage roads?

There is no sign that identities constructed through marriage roads are weakening, and payments to 'road link' people continue to be made. Indeed, over the colonial period and since, marriage 'roads' have lengthened, so that they now extend well beyond the Wahgi area. This extension of marriage 'roads' has proceeded in parallel with the proliferation of vehicular roads which both facilitate marriage at a distance while at the same time requiring social mechanisms to cope with the disconnection between kin which distance produces. The greater distances over which some Wahgi now marry has, in turn, to do with the central position they and their neighbours occupied in relation to colonial processes. Early on, the Australian Administration had established bases in the Western Highlands Province, which they used as their jumping-off point in the 'opening up' of the more remote Southern Highlands and Enga Provinces. Wahgi men, among others, were recruited as carriers and servants in this operation half a century ago, and took the opportunity to establish advantageous relationships with less-developed peoples in these areas. The Wahgi also possess land well-suited to cash-crop coffee, and the superior road system in the Western Highlands means that coffee produced there can be exported more cheaply.

These two factors, of earlier development and greater wealth, have allowed Wahgi men to pull in women, often as second wives, from less well-positioned communities in neighbouring Enga and Simbu provinces and from the Southern Highlands Province, with none of whom, traditionally, had there been any intermarriage. The institution of marriage 'roads' has been extended to cover this process. This is clearest (of the cases we know best) in the very early relationship which Wahgi men of Komblo Kekanem clan established with the people of Arumanda, one small part of Enga Province 50 miles distant. Kekanem youths, either working for the Australian Administration in Enga Province, or visiting their fellows there, initiated a marriage road to Arumanda in the 1940s, down which at least a dozen girls have subsequently come to other Kekanem men (or to close Kekanem relatives), the brides successively acting as 'road link' to each other. With marriage taking place at such a comparative distance, the support offered by the institution of marriage 'roads' would have been correspondingly more crucial for the otherwise isolated in-marrying Enga women.

Our data from the Arumanda end of this marriage road is unfortunately only fragmentary. Nevertheless, it is easy to see that in being creatively extended to cover inter-ethnic marriages, the practice of marriage roads has also been modified in at least one major respect. As we have seen, traditionally women tend to pass in both directions along a marriage road, the two-way passage being secured by sister exchange marriage and by the injunction that a man must find a bride for his mother's brother's son's son if so requested. However, in the case of the marriages contracted between Kekanem clan and Arumanda, the traffic has been exclusively one way. The comparative wealth of the Wahgi end is probably the major factor which has ensured that not a single

Kekanem bride has passed back in marriage to Arumanda for all the Arumanda girls who have come east to Kekanem men since the 1940s. When Wahgi girls marry out of the valley, they generally marry men with paying jobs in the government service, rather than villagers from elsewhere in Papua New Guinea. The Wahgi Valley has for long operated as a metropolitan magnet for valuables, whether the plumes and pelts used for elaborate decorated displays (Healey 1990), cult practices or (at least in the last half-century) wives. It is as though the landscape itself is tilted, with these things collecting in a Wahgi 'sink'. The institution of marriage roads has probably always been a strategy to cope with dis-connection, by locating substitute maternal kin within the clan, when the real ones were separated by warfare. The last 50 years has seen it being extended to cover the new circumstances of disconnection brought about by inter-ethnic marriage at a distance.

VEHICLES AS CONTEMPORARY DIALECTIC BETWEEN 'PLACE' AND 'ROADS' IN THE CONSTRUCTION OF LANDSCAPE-BASED IDENTITIES

From any reasonably lofty point on the side walls of the valley, Wahgi people will point out the massing of trees which mark clan ceremonial grounds. Sections of road will also be visible, where they are not obscured by the dip and rise of the land, or by trees. We have argued that 'places' and 'roads' constitute alternative and sometimes counterposed ways in which Wahgi identity is grounded in the landscape, and we have sketched how those identities have fared over time. We conclude by briefly hazarding one possible contemporary way in which these two identities may be brought together and sedimented in the landscape: and that is through the trucks, pick-ups and buses which venture out from 'places', ply the roads and eventually return to rest as skeletalising hulks.

To suggest that vehicles function in this way immediately engages two areas of Melanesian literature. The first is Munn's (1977) article, itself famous, on the 'Fame of Gawa', which analyses the way in which canoes are fabricated from heavy 'land' products, endowed with lightness and motion, and then detached and despatched on one-way voyages along 'paths' from which renown and shells return to their Gawan point of origin. The second literature is that which interrogates Melanesian artefacts as conjoining opposed or complementary principles. The principles thus detected vary, as do the artefacts themselves which range from axes (Battaglia 1983), netbags (MacKenzie 1991) and headdresses (O'Hanlon 1992) to canoes (Barlow and Lipset 1997). What these have in common however is that they are all 'traditional' artefacts: we know of no equivalent published analyses of introduced artefacts, such as vehicles.

Figure 8.2   Walking home with a netbag of sweet potato, a Wahgi woman passes by the roadside the decaying hulk of a truck, parked at its owner's settlement, adjacent to a grave

The broader anthropology of vehicles in Papua New Guinea – their use and localisation – is in fact relatively under-researched. We do not know of published examples equivalent, for example, to Diana Young's (2001) suggestive article on the life and death of cars in Pitjantjatjara, Southern Australia.[8] Young shows how Pitjantjatjara cars are, among other things, projections of their owning communities, reflecting their social order in seating arrangements and reinforcing their attachment to land. At the same time, the cars are also modified by the country through which they pass, taking on the colour of the orange desert dust.

But while there may not yet be equivalently full accounts for Papua New Guinea, and we ourselves have certainly made no special study of vehicles in the Wahgi, certain points are suggestive. Relatively few Wahgi have the financial capacity to purchase vehicles without contributions from others, and those others will often be clansmen, though by no means limited to them. Consequently, vehicles owned by villagers will tend to have a clan or 'place' identity, a point also noted by Finney (1973: 82) for the Eastern Highlands and by McLeod (pers. comm. 2001) for nearby Simbu, where the local car best known to McLeod was specifically named 'child of the place'. We do not know of cars being named in this way in Wahgi, though there the association between a vehicle and place is reinforced by the fact that the compensation has to be paid by the vehicle owner in the event of its injuring someone. Wahgi vehicles are also subject to ghostly agency, as they may be elsewhere in the Highlands (see e.g. A.J. Strathern 1984: 118). In the two instances we recorded it was also specifically the agency of agnatic ghosts, though we suspect that maternal kin are thought to be as capable of influencing vehicles as they are other aspects of Wahgi life. In the first of the instances recorded, plans were made for men to sacrifice a pig and to confess any harboured grievances in order to prevent their truck-owning clansman from crashing his vehicle. In the second instance, a man declined to get into a car with his son after the latter had insulted him; the father's fear was that his anger might lead – implicitly through ghostly mediation – to the car crashing.

If, then, Wahgi vehicles carry an agnatic or 'place' flavour (while not being free from other influences) as they venture forth, it is of course on roads that they are busy: not only on the paved highways and rough tracks along which coffee cherry is purchased, firewood transported to the tea factory at Kudjip, or passengers carried to and from town, but along 'roads' in that second sense of the ramifying links to maternal and affinal kin in other clans. At the same time, while they venture abroad, carrying the name of their owners, vehicles also potentially imperil clan enterprises. The Pig Festivals of Komblo's clans were almost thrown into chaos when, a few days before their climax in January 1980, a Komblo driver knocked down and killed a child from the major traditional enemy tribe of Kulaka. Only a hastily arranged and substantial compensation payment saved the Festivals and, perhaps, the peace (O'Hanlon 1989: 81–2).

Young (2001) comments that in the dry desert air of South Australia, abandoned cars rot extremely slowly. In fact, she observes that in certain respects cars never really die, since even as hulks they may carry forward and memorialise the identities of their deceased drivers. In the Wahgi, in contrast, cars in a sense die too soon. Despite the sometimes alarming ingenuity displayed by Wahgi mechanics, vehicles do not generally have long lives. Here a contrast might be drawn with those other Wahgi embodiments of place, the cult structures and the trees from which they are made. Whereas these latter never die, vehicles as spatially extended objectifications of place expire prematurely. But when vehicles do 'die', they are not generally abandoned by the roadside but parked up alongside the bush-materials houses of their owners. There, they serve as climbing frames for children, as improvised washing lines, and as sources of spares and of ironwork for miscellaneous purposes. Over time, the vehicle hulks skeletalise and start to sink into the ground, conjoining the two Wahgi modes of being in the landscape.

ACKNOWLEDGEMENTS

Catherine Allerton, Bob Barnes, Ira Bashkow, Josh Bell, James Carrier, Chris Gosden, Eben Kirksey, James Leach, Abby McLeod, Adam Reed, Laura Rival, Alan Rumsey, Pamela Stewart, Andrew Strathern and Karen Sykes all kindly provided criticisms, comments and references which we have attempted to address, with only partial success.

NOTES

1. A later and darker version than Simpson's of colonialism as mediated through road construction appears in one of Shearston's short stories on Papua New Guinea from the 1970s. In 'End of a Road' (1979), the dissipated administration officer directly slays the Highlander in charge of a gang of road workers.
2. This gathering darkness is best reflected in the death of Makis, Read's informant. His charismatic presence presides over Read's (1965) early ethnography of the Highlands. By the time of Read's return to the 'High Valley', Makis is dead, knocked down drunk on the road (1986: 32–3).
3. See O'Hanlon (1989: 27) for a more detailed account of the relationship between clan, ceremonial ground and *bolyim* house/*mond* post.
4. This practice has mistakenly been categorised as prescriptive second-cross-cousin marriage. It is not: a man has to find a bride for his mother's brother's son's son only if asked, and the girl in question need not be his own daughter (O'Hanlon and Frankland 1986).
5. Here, too, kinship terminology is adjusted appropriately, as it is in equating maternal kin and 'road link' people. Kinden calls his clansman Bumbye by the term for 'wife's father' (because Bumbye is the husband of the woman who, as the 'road', provided Kinden's wife).
6. See also Allerton (n.d.) on marriage in Manggarai (Flores) where the idiom of marriage 'roads' or 'paths' is similarly elaborated, as is the importance of remembering origins in order to ensure health and success in life.
7. People on the same marriage road call each other by a specific term *kol ding wol* ('one road') whether or not they are in the same clan.
8. Though see Sykes (n.d.) for a stimulating analysis of the magic-imbued trucks on New Ireland which uneasily conjoin the moieties of 'father' and 'children', an argument with parallels to our own.

REFERENCES

Allerton, C. (n.d.) 'The Path of Marriage: Journeys and Transformation in Manggarai, Eastern Indonesia', MS.
Barlow, K. and Lipset, D. (1997) 'Dialogics of Material Culture: Male and Female in Murik Outrigger Canoes', *American Ethnologist* 24(1): 4–36.
Battaglia, D. (1983) 'Projecting Personhood in Melanesia: The Dialectics of Artefact Symbolism on Sabarl Island', *Man* (n.s.) 18: 289–304.
Clifford, J. (1997) *Routes: Travel and Translation in the Late Twentieth Century.* Cambridge, MA: Harvard University Press.
Feil, D.K. (1978) 'Straightening the Way: An Enga Kinship Conundrum', *Man* 13(3): 380–401.

—— (1987) *The Evolution of Highland Papua New Guinea Societies*. Cambridge: Cambridge University Press.

Finney, B.R. (1973) *Big-men and Business*. Canberra: Australian National University Press.

Gitlow, A.L. (1947) *Economics of the Mount Hagen Tribes, New Guinea*. New York: J.J. Augustin.

Gupta, A. and J. Ferguson (1997) 'Discipline and Practice: "The Field" as Site, Method, and Location in Anthropology', in A. Gupta and J. Ferguson (eds) *Anthropological Locations*. Berkeley: University of California Press.

Hayano, D.M. (1990) *Road Through the Rain Forest: Living Anthropology in Highland Papua New Guinea*. Illinois: Waveland Press.

Healey, C. (1990) *Maring Hunters and Traders: Production and Exchange in the Papua New Guinea Highlands*. Berkeley: University of California Press.

Hirsch, E. (1994) 'Between Mission and Market: Events and Images in a Melanesian Society', *Man* 29(3): 689–711.

—— (1995) 'Between Place and Space', in E. Hirsch and M. O'Hanlon (eds) *The Anthropology of Landscape: Perspectives on Place and Space*. Oxford: Oxford University Press.

Humphrey, C. (1995) 'Chiefly and Shamanist Landscapes in Mongolia', in E. Hirsch and M. O'Hanlon (eds) *The Anthropology of Landscape: Perspectives on Place and Space*. Oxford: Oxford University Press.

LiPuma, E. (1988) *The Gift of Kinship: Structure and Practice in Maring Social Organisation*. Cambridge: Cambridge University Press.

Luzbetak, L.J. (1954) 'The Socio-religious Significance of a New Guinea Pig Festival', *Anthropological Quarterly* (n.s.) 2: 59–80, 102–28.

MacKenzie, M.A. (1991) *Androgynous Objects: String Bags and Gender in Central New Guinea*. Switzerland: Harwood Academic Press.

Meigs, A.S. (1984) *Food, Sex, and Pollution: A New Guinea Religion*. New Brunswick, NJ: Rutgers University Press.

Munn, N.D. (1977) 'The Spatiotemporal Transformation of Gawa Canoes', *Journal de la Société des Océanistes* 33: 39–54.

Nengo, P. (1991) *Tinpis run*. France/Belgium/PNG: J.B.A. Productions.

O'Hanlon, M.D.P. (1989) *Reading the Skin: Adornment, Display and Society Among the Wahgi*. London: British Museum Publications.

—— (1992) 'Unstable Images and Second Skins: Artefacts, Exegesis and Assessments in the New Guinea Highlands', *Man* 27(3): 587–608.

—— (1993) *Paradise: Portraying the New Guinea Highlands*. London: British Museum Press.

O'Hanlon, M.D.P. and L.H.E. Frankland (1986) 'With a Skull in the Netbag: Prescriptive Marriage and Matrilateral Relations in the New Guinea Highlands', *Oceania* 56: 181–98.

Read, K.E. (1965) *The High Valley*. New York: Charles Scribner's Sons.

—— (1986) *Return to the High Valley: Coming Full Circle*. Berkeley: University of California Press.

Reay, M.O. (1959) *The Kuma: Freedom and Conformity in the New Guinea Highlands*. Melbourne: Melbourne University Press.

—— (1981) 'Some Aspects of Social Change in the Minj Area, Western Highlands Province, Papua New Guinea' (report submitted to the Jiwaka area government). Canberra: Research School of Pacific Studies, Australian National University.

Shearston, T. (1979) 'End of a Road' in *Something in the Blood*. Queensland: University Press.

Simpson, C. (1962) *Plumes and Arrows: Inside New Guinea*. Sydney: Angus and Robertson.

Sinclair, J.P. (1966) *Behind the Ranges: Patrolling in New Guinea*. Melbourne: Melbourne University Press.

Stewart, P.J. and Strathern, A.J. (2002) *Remaking the World: Myth, Mining, and Ritual Change Among the Duna of Papua New Guinea.* Washington: Smithsonian Institution Press.

Strathern, A.J. (1984) *A Line of Power.* London: Tavistock.

Strathern, A.J. and Stewart, P.J. (2003) 'Conflicts vs. Contracts: Political Flows and Blockages in Papua New Guinea', in R. Brian Ferguson (ed.) *The State, Identity, and Violence: Political Disintegration in the Post-Cold War World.* New York and London: Routledge.

Strathern, A.J. and Strathern, M. (1971) *Self-decoration in Mount Hagen.* London: Duckworth.

Sykes, K. (n.d.) '*The Snatcher* on the Road to Regional Development in New Ireland: Possessive Individualism and the Reach of the Entrepreneur.' MS (paper given at AAA meetings, Atlanta, Georgia 1988).

Young, D. (2001) 'The Life and Death of Cars: Private Vehicles on the Pitjantjatjara Lands, South Australia', in D. Miller (ed.) *Car cultures.* Oxford: Berg.

9 'ISLAND BUILDERS': LANDSCAPE AND HISTORICITY AMONG THE LANGALANGA, SOLOMON ISLANDS[1]

Pei-yi Guo

A unique feature of Malaita are [*sic*] the artificial islands of Langalanga and Lau lagoons, built laboriously by the saltwater people. These islands of coral rock, constructed over centuries to escape the frequent raids by headhunters, are also the traditional home of the manufacture of shell money.
(Solomon Island Tourist Authority 1996)

The Langalanga of the Solomon Islands used to construct and dwell on tiny artificial or semi-artificial islets for generations in the Langalanga Lagoon on the island of Malaita. After many generations of residence on the artificial islets, the majority of the Langalanga people have moved onshore to build new settlements along the coastline of mainland Malaita over the past few decades, as a result of a series of historical developments. Although the majority of Langalanga people no longer live on artificial islets, many people still introduce and present themselves as the 'island builders'.

This chapter aims to understand how the Langalanga people conceptualise and appropriate their landscape, especially in relation to their historicity. I argue that landscape is a key component of how Langalanga people perceive, memorise and represent history, and configure their sense of self. Although landscape is better seen generally as cultural process in Langalanga, it is inscriptive in some circumstances, especially in the Langalanga interactions with the gazes of outsiders. The colonial and postcolonial (tourist) gazes have highlighted artificial islands as a locus of special interest (Guo 2001b). It is through this culturally patterned mode of organisation of memories of the past and its entanglement with a wider range of powers and relations in a historical context that the artificial islands become the dominant symbol in the process of

189

differentiation and representation of self and other, and landscape is transformed from cultural process to inscription.

THE LANGALANGA AND THEIR LANDSCAPE

The Langalanga live by the west coast and on tiny offshore islets of the Langalanga Lagoon on Malaita Island. The population of the Langalanga was approximately 5,000 in 1997. Langalanga subsistence is largely based on food crops of root vegetables, as well as fishing and wage labour. However, their major cash income depends on manufacturing shell money, which is used by many groups in the Solomon Islands for bridewealth, compensation, body decoration and sometimes payment in land transactions.

The emergence of the Langalanga is a result of multiple waves of migration. They first came down from the Kwara'ae and Kwaio mountains of Malaita Island to the Langalanga coast, and later moved to offshore islets or even built their own artificial islets in the lagoon. Some Langalanga people attribute the introduction of shell money manufacture as the prime reason for such movement, because materials for shell money production are more accessible by the sea. Others consider reasons such as refuge-seeking as possible motives for the adoption of the specific residential form. The new residence then attracted people from the mountains of Malaita and other islands in the Solomon Sea to join in.

Langalanga artificial islands are built on reefs and shallow places in the sea, with man-made foundations. They first make a big raft of logs that floats and then load it with rocks. The raft is ferried to the desired location, then coral rocks are put on the raft to sink it under the sea. People then heap up coral rocks to build the permanent landmass. Usually it is built to a level slightly above the high tide mark. Soils are added later to fill in the holes and form the land. Some trees are planted on top afterwards. From the material perspective, an islet is built technically by heaping rocks on reefs and shallow places in the sea. On the other hand, supernatural power is needed to ensure the strength of the islet. Rocks symbolise the power in many ways: the first rock for a new islet is placed by the *kastom*[2] priest to acquire the power of the shark; a latecomer adds new rocks around the existing islet, and he needs to obtain a rock from the founder of the islet to be incorporated in the foundation of his own section as a sign of entering into membership; a man who wants to construct a new islet of his own usually takes a rock from his clan islet as a way to transmit the power from his ancestors to the new settlement.

After more than 300 years of residence on the artificial islets, the majority of the Langalanga people moved onshore over the past few decades. The British colonial policy of pacification reduced the tension between the Langalanga and their neighbouring bush population; missions encouraged both bush and saltwater people to reside together in coastal mission villages; the Masina Rule (Keesing 1992) after the Second World War proclaimed a single Malaita identity, bringing to an end the traditional antagonism between the saltwater and the bush people. Therefore coastal land became more accessible to the Langalanga. When several cyclones in the late 1960s and the early 1970s caused severe damage to their tiny islets, the Langalanga abandoned their old homes and moved to build new settlements onshore.

Through local people's accounts of their lives on the artificial islands, we notice that features of the islands play an important role in their memory. In those narratives, people constantly compare their lives on the islets in the past to their present lives, and they are concerned about how the special residential form affects their *genre de vie*. Summarising the migration narratives of the Langalanga people, the central theme in their rhetoric was 'new place, new landscape and new life'. People started to construct their new sense of place in the new settlements. When people talked about their initial reluctance to move onshore and the amount of hard work it took to set up the village there, the characteristics of the landscape and its transformation were always main themes in their narratives. People love to talk about how swampy and bushy the piece of land used to be, and how mosquitoes and mud made their lives miserable, and how the whole landscape was changed by their efforts. In the history of the development of the village, the landscape continued to change. The church was built, the school had been moved and rebuilt twice, damage was caused by cyclones, houses were relocated and rebuilt and some were newly established.

The coastal Langalanga people today emphasise that the most significant changes after their recent migration were that they were closer to the land they cultivated, and spent less effort on paddling between offshore islets and mainland Malaita. As a result, their relation to their landscape changed dramatically. The majority of the Langalanga people were content with their life onshore because it is convenient to go inland to their gardens as well as to carry out seaward activities (Guo 2001a).

So far I have set the stage for a contextualised understanding of the interweaving of the landscape, the past and Langalanga migration history. I now turn to explore the poetics of landscape in Langalanga – the local conceptualisation of landscape.

THE POETICS OF LANDSCAPE

In order to understand why artificial islands are used as the cultural representation of the Langalanga people, we need first to ask: why artificial islands? Why do the Langalanga choose a feature of the landscape instead of something else to represent them? What is the relationship between the Langalanga and their surroundings? This is a question of local conceptualisation.

Different people may use different things to represent themselves in relation to others – such as cloth in India (Bayly 1986), or a kind of staple food, such as rice, in Japan (Ohnuki-Tierney 1993). But why those things? Researchers have shown that the dominant symbol(s) that is used to present and represent the people usually plays a prominent role in their culture, for example, 'We are what we eat.'

And for the Langalanga, 'We are where we live (and lived).' Landscape is a 'dominant symbol' in Langalanga: 'it occurs frequently, or its presence, both itself and its iconic representations, is quite conspicuous' and 'it serves as a "window"', revealing something important about the culture (Ohnuki-Tierney 1993: 5). In this section I will examine the local view of landscape, that is, how landscape is conceptualised and appropriated by the Langalanga, and how and why artificial islands, a specific feature of the landscape, become the representation of the collective self.

My research on the Langalanga shows that one important key to the question lies in their specific 'mode of organization for memories of the past' (Fox 1997a: 17). The reason that artificial islands become their cultural marker is strongly connected to the way they view them as the representation of 'tradition' and 'the past'. In order to understand why features of the landscape are appropriated as the cultural marker of the Langalanga people, it is necessary to elucidate the role landscape plays in their historical memory and the memory process of the past. This is the question of historicity, that is, 'the culturally patterned way or ways of experiencing and understanding history'(Ohnuki-Tierney 1990). Since Renato Rosaldo's study of Ilongot society (1980), the 'spatialization of time' – that is, how people remember, write or locate their history in geographical forms, often in their journeys or movement through the landscape – has caught the attention of many anthropologists (e.g. Rappaport 1989; Santos-Granero 1998). The argument is not that the notion of space replaces time in these societies, but that it represents a 'different mode of organization for memories of the past'. Studies have shown that such a mode is widely found among the Austronesians (e.g. Fox 1997b), non-Austronesians (e.g. Feld 1996;

Weiner 1991), Aborigines in Australia (e.g. Morphy 1993, 1995; Munn 1986), and American Indians (e.g. Basso 1984, 1988, 1996; Rappaport 1985, 1989).

Similar phenomena are found among the Langalanga, an Austronesian group. The practice of 'spatialization of time' can be found in their historical narratives and legends, especially in the form of 'topogeny' – the recitation of an ordered sequence of place names (Fox 1997a). Although many Langalanga abandoned the artificial islands and moved onshore, in their memory and discourse about the past, the special landscape of the artificial islands, which they built with their own labour and experience as the core of living space in the past, is constantly used as the metaphor of the past, their preceding ancestors and their activities.

By exploring the conceptualisation and appropriation of landscape among the Langalanga, we find that landscape is a key component of how people perceive, memorise and represent history (i.e. their historicity), and how they configure their sense of selves. Through the studies of local views of landscape, this section looks at the triangulated relationships between humans (self, collective selves, identity), history (ancestral past, shared past) and landscape (place, landmarks, surroundings).

Humans → Landscape

People may have direct relationships with their surroundings through their labour. For example, the Zafimaniry people change their land by building houses or constructing megaliths; through their acts, they become part of the land. Landscape is used as their ethnic marker because it is what one does (Bloch 1995). On the other hand, land (and sea) provides subsistence materials for people and thus empowers them. For example, Fijian villagers believe that humans are the product of place; they emphasise the 'direct embodied experience of the land: seeing, touching, hearing and smelling' (Toren 1995).

Landscape also plays a role in the relationships between humans. In the Amazon, kinship can be perceived directly from the surroundings because personal kin contribute to landscape modification (e.g. house building, garden making) (Gow 1995). Similarly, kinship (moiety, clan) is mapped on to landscape and expressed through perceptions of landscape among the Australian Aborigines (Morphy 1995). In many societies, people use place names to refer to or represent one another (e.g. Basso 1996: 110). Sometimes, people connect to the landscape indirectly – through a form of representation of the landscape, for example, maps and landscape paintings.

In Langalanga, the direct interactions between humans and landscape include the utilisation of landscape for subsistence. Landscape is used for gardens, fishing grounds, and as a source of firewood and water. On the one hand, the land and the sea provide what the Langalanga need for subsistence. On the other hand, landscape shapes human experiences and is also shaped by human experiences (Bender 1993). As Barrett (1991: 8) points out, 'landscape is the entire surface over which people moved and within which they congregated.... Thus landscape, its form constructed from natural and artificial features, became a culturally meaningful resource through its routine occupancy' (cited by Knapp and Ashmore 1999: 6–7).

People make use of some features of the landscape as boundary markers that separate people into different groups. For instance, rivers and trees are seen to set boundaries between land owned by different owner groups or kinship groups. In addition, features of landscape are also employed as labels to categorise different kinds of people – the most significant of these is the contrast between the bush people (*ioi i tolo gi*) and the saltwater people (*ioi i asi gi*).

Features of landscape are also reference points when people describe their actions and directions. For example, *rae fali tolo* means 'up to the bush' (*rae* means 'raise', *fali* means 'till' and *tolo* means 'bush') , while *sifo fali asi* means 'down to the sea' (*sifo* means 'down') . Features of landscape also play roles in the conceptualisation of time, as evidenced in the local names of months, in which the specific scenes in their landscape are often portrayed. For example, in explaining the meaning of the *kora'asi* month, an old man told me that in the *ara* season, the wind was strong and broke the waves, which were vaporised into the air like dust. (*Kora* refers to the white part in broken waves, the foam.) In another explanation, another man said it was called *kora'asi* because the sea was dirty at this time as a result of the strong *ara* wind (*kora* means 'dirty').

Landscape → History

Landscape and landmarks are often used as codes of memory of the past through myth, legends and stories (Basso 1996; Tilley 1994). Küchler argues that in Western tradition, landscape is an inscribed surface, 'the most generally accessible and widely shared *aide-mémoire* of a culture's knowledge and understanding of its past and future' (1993: 85). Sometimes landscape is used as the symbol of the past. For example, when Jewish people from Europe and elsewhere established settlements in Palestine, they used farms as the symbol of the renaissance of Jewish culture: they related farmers to ancient Hebrew farmers, as the sons of the soil, and the land as the link to God. Giving meanings to the landscape became the way to rebuild human links to God in the twentieth century (Selwyn 1995).

The relationships between landscape and ancestral past can go beyond representation and symbolisation. Morphy (1995) argues that a characteristic feature of Australian Aboriginal cultures is the 'subordination of time to space'. As ancestral beings are thought to have travelled and left evidence on the landscape, their own forms became parts of the land, and became fixed in it in a timeless way, so that today they still serve as reference points. The flow of action was fixed by its transmission to landscape.

There are two major dimensions in the relationships between landscape and history in Langalanga. First, landscape features are markers of the past. For example, the Langalanga distinguish the artificial islets that were inhabited (*faluaua tolea*) from the artificial islets which were once occupied but have been abandoned (*faurara*) by the time the conversation takes place (Guo 2001b).[3] Whether there is anyone residing on the artificial islet is particularly singled out as a way to distinguish different categories. Though people are originally seen as expanding and building more and more artificial islet settlements, some islets are described as having been abandoned in recent migration history, especially after the cyclones. Some artificial islets are left with nothing but islet foundations. Some settlements have almost totally disappeared. People who had lived in them are still alive and recall their past there. These islets are referred to as *faurara*: *fau* means 'stones' and *rara* means 'shore'. Nobody lives on them anymore; what are left are the foundation stones (coral rocks) of the artificial islets. They mark the part of the history in the past.

Landmarks or signs on the landscape are sometimes seen as the symbols of the ancestral past; they can be seen as the codes of memory presented in myths or legends. Some features of landscape are evidence of ancestral activities. These are called *tafurae*, signs left by ancestors, including stone walls, houses, trees and sacrificial stones.

Things on the surface of the land are important features of landscape. They are often related to settlement history and land ownership. For example, a Langalanga man talked about the strip of ground by the sea: 'For many generations, I and my people before me have used the timber and native string and native putty which grow on this ground for our canoes.' Things growing on the ground of a piece of land and the access to use of those things indicate (if not stand for) an ancestral connection or affinal connection to the land. In historical narratives, people often recall the trees their ancestors planted; the most important thing is to link these plants with ancestral history, and thus land ownership. In the context of frequent land disputes and the introduction of a court system, which favours certain material 'evidences' these *tafurae* are exploited as a 'resource' (compare Stewart and Strathern 2000 on the concept of *malu* among the Duna people of Papua New Guinea). They are used as evidence of ancestral activities in arguing the authenticity of their 'history' for the claims of ownership.

However, when the ancestors left their signs that are related to super-natural power on the landscape (e.g. sacrificial places, *fera*), their power was transformed into a part of the landscape. These features of the landscape are more than the evidence of spiritual continuity, they are 'the way in which spiritual continuity is constructed' (Morphy 1993: 226). This is the second dimension in the relationship between landscape and history in Langalanga. Supernatural power is involved in the rela-tionships between ancestral history and landscape. A person maintains the relationship with the ancestors (*agalo*) through sacrifices to secure land rights and prosperity. Particular clans possess and perform certain magic to calm the sea, increase agricultural productivity, and attract fish and dolphins. There are *kastom* taboo places for the practices of ancestral worship, such as the trees and reefs under taboo of exploitation, and places where the landscape has been shaped by supernatural animals, which are conceived of as ancestors. Some 'sacred' animals play important roles too. Among them the shark[4] is the most significant and is related to the building of artificial islands. For instance, when a person wants to build a house on an artificial ground, the first few stones need to be put in a special way by a *kastom* priest (*fata abu*). He would place the first stone for sharks in order to obtain power from them, so when cyclones or rough seas come, the island would not be destroyed. Sharks gave power to humans to transform the landscape in building artificial islets. When a section of the landscape was articulated with supernat-ural power, it was in fact articulated with the ancestors and their power.

Humans → History → Landscape

In the discussions above, we see that Langalanga people are often articulated with landscape through their ancestral history and ancestral past (humans → history → landscape). In addition to the examples above, another way for people to appropriate landscape is through naming (Basso 1984, 1988, 1996). Naming is more than giving a linguistic sign to a particular place or landmark; the names usually record historical events. Another possibility is that people are connected to land because of what their ancestors have done.

Personal names are connected with ancestors and history. In general, Langalanga people use the names of their ancestors as a way for remembrance. However, many Langalanga names are invented after events – usually to commemorate a relative or an elder from the past. Names for such a purpose usually use the location name as a suffix, combined with the prefix *ani* (crying).[5] When a relative died, people used the name of the place where they had heard the bad news and wept to name a newborn baby. Names are linked to ancestors and the past through historical events, especially the sad experience of eternal separation from an ancestor. For instance, the name 'Anitulagi' comes from the event when a woman heard someone crying at Tulagi because the latter had heard the bad news of a relative's death. The name 'Anisitolo' came from an unforgettable event. Some Langalanga people went for a long-distance trip and experienced bad weather. Anisitolo recalled:

Our grandfathers started to cry for any signs of the island so that the sky might be clear. They cried for the ancestral spirits. They cried for any signs of the islands; they wanted to see the *tolo* (i.e. mountain), so they cried to the spirit. All of a sudden they arrived at the west coast of this island, Tobaita, just along the shore. When they arrived at Laulasi, my mother delivered me. And the men asked, 'Is it a boy or a girl?' 'Oh, it's a boy.' 'Well, we want to name him after what we have done, "Anisitolo".' Because they were crying to see an island when it's dark all over. That's why they named me Anisitolo after that event.

In this way, people are connected to ancestors through the event of the ancestor's death; and the event is described from the perspective of relatives of the deceased, who cried when they heard the bad news. The dead and the sorrow for the death are then recorded by the name of the location where the relatives heard the news. Human names are connected to history through a spatial location as reference.

History in Langalanga is not only recorded in human names, but also place names. Some place names are descriptions of the landscape in the place; for example, 'Gwaelaga' means 'group' (*gwae*) of sea grass (*laga*), 'Foufala' means 'that round (*fala*) stone (*fou*)'. Such names are seen as the description by an important ancestor of an important situation in the past. For instance, 'Talakali' means that 'the road (*tala*) is guarded (*kali*, protection)'. When explaining the naming of Talakali, people would point out that in the past, when the bush people and saltwater people were in tension, the saltwater people dared not come onshore. They could only do so when a *ramo* (warrior-leader) was around to protect them, and this piece of land (where the saltwater people anchored onshore) was named after this history. 'Maemadama' (a pool at Loa River) was named not only because the shape was as round as a moon (*madama*). The most significant thing pointed out by narrators is the memory of an ancestor, and the time he saw his image in the pool and came up with the name.

When Langalanga people name a place or talk about a place name, they need to make reference to the historical events or ancestral activities associated with the landscape. When a place name is mentioned, the emphasis is on the ancestors who initiated the name or on how the name is linked to a particular ancestor. For instance, when referring to the name of 'Laulasi' Island, the most important thing for the informants is to talk about the story when the woman who introduced shell money to the lagoon finally settled down by the sea, and said, *Lau nasi* ('I'll stay here') when she travelled down from the mountain and saw the sea.

HUMANS → HISTORY: HUMANS → LANDSCAPE → HISTORY

The relationships between humans, human culture and history have been widely studied by anthropologists. People often remember, recall and reconstruct their past through legends, narratives, songs, rituals or genealogies. In many societies, landscape is significant and plays a key role in peoples' mode of historicity (humans → landscape → history). In Fiji, the power of stories lies in their reference to known landmarks because they thus emphasise material and manifest continuity between the present and the past (Toren 1995).

Studies have shown that the 'spatialization of time' (Fox 1997a: 17), or the 'spatial conception of time' (Basso 1996: 34) – history as described in terms of landscape, place names, and migration paths – are widely seen in many cultures (e.g. Fox and Sather 1996; Jorgensen 1990). One form, as already noted, is what Fox called 'topogeny', the recitation of an ordered sequence of place names. It is widely found among Austronesian societies (Fox 1997b), but also in Australia, Papua New Guinea, and the Amazon,[6] and we find similar practices in Langalanga. Stories of journeys are a major type in Langalanga historical narratives, which are characterised by the constant appearance of place names and features of landscape. For example, in the story of a snake migrating north from South Malaita:

Then it moved, drifted and landed at Maka, asked to stay but was given a 'no' again. The snake drifted. It went ... it went and asked to live at Ufu and received a 'no' again. It came. The snake drifted ... and landed at Rohinari, and the place was full again. So the snake came and drifted along the island [coast]. It came and arrived at the water mouth of Diua. The man at Diua told him, 'Oh, it full here and you try over there.' So it came to Tafoka, asked at the water mouth of Tafoka, and they told him 'no' again. So it came to Onepusu. When it arrived at Onepusu, it asked the man there and he said, 'This place is full already. Try over there.' Then it came to Kiu. Arriving at Kiu, it asked them and they said, 'Oh, it's full, try another side from us.' So it came to Wairaha, arrived at the water mouth of Wairaha and asked, but it was just the same – 'It's full already ...' (narrated by Bennie, author's fieldnotes)

The same pattern goes on in the rest of the legend, which details the journey of the snake. This is typical of Langalanga migration narratives. In historical narratives, people often mention the places where the ancestors stayed, passed by, or did some kind of activity. Knowledgeable informants would often explain the meaning of those place names and the events they were named after. In a famous story, which describes the journey of the woman who introduced shell money to Langalanga and the man who found her, we can see that naming of places is central to Langalanga historical narratives.

At first they lived at Fougwari (*fou*, stone; *gwari*, cold) near Loa. They tried to heat a stone there to change the colour of the shell but failed, so she said it was 'Fougwari'. Then they moved down to Furafai. *Fura* is a unit of *galia* (shell money), and *fai* (four) *galia* is called a '*fai*'. Then they moved down to Kwaioe (the *kwai* [river], of their son Are'oe). Then to Oreore land – *ore* means cut off, and Afelaua said, '*Lau ore lo*' (I cut off from my original land).... Later Afelaua and Lomo moved to Bubuitolo (means 'look to the bush', *tolo* means bush). (by Tofe and Jonathan)

The mainstream migration narratives in the Langalanga traced their ancestral origins[7] in the central mountainous area (*tolo*, bush) of Malaita Island and detailed the paths their ancestral heroes took in their journey from the mountain to the seacoast (*asi*, sea). Discovery is always seen as a process, which is recorded in landscapes and landmarks (see Burt 1994) – and in a linear way. In most narratives, the founding hero moved from one settlement to another before arriving at the final destination. From a geographical perspective, they moved down the hill step by step and migrated towards the sea. It is essential to list the places where the founding hero had been.[8] Place names and features of the landscape, including the places where the ancestors made stops, the houses or shrines the ancestors built and then abandoned, the trees they planted and the places they gave names to, are presented in a lineal pattern. This 'spatialization of time' – found also in many Austronesian and non-Austronesian cultures in Oceania (see Rumsey and Weiner 2001) as well as Native American cultures – articulated humans to history through the features and transformations of landscape.

LANDSCAPE AS TEXT OR PROCESS?

There are two major genres of models in landscape studies: the inscriptive model and the processual model. The former, initiated by cultural geographers, sees landscape as a pictorial way of representing or symbolising surroundings and as the materialisation of memory. 'New Cultural Geography' scholars (see Duncan 1990) visualised landscape as a 'cultural image' (Knapp and Ashmore 1999: 3), and initiated the metaphor of landscape as text.[9] For example, in the introduction of *The Iconography of Landscape*, Daniels and Cosgrove point out that although geographers used to treat landscape as the object of empirical investigation, they also liken landscape to a text and its interpretation to 'reading' (1988: 1).

The text metaphor or the inscriptive model is well liked by some anthropologists too (Selwyn 1995: 132). For instance, Santos-Granero (1998) argues that the Yanesha in Peruvian Central Andes 'write' history into the landscape – an act which he calls 'topographic writing', a communicational system based on 'topograms' (individual elements of the landscape). Rumsey (2001) points out that many examples in the volume *Emplaced Myth* (Rumsey and Weiner 2001) share the idea that 'the earth is interpreted as a surface of inscription' (Rumsey 2001: 32), and the trend in the discipline of anthropology favours 'notions of inscription, repetition or mimesis' (Rumsey 2001: 35–8).

However, several anthropologists find the text metaphor popular but unanalysed. Green (1995) points out that the text analogy or text-based paradigm leads us to think of an image as fixed and thus narrows the possible ways that we might envisage the visual. Küchler, as mentioned earlier, (1993) argues that the 'Western' view, which originates from landscape art since the Renaissance, treats landscape as an inscribed surface, as an 'aide-mémoire' of cultural knowledge and understanding of its past and future (1993: 85). In contrast, in New Ireland, landscape is not the inscription of memory or encoding of memories, but the process of remembering. The 'Western' conceptualisation – 'landscape of memory' – sees landscape as a fixed, objectifiable and measurable description of a surface, while the Melanesian conceptualisation – 'landscape as memory' – sees landscape as something that is affected by the project of its representation and remembrance, as part of a process of remembering. Gow (1995) also opposes the reading metaphor for several reasons: that it is a cultural practice of the West, and that there is a presumption of encoding/decoding and sender/receiver. Landscape is thus reduced to representation only (see also Humphrey 1995). On the contrary, he argues, the Amazon people see local environment as a lived space, as a cultural process.

A processual approach is also seen in Morphy's study, which contrasts the view of landscape of the European settlers with that of the Australian Aborigines (Morphy 1993). For the white colonisers, landscape is given a value by its place in history and economic potential. Place names record historical events and the roles of human agents in the development of the land. However, for the Aborigines, place names refer to spiritual forces. What is involved here is not the evidence of spiritual continuity, but 'the way in which spiritual continuity is constructed' (Morphy 1993: 226).[10] While studies of Australian Aborigines used to treat landscape as part of the ethnographic description, and ignored its role in the process of social reproduction, Morphy argues that landscape is a key concept and a regional characteristic among Australian Aborigines – it is integral to the development of concepts of Self and Other, as well as to the adaptive relations between people and land (1993: 205–6).

In the processual model, landscape is more than a space alive with meanings (Gow 1995: 47), or the representation of place or environment; the relationships between people and landscape are more intertwined. Humphrey (1995) explores how the Mongolians see landscape as something with energies far greater than those of humans, and as something to interact with. Toren, as already mentioned, argues that 'Fijian villagers emphasize direct embodied experience of the land: seeing, touching, hearing and smelling' (1995: 176). Bloch (1995) and Selwyn (1995) examine the practice of using features of the landscape as markers of ethnic identity in Madagascar and the Israeli state. Similar views are found in Knapp and Ashmore (1999), who talk about 'ideational landscapes'. Their idea resembles Johnston's 'inherent perspective' where 'landscape is not separately perceived but embedded within ways of living and being' (1998: 13).

Hirsch (1995) criticises the text metaphor of landscape – as used by cultural geographers – for being too static and limited to the representational, objective and outer aspects. Such views suggest that the notion of landscape implies a denial of process, because they take landscape as a static and restrictive way of seeing which sustains a radical split between insiders and outsiders. It confuses artistic representations and everyday practice (Hirsch 1995: 22–3). In the processual view that Hirsch proposes, landscape is an in-between and unstable concept – there is no 'absolute' landscape: landscape as cultural process is dependent on the cultural and historical context (1995: 23). Peter van Dommelen (1999) and Knapp and Ashmore (1999) also point out that landscape is not only the background of human actions but the outcome of the engagement between people and world in particular historical and local conditions.

BETWEEN PROCESS AND INSCRIPTION

In the inscriptive model, landscape can be alienated from the people, while in the processual model, landscape is embodied in the people, and the relationship between people and landscape is more intertwined and dynamic in some societies than the inscriptive model may suggest. For the Langalanga, both models have explanatory power. Although landscape is better seen generally as cultural process for Langalanga, it is inscriptive in some circumstances, especially in juridical cases of land dispute, and during Langalanga interactions with the gazes of outsiders. Below I will discuss the dialectical relationships between the inscriptive and processual conceptualisations.

Langalanga people make a bodily analogy in describing landscape. For example, in illustrating a river, they use terms such as *gwau kwai* (head of river) and *abolo kwai* (the body of river, the middle of river). However, the most salient emphasis is on the human impact on landscape. Human or body parts transformed into parts of landscape are rarely seen in Langalanga legends (see Sikkink 1999). When the Langalanga talk about landscape features, the most frequently mentioned are the result of human actions, for example, houses, artificial islets, and *tafurae* (signs left by ancestors). In Langalanga language, the notion of 'path' is expressed as 'foot print' (*fuli aela*), the human impact on landscape. Some features, such as rivers, might also relate to actions of supernatural beings. For example, it is believed that a shark born of a woman caused the creeping course of the Loa River, while a snake born of a woman drank the water in another river and made it dry in the middle. People continue to make changes to their landscape and embed landscape as part of their life today. In the narratives of recent migration, Langalanga people talk about the transformation of landscape – their efforts to dry the swampy coastal land – as one of the most important pages of their history. Women, especially, contribute much to the construction of new landscapes, and thus build up a strong identity with places. People consider their new settlements, new gardens, and new relationships to land and sea as the most significant characteristics of their new life.

Landscape features left by ancestral activities are acts of human (and supernatural) beings and are thus seen as containing the power of ancestral or supernatural spirits. Through those actions, power transforms landscape, and is transmitted to their descendants.

Sometimes, landscape features are seen as containing power through people's connections to ancestral activities. For instance, land (*wado*) is an important resource for the Langalanga. Its position in relation to the 'discoverer' or the 'founder' of the clan is a central theme concerning a piece of land. For example, a Langalanga man, Silas Waletofe, explained that:

'Tribal land' is *fuiwale*, the customary land that is owned by the 'tribe' (i.e. clan). The discoverer, founder of the land, then put a sacrifice ground there, and planted nut trees (*nali*, nuts) and bread fruit trees (*baleo*). After the founder died, his children then named parts of this land after their own 'tribe'. They used this person's name for something on the land, for example, the river they used, or the piece of ground where he put his sacrificial altar. They also needed to know the boundary, to let their neighbours recognise and know them. (Silas Waletofe)

Ancestral actions (discovering the piece of land, using the water in the river, and naming the place) and their transformations of the landscape (by planting trees, making gardens, and building houses and sacrificial grounds) empower their descendants, giving them the right to the land.

A given area and its landscape can be cut off from the people, and may no longer provide their daily needs, but it is still the result of human actions in the past. Through the transformations of landscape, humans (especially ancestors) became a part of the landscape, and the landscape becomes a symbol for the humans. Therefore, people are classified as 'bush people' and 'saltwater people', and artificial islands become the cultural representation of the Langalanga.

Landscape entails codes of memory in other contexts. *Tafurae* (signs) left by ancestors: that is, the places they passed by and named, the sacrificial grounds, the *fera*, and the houses they built, and the trees they planted, are seen as symbols of the ancestral past, and are appropriated as sources of legitimate land claims. For example, *fera*, the sacrificial houses built by ancestors, are considered important indications of the past. The locations of ancient *fera* are remembered by knowledgeable informants. It is important to point out where their ancestors set up a *fera*, or where the *fera* was moved to in the course of migration. The more information there is, the more accurately locations can be recalled, the 'truer' the migration narratives are considered. History is evaluated by the names and locations of ancient sites.

The names of places and people were markers or codes of memory of the past, on the one hand. But, on the other hand, as discussed above, the act of an ancestor naming a place also transferred power to the place. Place names often record events in the past; they describe the actions of ancestors in the landscape. As mentioned, people's names often record the scene of hearing of the death of ancestors, and so the place names are used to commemorate the ancestors involved. Knowledge of names and naming is often viewed as proof or evidence that assures the authenticity of narratives. This implies a shared recognition that naming has the function of recording historical events or historical figures. In land disputes, such knowledge transforms landscape from process to inscription. The name of a place is not only the record of how an ancestor gave power to the landscape, but also legitimates the claims made by people in disputes over land.

This chapter has examined why a unique feature of landscape – the artificial islands – has become the expression of identity (see Stewart and Strathern in Chapter 1 of this volume) for the Langalanga. There is a symbolic-cultural significance of landscape for the Langalanga, while 'the meanings are deeply embedded in broader socio-cultural context as well as long-term historical processes' (Ohnuki-Tierney 1993: 5).

Basso points out that people's sense of place, their sense of their tribal past, and their sense of themselves are intertwined (1996: 35). Kahn also argues that, for the Wamirans of Papua New Guinea, 'features in the landscape and other markers ... resonate deeply as they link people to ancient myths and current history. They represent connections between people and their common past, links between individuals and their group, or sources of individual identity' (Kahn 1996: 194). The entanglement between humans, landscape and history is valuable for understanding the concept of the self. Through the exploration of this triangle of relationships, we are able to comprehend why landscape is seen as an ethnic marker for the Langalanga; we are able to understand why landscape is picked by the Langalanga as the metaphor to separate Us (artificial islanders) and Them (neighbours from the mountains, colonisers and tourists). Through the exploration of the entanglement between humans, landscape and history, we are able to comprehend the position of landscape in the Langalanga culture, and why it is sensible for them to make use of a particular feature of landscape to represent themselves. Such representation usually happens in the context of land disputes, and during encounters with others – giving rise to the inscription of landscape.

I have argued elsewhere (Guo 2001a, 2001b) that artificial islets have been portrayed by colonial officers and tourists as a curiosity and the trademark of the Langalanga. By analysing the data from colonial archives, I found that the colonial officers paid special attention to the geographical characteristics in the early reports, especially the artificial islets in the Langalanga Lagoon. The special residential form of the Langalanga was seen as the most fundamental characteristic of the group. For example, the 1934 report states, 'the lagoon contains numerous islets built up by the hands of man upon the outer coral reefs. These islets are heavily populated by a virile race of fisherman' (BSIP 1930–7). In reviewing these early reports, it is clear that the term 'artificial islands/islets' was attached to the Langalanga group whenever they were mentioned for the first time and thus it became their cultural label. 'Langalanga' was not only a geographical lagoon or a group of people, but also a lagoon with artificial islands, or a group of people who built and dwelt on artificial islets. Island life was viewed as a cultural trait, a kind of custom for the Langalanga.

However, the most influential gazes in contemporary times come from the tourists. In advertisements for tourism, the special scenery in the Langalanga Lagoon – the artificial islands – was the main attraction. The 'traditional' residential form on the artificial islets was portrayed as ancient and exotic, and was seen as the result of seeking refuge from the bloody tribal wars onshore.

The Langalanga were keen to pick up these images seen through the gazes of outsiders. They knew the advantage of presenting and selling those elements to tourists, and were not reluctant to do so. For the Langalanga people, landscape is more like a cultural process in their daily lives, and there is a mutual embodiment between landscape and people. However, in the process of the Langalanga engagement with colonisers, scholars and tourists, landscape is transformed into their cultural image and their cultural representation. Landscape is used to express a sense of people's social identity (Knapp and Ashmore 1999: 14–16). Landscape is turned into inscription, which marks and encodes them as a particular group of people. The Langalanga people identify themselves as 'the island builders', the image which has been created through external gazes and internal transformation in their particular historical and political context.

Such gazes contribute to the process and local discourse of cultural reshaping; it is in this context that we are able to understand why, through narratives of recent migration and recounting of island life, Langalanga identification and attachment to the old landscape remain strong.

The 'artificial islands' were more than the source of tourism income for the local people. For coastal Langalanga people, the artificial islands are polysemic. On the one hand, they provide a constant contrast to their way of life today: they are within observable distance, and are within the space of their daily life. People often compare their lifestyle on the coast with that of their neighbours on the islets when they make comments about their own lives. On the other hand, they also point to artificial islets as their past, as the symbol of the time before they moved onshore. I was constantly reminded that coastal Langalanga people migrated from the artificial islets to the shore not too long ago. In personal life history and in historical narratives or legends, the artificial island is surely the key component in the illustration of the past.

Yet, for many coastal Langalanga, the artificial island not only represents 'the other' and 'the past', it also represents the way of 'tradition' and the way of the ancestors, and thus makes it the way of 'the Langalanga'. It is regarded as their cultural marker, though they themselves have migrated and adopted a different mode of residence.

NOTES

1. This chapter is partly rewritten from my PhD dissertation, 'Landscape, History and Migration among the Langalanga, Solomon Islands' (Guo 2001a). I would like to thank the Langalanga people for their help in my fieldwork, and Dr Andrew Strathern and Dr Pamela J. Stewart for their useful suggestions and editorial work on the text.

2. This is a Melanesian way of saying 'custom'.

3. In the Langalanga language, there are three words that refer to 'island'. The term *kokomu* refers to natural islets and all islets in general. On the other hand, other terms are used particularly in referring to artificial islets: *faurara* and *faluaua tolea*. The former means an artificial islet that is no longer inhabited; the latter means 'an inhabited artificial islet'. The Langalanga distinguish islands that are naturally formed from those that are human-built. In their cultural conception of landscape, a person's (or an ancestor's) body movements and physical impacts on landscape are emphasised. It makes perfect sense, therefore, that they stress whether an island is natural or whether it is the work of human labour. However, they do not have a single phrase to correspond to the English term 'artificial island'. When necessary, the Langalanga now use Solomon Pijin, *aetifisio aelan* (see Guo 2001b for a detailed discussion).

4. Sharks are links to ancestors. *Alo are* is the spirit of the ancestor; it can possess sharks or flying foxes, etc. to give signs to people and tell them to make sacrifice to ancestors. People believe that the shark is a strong animal and possesses power to protect people, but it also has power to kill. Some believe that the Langalanga are particularly connected to sharks because some sharks are ancestors. Another popular story illustrated a woman who violated a taboo and gave birth to a shark. Thus the shark is the offspring of a Langalanga woman and is related by blood to the Langalanga people.

5. Some names do not record the news of a death but still use features of landscape in their description. For example, 'Waleoloinamo' means 'come to shore': *wale* means man, *namo* means reef.

6. For example, Waterson (1997) describes how house, genealogies, myth and histories are all closely bound up together and embedded in local landscapes for the Tana Toraja of Sulawesi. Morphy (1993, 1995) points out that the cultural core for Australian Aborigines is 'the attachment of people to place through the mediating process of the ancestral past' (1995: 186). Wassmann (1990) argues that for the Nyaura in the Sepik area, history is most precise when it is geography, organised spatially rather than temporally. Rappaport (1989) finds the Paéz in Colombia use geographical sites not just to encode historical events, but also to make sense of the past. In this mode of historicity, each site is associated with a short episode or fragment, and the chronological character of history is broken.

7. Fox and Sather (1996) point out that the 'origin' concept is shared among Austronesians. However, in Langalanga, those who claimed to migrate from the same origin place did not necessarily share a common identity. People think they might be related somehow in the ancient past, but it is not remembered anymore. Whether they view it as of special cultural meaning needs further study.

8. One reason for detailing all previous settlements and *fera* is to secure their claimed boundary by saying the founder had been to all these places.

9. The article by Duncan and Duncan in 1988, '(Re)reading the Landscape' as well as the book *The City as Text* by Duncan (1990), are the first systematic attempts to examine the 'text-like' quality of landscape.

10. The former resembles what Küchler (1993) called 'landscape of memory', while the latter echoes 'landscape as memory'. Cf. above, pp. 196, 200.

REFERENCES

Barrett, J.C. (1991) *Landscape, Monuments and Society: The Prehistory of Cranborne Chase*. Cambridge: Cambridge University Press.

Basso, K.H. (1984) '"Stalking with Stories": Names, Places, and Moral Narratives among the Western Apache', in E.M. Bruner (ed.) *Text, Play and Story: The Construction and Reconstruction of Self and Society*. Washington, DC: American Ethnological Society, pp. 19–55.

—— (1988) '"Speaking with Names": Language and Landscape among the Western Apache', *Cultural Anthropology* 3: 99–130.

—— (1996) *Wisdom Sits in Places: Landscape and Language Among the Western Apache*. Albuquerque, NM: University of New Mexico Press.

Bayly, B.A. (1986) 'The Origins of Swadeshi (Home Industry): Cloth and Indian Society, 1700–1930', in A. Appadurai (ed.) *The Social Life of Things: Commodities in Cultural Perspective*, Cambridge: Cambridge University Press, pp. 285–321.

Bender, B. (1993) 'Introduction: Landscape – Meaning and Action', in B. Bender (ed.) *Landscape: Politics and Perspectives*. Oxford and Providence, RI: Berg Publishers, pp. 1–17.

Bloch, M. (1995) 'People into Places: Zafimaniry Concepts of Clarity', in E. Hirsch and M. O'Hanlon (eds) *The Anthropology of Landscape: Perspectives on Place and Space*. Oxford: Clarendon Press, pp. 63–77.

BSIP (British Solomon Islands Protectorate) (1930–7) #27 VI – District Annual Reports and associated correspondence, Malaita District Office 1930–1937. Stored in the Solomon Islands National Archives.

Burt, B. (1994) *Tradition and Christianity: the Colonial Transformation of A Solomon Islands Society*. Switzerland: Harwood Academic Press.

Daniels, S. and D. Cosgrove (1988) 'Introduction: Iconography and Landscape', in S. Daniels and D. Cosgrove (eds) *The Iconography of Landscape: Essays on the Symbolic Representation, Design and Use of the Past Environments*. Cambridge: Cambridge University Press, pp. 1–10.

Duncan, J. (1990) *The City as Text: The Politics of Landscape – Interpretation in the Kandyan Kingdom*. Cambridge: Cambridge University Press.

Duncan, J. and N. Duncan (1988) '(Re)reading the Landscape', *Environment and Planning D: Society and Space* 6: 117–26.

Feld, S. (1996) 'Waterfalls of Song: An Acoustemology of Place Resounding in Bosavi, Papua New Guinea', in S. Feld and K.H. Basso (eds) *Senses of Place*. Santa Fe, NM: School of American Research Press.

Fox, J.J. (1997a) 'Place and Landscape in Comparative Austronesian Perspective', in J.J. Fox (ed.) *The Poetic Power of Place: Comparative Perspectives on Austronesian Ideas of Locality*. Canberra: Australian National University, pp. 1–21.

—— (ed.) (1997b) *The Poetic Power of Place: Comparative Perspectives on Austronesian Ideas of Locality*. Canberra: Australian National University Press.

Fox, J.J. and C. Sather (eds) (1996) *Origins, Ancestry and Alliances: Explorations in Austronesian Ethnography*. Canberra: Austronesian National University.

Gow, P. (1995) 'Land, People, and Paper in Western Amazonia', in E. Hirsch and M. O'Hanlon (eds) *The Anthropology of Landscape: Perspectives on Place and Space*. Oxford: Clarendon Press, pp. 43–62.

Green, N. (1995) 'Looking at the Landscape: Class Formation and the Visual', in E. Hirsch and M. O'Hanlon (eds) *The Anthropology of Landscape: Perspectives on Place and Space*. Oxford: Clarendon Press, pp. 31–42.

Guo, P. (2001a) 'Landscape, Migration and History among the Langalanga, Solomon Islands', PhD thesis, Department of Anthropology, University of Pittsburgh.

—— (2001b) 'External Gazes and Cultural Representation: Langalanga People and Their "Artificial Islands"', paper presented at the 'Representation and Boundary' Conference held on 22 June 2001 at the National Museum of Natural Science, Taichung, Taiwan.

Hirsch, E. (1995) 'Landscape: Between Place and Space', in E. Hirsch and M. O'Hanlon (eds) *The Anthropology of Landscape: Perspectives on Place and Space*. Oxford: Clarendon Press, pp. 1–30.

Humphrey, C. (1995) 'Chiefly and Shamanist Landscapes in Mongolia', in E. Hirsch and M. O'Hanlon (eds) *The Anthropology of Landscape: Perspectives on Place and Space*. Oxford: Clarendon Press, pp. 135–62.

Johnston, R. (1998), 'Approaches to the Perception of Landscape: Philosophy, Theory, Methodology', *Archaeological Dialogues* 5: 54–68.

Jorgensen, D. (1990) 'Placing the Past and Moving the Present: Myth and Contemporary History in the Telefomin', *Culture* 10: 47–56.

—— (1997) 'Who and What Is a Landowner? Mythology and Making the Ground in a Papua New Guinea Mining Project', *Anthropological Forum* 7: pp. 599–627.

Kahn, M. (1996) 'Your Place and Mine: Sharing Emotional Landscapes in Wamira, Papua New Guinea', in S. Feld and K.H. Basso (eds) *Senses of Place*. Santa Fe, NM: School of American Research Press, pp. 167–96.

Keesing, R.M. (1992) *Custom and Confrontation: The Kwaio Struggle for Cultural Autonomy*. Chicago: University of Chicago Press.

Knapp, B. and W. Ashmore (1999), 'Archaeological Landscapes: Constructed, Conceptualized, Ideational', in W. Ashmore and B. Knapp (eds) *Archaeologies of Landscape: Contemporary Perspectives*. Malden, MA: Blackwell Publishers, pp. 1–32.

Küchler, S. (1993) 'Landscape as Memory: The Mapping of Process and its Representation in a Melanesian Society', in B. Bender (ed.) *Landscape: Politics and Perspectives*. Oxford: Berg Publishers, pp. 85–106.

Morphy, H. (1993) 'Colonialism, History and the Construction of Place: the Politics of Landscape in Northern Australia', in B. Bender (ed.) *Landscape: Politics and Perspectives*. Providence and Oxford: Berg Publishers, pp. 205–43.

—— (1995) 'Landscape and the Reproduction of the Ancestral Past', in E. Hirsch and M. O'Hanlon (eds) *The Anthropology of Landscape: Perspectives on Place and Space*. Oxford: Oxford University Press, pp. 184–209.

Munn, N.D. (1986) *The Fame of Gawa: A Symbolic Study of Value Transformation in a Massim (Papua New Guinea) Society*. Cambridge: Cambridge University Press.

Ohnuki-Tierney, E. (1990) 'Introduction: The Historicization of Anthropology', in E. Ohnuki-Tierney (ed.) *Culture Through Time: Anthropological Approaches*. Stanford, CA: Stanford University Press, Stanford, pp. 1–25.

—— (1993) *Rice as Self: Japanese Identities through Time*. Princeton, NJ: Princeton University Press.

Rappaport, J. (1985) 'History, Myth and the Dynamics of Territorial Maintenance in Tierradentro, Colombia', *American Ethnologist* 12: 27–45.

—— (1989) 'Geography and Historical Understanding in Indigenous Colombia', in R. Layton (ed.) *Who Needs the Past: Indigenous Values and Archaeology*. London: Unwin Hyman, pp. 84–94.

Rosaldo, R. (1980) *Ilongot Headhunting 1883–1974: A Study in Society and History*. Stanford, CA: Stanford University Press.

Rumsey, A. (2001) 'Tracks, Traces and Links to Land in Aboriginal Australia, New Guinea and Beyond', in A. Rumsey and J. Weiner (eds) *Emplaced Myth: Space, Narrative and Knowledge in Aboriginal Australia and Papua New Guinea*. Honolulu: University of Hawaii Press.

Rumsey, A. and J. Weiner (eds) (2001) *Emplaced Myth: Space, Narrative and Knowledge in Aboriginal Australia and Papua New Guinea*. Honolulu: University of Hawaii Press.

Santos-Granero, F. (1998) 'Writing History into the Landscape: Space, Myth and Ritual in Contemporary Amazonia', *American Ethnologist* 25: 128–48.

Selwyn, T. (1995) 'Landscapes of Liberation and Imprisonment: Towards an Anthropology of the Israeli Landscape', in E. Hirsch and M. O'Hanlon (eds) *The Anthropology of Landscape: Perspectives on Place and Space.* Oxford: Clarendon Press, pp. 114–35.

Sikkink, L. (1999) 'Landscape, Gender and Community: Andean Mountain Stories', *Anthropological Quarterly* 72: 167–82.

Stewart, P.J. and A. Strathern (2000) 'Naming Places: Duna Evocations of Landscape in Papua New Guinea', *People and Culture in Oceania* 16: 87–107.

Tilley, C. (1994) *A Phenomenology of Landscape: Places, Paths and Monuments.* Oxford: Berg.

Toren, Christina (1995) 'Seeing the Ancestral Sites: Transformations in Fijian Notions of the Land', in E. Hirsch and M. O'Hanlon (eds) *The Anthropology of Landscape: Perspectives on Place and Space.* Oxford: Clarendon Press, pp. 163–83.

van Dommelen, P. (1999) 'Exploring Everyday Places and Cosmologies', in W. Ashmore and B. Knapp (eds) *Archaeologies of Landscape: Contemporary Perspectives.* Malden, MA: Blackwell Publishers, pp. 277–85.

Wassmann, Jurg (1990) 'The Nyaura Concepts of Space and Time', in N. Lutkehaus, C. Kaufmann, W.E. Mitchell, D. Newton, L. Osmundsen and M. Schuster (eds) *Sepik Heritage: Tradition and Change in Papua New Guinea.* Durham, NC: Carolina Academic Press, pp. 23–35.

Waterson, Roxana (1997) 'The Contested Landscapes of Myth and History in Tana Toraja', in J.J. Fox (ed.) *The Poetic Power of Place: Comparative Perspectives on Austronesian Ideas of Locality.* Canberra: Australian National University, pp. 63–90.

Weiner, James F. (1991) *The Empty Place: Poetry, Space and Being Among the Foi of Papua New Guinea.* Bloomington: Indiana University Press.

10 BIOGRAPHY, ECOLOGY, POLITICAL ECONOMY: SEASCAPE AND CONFLICT IN JAMAICA

James G. Carrier

This chapter is concerned with the meanings of the coastal waters for different sets of people in Negril and Montego Bay. These are tourist towns, visited primarily by North Americans but also by Europeans, and as tourism in Jamaica grew sharply in the last three decades of the twentieth century, so have they. Moreover, during these decades the Jamaican government, under external pressure, introduced structural adjustment and free trade policies that weakened much of the rest of the economy. So, while tourism grew, more conventional sections of the economy shrank and the country's reliance on tourism accelerated. Thus it is that, looking at Negril and Montego Bay, one could see the consequences of powerful forces at work on the country.

These forces did not shape only the obvious, built features of these two towns, the roads, hotels, airports, bars, piers and the like. In addition, they shaped the geographical environment, the land and, my concern in this chapter, the coastal waters. They shaped the population, which grew sharply as more and more Jamaicans went to these towns in search of work. They shaped what these people did once they arrived. Even people who found themselves in these places for reasons divorced from these national and international forces, confronted places and lived lives that were affected by them.

Many different sorts of people experienced the waters of these two places. In this chapter I will consider two. One set is conservation activists, especially a handful of people who worked to establish marine parks, national parks intended to protect and enhance the quality of the coastal waters in these two places. Because there are only a few of these, I consider them primarily as individuals and in terms of their individual histories. The other set is fishers, the local people who fished in those

210

waters. Because there are substantial numbers of these, I will deal with them in more general terms. These two sets of people confronted the same environment, the waters of Negril and Montego Bay. However, these bodies of water meant different things to them, and these different meanings brought these different people into conflict with each other.

My purpose in this chapter is to sketch the nature and bases of these different meanings. As I hope to make clear, many of them sprang from the direct experiences these people had with or in the context of those waters, the memories encoded in the sea, which made these waters part of the 'foreground' (see Hirsch 1995: esp. 4) of their lives. However, more than direct experience was at work. In addition to the collective values and identities that affected how people appear to have understood those waters, the national and international forces that I have mentioned had an important part to play. They affected how those waters were used and their material condition, and they imposed new meanings on them, which people had to confront. These meanings tended to construe these waters as a 'background' (again, see Hirsch 1995), which had certain potentialities waiting to be realised.

These old and new meanings did not simply endow these waters with sense and significance. In addition, they peopled those waters, because they defined certain sorts of people and certain sorts of activities and relationships as appropriate for those waters, and others as inappropriate. More is at stake here, then, than what went on in people's heads or even their personal experiences, for those thoughts and experiences existed in a world of powerful institutions and forces, forces that put pressure on these people to modify what went on in these waters in order to bring out the potential contained in them when viewed as background. In presenting this tale of people, landscape and meaning, then, I necessarily present as well a tale of the larger world that impinged upon Negril and Montego Bay.

CONSERVATION ACTIVISTS

The activists seeking to establish these marine parks had lived in Jamaica, some of them for decades. However, they went there as adults from Europe and the United States. These are only some of the people involved in establishing and running these parks, but they are distinctive because they were the leaders in the efforts to set up these parks. I will deal with them in two different ways. In this section, I will focus on two individuals who were, by general consent, the founding figures of these parks. In the next section I will deal with park managers in general, those who were in charge of these parks after they were established. I begin with Negril.

Negril

The Negril park is the result of agitation by the Negril Coral Reef Preservation Society (NCRPS). This was a local conservationist organisation originally dominated by a handful of Europeans and North Americans who were active in commerce in general, and the tourism industry in particular. There had been a precursor organisation, a section of the Negril Chamber of Commerce, agitating since about 1980. The NCRPS itself was established in 1990, and the Negril park was declared by the Jamaican government in 1998. I will describe the woman who was central to the NCRPS, and through it the formal establishment of the park. I will call this woman X. She is from the United States and was born around 1950. She was effectively the founder of the NCRPS and was long its president.

X was a conservation activist, and I begin with her understanding of 'the environment'. For her, it was essentially the coastal waters in the immediate area of Negril. She was concerned with the increasingly unhealthy state of this environment, and a central aspect of this for her, as both cause and effect, was the deterioration of the coral in the area. One of her recurrent concerns was the shrinking of Negril's sandy beach, which she said was caused by that deterioration. As this may suggest, X saw her surroundings in environmental-scientific terms. She was knowledgeable about coral in itself and as it relates to the coastal environment; she was knowledgeable about coastal ecosystems, especially the effects of terrestrial run-off, which appeared to be important in Negril.[1]

However, environmental science was not the only way she saw things. In fact, her approach was clearly and strongly emotional, and stands in contrast to the tone of some of the marine biologists who have done work in Jamaica, people who could be passionate about their science but who were dispassionate about the waters they studied and the processes they discerned. X not only saw her surroundings in emotional terms, she saw that emotion in others as well. For example, she described how she showed local people photographs of the Negril beach in the 1950s, when, she says, it was about 100 yards wide, much wider than it is now. She said older fishermen cried when they saw how much things had changed for the worse.

This sense of loss was pronounced in one conversation that I had with X. Driving through Negril she spontaneously started to talk about what things were like when she first lived there, and her tales and her tone were a mixture of affection and aggravation: the absence of any serviceable road link to the outside world; there was only one telephone in the town, and it took her all day to make a call; the handful of hippie hotels in town and the goings-on of their owners and friends; and how all this changed with the construction of Norman Manley Boulevard along Long Bay to the north, the partial filling of the Great Morass (the swampy area that lay just behind the shoreline) and the building of tourist hotels along the new road. So her view of the place was also shaped by the history of Negril and by the events of her life there. To understand better how she thought of her surroundings, then, it is necessary to understand what brought this woman to Negril, and what she did once she arrived.

In the 1970s, X was married and living in the American Midwest. Late in that decade she became gravely ill, was treated and recovered. At that time she also divorced, and it seems that the strain of the disease and treatment was instrumental in ending her marriage. She said that she had been to a party where one of the guests had shown pictures of Negril. Although she had never been to Jamaica before, she decided to go there to recover from her illness and from the collapse of her marriage. When she first moved to Negril, she did not work, but lived on her divorce settlement, which lasted her for about five years.

During this period she swam several miles each day, up and down the waters off the shore of the area of Negril called the West End, the part of town that was built before the tourist boom. She was not exploring the coastal waters, for her route did not vary. Instead, as she described it, she was passing her days, recovering from the disastrous events that had befallen her, gradually rebuilding herself physically and mentally, and figuring out her life. She told me stories of octopuses changing colour, and other curious things she saw during her swims, and she said that gradually she got to know what she described as the personalities of different sorts of marine life. For her, then, the waters were populated primarily by marine life and by people who valued that life. And her growing interest in and engagement with marine life led her to find books on the subject.

After she had used up her divorce settlement, she took a job in a nearby town, soon abandoned this as unsatisfactory, and ended up working for her landlady, who owned a dive shop in Negril, a small business that rented and refilled air tanks, taught people how to dive and provided boats to take people out on dives. X said that this woman was wearing herself out running her dive shop, and complaining that she needed an additional instructor. X volunteered, to assist her friend and to earn some money. She was quickly trained, first as a diver and then as an instructor. While doing this work, she became increasingly involved in marine conservation activities.

For X, then, the marine environment was not something to be apprehended only as a space construed in terms of the abstract frames of science. While this woman could discuss run-off and its effects on nitrogen levels in coastal waters, those waters were more than just the marine environment. In addition, they were the place where she had recovered from her illness and from the collapse of her marriage, where she built a life in a place she had never been before. And in her tale, personal and public history intersect in consequential ways. Her recovery coincided with the growth of tourism in the area, a growth that profoundly changed Negril in ways that dismayed her and that helped lead her to her environmentalism. This sort of intersection occurs as well for the main activist in Montego Bay.

Montego Bay

In its present form, the Montego Bay Marine Park is the result of the activities of the Montego Bay Marine Park Trust. This was set up in the 1970s, when a small marine protected area was declared in the bay, and it was dominated by a small number of Europeans who had moved to Montego Bay in the previous few decades. Thus, the park and its Trust have a longer history than the Negril park and the NCRPS. Also, agitation for a park in Montego Bay appears to have been more of a collective affair than was the case with Negril, where X's position was pre-eminent. However, generally those who were active in Montego Bay late in the 1990s saw one man as the most important early force. He is Y. Although he left Jamaica around 1995 to return to his country of birth, senior people in the park and trust referred to him frequently while I was in Jamaica, and he regularly returned to Montego Bay, which is where I met him.

As with X, for Y 'the environment' was effectively the marine environment, here the waters of Montego Bay. He was aware of scientific findings about Montego Bay and had worked with marine biologists in Jamaica. However, like X, he was no scientist. Also like X, he said that much of the cause of the deterioration of the bay is land-based. He referred to dredging and other alterations to the beachfront in the 1970s, a part of the extraordinary growth of Montego Bay as a tourist area in the last third of the twentieth century. He also referred to changes in the run-off going into the bay as a result of the clearing of forest and the spread of farms in the area. However, and yet again like X, Y's scientific orientation is only one aspect of his approach to his surroundings. The other important aspect springs from his personal history. This is less striking than X's, but illustrates the same intersection of personal history and broader historical changes affecting the country.

Y went to Jamaica in 1957, to Kingston. In 1964, he transferred to Montego Bay and formed a divers' group with two others in the town, one of whom ran a dive shop. Around 1970, Y and his fellows decided to form their own dive company. They did so because they knew that a group of British divers wanted to go to Montego Bay, a group that was larger than could be accommodated by the city's existing dive organisations. Although forming this company was a commercial decision, it was apparent from what Y said that it was by no means purely commercial. He enjoyed the bay as a place to dive, took pride in it, and wanted others to enjoy it as well.

However, that pride and pleasure were under threat, for at about the same time the editor of a popular American diving magazine wrote that the waters of Montego Bay were not as clear as they had been. Y decided that the editor was correct. As a result of this, he and some other interested people organised a workshop around 1974 to try to address the problem. Emerging from the workshop was a proposal for a marine protected area, relatively small, to the north-east of Doctor's Cave Beach in Montego Bay. This was officially recognised by the Jamaican government late in 1974 (O'Callaghan et al. 1988).

From this brief sketch, it should be clear that Y's involvement with the marine environment in Montego Bay was less intense than was X's involvement in Negril. Y was recovering from no personal crisis in the midst of Montego Bay's waters, and one central element of his involvement was diving as a commercial enterprise. Thus, for Y the marine environment effectively was, among other things, a commodity, the consumption of which his company sold to tourist divers. However, it is also clear that this does not capture his thinking adequately, any more than does X's scientific approach to Negril's coastal waters.

Y's commercial interest in the bay both sprang from and fed into his personal involvement with the marine environment. As I have said, Y formed his dive company partly out of his pleasure and pride in diving in Montego Bay. Equally, the pragmatics of running the dive company meant that the bay's waters shaped his dealings with others. This is apparent in things like the workshop around 1974, and his repeated involvement with efforts to protect and improve the bay's waters. And, of course, the sheer fact that he was living and diving in Montego Bay for so many years meant that those waters would figure in important events in his life. For instance, around 1970, when the editor of the American diving magazine wrote his letter, two of Y's friends tried to set personal depth records. Neither came back, though both bodies were recovered eventually, one from a depth of over 300 feet. Not surprisingly, he said that this helped to change the way that he thought about the waters at Montego Bay.

So, Y's practical engagement was not simply utilitarian. He liked to dive and was involved in the dive business, which meant that he had both a personal and a practical relationship with the environment. This led him to take a personal interest in the state of the waters and in what people said about it. Thus, he was proud of the way that his early dive business enabled visitors from the British Isles to swim and enjoy a body of water in which he took a proprietary interest. Similarly, he was unsettled by the reaction of the editor of the American diving magazine to the waters of Montego Bay, and unhappy when he recalled his own growing sense that the quality of the waters noticeably deteriorated around 1970. Although his orientation to those waters was less intense than X's orientation to the waters of Negril, Montego Bay was part of his world and work, and what affected it affected him, both professionally and personally.

I have sketched the stories of X and Y with only a modest end in view. That is to show how important aspects of both of their biographies were played out in the context of these bodies of water, a process that gave these waters personal meanings and attachments. Thus, for them and for other activists I have not described, the coastal waters were not just neutral spaces where the forces defined by environmental science were manifest. X and Y were conversant with that science and had worked with specialists. However, their ability to construe those places in these scientific terms reflected personal histories that led them to become environmental activists.

I have presented X and Y in the personal way that they presented themselves, playing down the larger historical forces that affected their surroundings. Though their stories did not centre on them, X and Y were aware of those forces, which were important in the ways that they affected the marine environment, and so made for the degradation of Negril's coral that concerned X and for the loss of clarity of Montego Bay's waters that caused Y concern. These broader forces were important in other ways as well. Aspects of them became particularly apparent when X in Negril and Y's fellows and successors in Montego Bay sought to protect the surroundings that concerned them. The aspects that became apparent were political-economic, and I turn to them now.

NEOLIBERAL LANDSCAPES

When X, Y and the others who sought to protect these bodies of water acted to conserve the marine environment, they came into contact with a set of institutions. These include the Jamaican state in various forms and arms, NGOs in Jamaica and elsewhere, and national and supranational agencies, but in Negril and Montego Bay the most noteworthy of these was the United States Agency for International Development (USAID). These institutions were important because of the political-economic ideology of neoliberalism. This ideology is based on an idealisation of the free market (see Carrier 1997), and was expressed as a kind of virtualism, efforts by powerful institutions to make the world conform to the virtual reality defined by that idealisation (see Carrier and Miller 1998).[2] One aspect of this ideology was the way that it construed the coastal waters and the people and organisations involved with them.

At the core of neoliberalism is a rejection of the state as a political entity and as an economic entity. Politically, neoliberalism marks a declining faith in the efficacy of state agencies and a growing faith in local institutions and organisations, 'the community'. Central governments are seen as lethargic, grossly inefficient and unresponsive, if not actually corrupt; local groups are seen as energetic and efficient. Economically, neoliberalism marks a growing pressure to curtail state financial power and regulation. For poorer countries like Jamaica, this meant rejection of state-based models of economic development and the rise of market-based models (see Bromley 1994; McMichael 1998; especially for Jamaica, see Edie 1991).

The Jamaican government agency that oversaw environmental and conservation projects was the Natural Resource Conservation Department, and it illustrates these two strands of neoliberalism. Early in the 1990s, and largely in response to pressure from the USAID, this was transformed into the Natural Resource Conservation Authority (NRCA). This was the transformation of a government agency into a quasi-autonomous organisation, intended to take conservation out of the political hands of the state and put it in the supposedly non-political hands of local activists and specialists. However, the NRCA's independence from politics was somewhat illusory, for it was dominated by the USAID, which occupied the top floor of the building that housed the NRCA and was involved in extensive guidance and training of NRCA staff under the rubric of 'capacity building'.

The political strand of neoliberalism was clearly reflected in NRCA policy; the agency's thinking and its associated justification were summarised by some environmental activists (Goreau et al. 1997: 2093):

The Natural Resources Conservation Authority (NRCA) ... recognizes that officials in the capital are less able than locally based organizations to identify local problems, propose solutions, or implement them. Central control over environmental policy has historically resulted in decisions favouring short-term financial interests of individuals and institutions which are well connected in the capital. Decision making is often protracted and may not address local concerns. Residents of the area feel increasingly dispossessed and powerless to control access to resources or halt degradation from development that adversely affects their quality of life, causing increasing alienation from the political process. NRCA has decided to increase the power of local communities to decide which forms of development, conservation, and environmental management best meet their long-term needs.

This echoed the growing global stress on participatory or community conservation, part of a rhetoric of 'empowering' people (see Adams and Hulme 1998; Adams and McShane 1996; Christie and White 1997; Leach and Mearns 1996).

The economic strand of neoliberalism meant that state spending should be kept to a minimum, so that conservation groups would have to find money for themselves. So, the 1990s saw a drop in the money that the NRCA spent on support for conservation activities, a consequence of cuts in its own budget. For the Montego Bay park, this meant that NRCA funding fell from J$2.7 million in 1997 and again in 1998 (about £50,000), to J$450,000 (about £7,000) in 1999 and 2000, supplemented by about J$125,000 (about £2,000) from an NRCA fund based on user fees collected at the installations that the NRCA oversaw (this was about a quarter of what the NRCA collected at the Montego Bay park; J. Williams, pers. comm.).

These two sides of neoliberalism shaped the institutional setting of those involved in these parks, and they imposed new historical meanings on the landscape that these people confronted. Waters that had meaning in terms of the biographies of people like X and Y, and in terms of the impersonal models of environmental science, took on meaning as a resource to be managed and exploited. This meaning sprang from the two different ways that these parks sought to raise money: applying to international donors for support; charging people, directly or indirectly, to enter the parks.

The USAID was the most important international donor agency for environmentalist organisations in Jamaica. Dealing with it obliged these organisations to understand and present themselves in distinctive ways, though the pervasiveness of neoliberalism made it likely that any substantial donor would have expected the same sort of understanding and presentation. Overwhelmingly, the discourse or rhetoric that the USAID required obliged the parks to construe and present themselves as bureaucratic, rational organisations. One concrete form this took was the development of management plans and business plans, annually in the last part of the 1990s. The 1998 management plan for the Montego

Bay park is around 70 pages. It begins with the management plan 'goals', followed by the park's 'mission' and 'vision', and contains a set of 'action plans' that form the vast majority of the management plan: 'Marine ecosystem management', 'User management', 'Community relations', 'Administration', 'Financial sustainability'. Each of these comes with a set of associated 'strategies', themselves containing a set of 'activities'. The Negril management plan for 1998 is about twice as long, but is roughly the same.

Management plans require that the people who draw them up translate their initial motivations and understandings into a particular form, one made powerful by the requirements of agencies like the USAID (see Carrier 1997: 47–54; 2001). The management plan for the Negril park could not begin with X's illness, divorce and years spent swimming off the West End; the management plan for the Montego Bay park could not refer to people who died trying to set depth records, or even Y's pride in helping divers enjoy the bay's waters. Preparing these plans obliged these activists to silence, and hence deny, their personal histories, histories in which local waters played an important part. Rather, it obliged them to think of themselves and their goals in terms of things like biodiversity, management structures, consultative groups and the like.

Moreover, in obliging them to think of themselves and their goals in this way, it obliged them to see the coastal waters in terms of a new set of meanings. The older personal and scientific meanings recurred in these people's casual talk as they referred to places where important events in their own and their friends' lives had occurred, and as they pointed out how this or that feature of their waters was shaped by the sorts of processes that were important to environmental science. However, while these older meanings did not disappear, these waters were overwritten with a new set of meanings, and consequently became associated with new sets of imperatives and actors. One set of actors was tourists, together with the commercial organisations that catered to them.

I said that the other avenue for securing funding was charging people to enter or benefit from the parks; in effect, attracting ecotourists. Ecotourism fits neoliberalism: if an aspect of the environment is valuable, people will pay to see and experience it – with the corollary that the willingness to pay is the legitimate measure of value (see Watts 2000: esp. 44–6). But regardless of this conceptual fit, for some years ecotourism had been a sort of pot of gold at the end of the conservationist rainbow. For instance, estimates for the number of ecotourists in the world for as long ago as 1988 range between 157 and 236 million; estimates for the revenue they generated ranged up to about US$1.2 trillion (Ceballos-Lascurain 1996: 46–8). In the Caribbean, X and Y, environmental activists and conservation administrators had ecotourism success stories presented to them, especially Saba Marine Park and Bonaire Marine Park (see Dixon et al. 1993), both in the Netherlands Antilles, where fees charged to divers generated substantial income and even financial independence (for detailed analyses, see Framhein 1995 for Saba, and Scura and van't Hof 1993 for Bonaire).[3]

Ecotourism loomed large in a study carried out late in the 1980s, funded by the Organisation of American States, that reviewed possible sites for marine parks in Jamaica. That report's assessment of the ecotourism potential of Montego Bay was an important reason why it was selected as a park site, even though some had argued that it was so degraded that it could not effectively be protected with the limited resources likely to be available. After all, Montego Bay was and remains the prime tourist location in Jamaica. In the late 1990s it was the country's second largest city, with 56 hotels and over 5,000 rooms (Bunce and Gustavson 1998: 75). That report on possible park locations in Jamaica made the obvious point:

> marine parks can be pretty much self-supporting through a number of activities: snorkelling, SCUBA diving, glass-bottom boat tours arranged for a fee. Usually the marine park organization will leave most of these activities to commercial diver operators and watersport centers. In that case, however, substantial revenues may be obtained from concessions. (O'Callaghan et al. 1988: 37)

So, the spreading influence of neoliberalism in the larger world meant that these parks were obliged to present themselves not just as bureaucratic, rational organisations, but as bureaucratic, rational, commercial organisations, so that the bay's waters became a commercial resource to be populated by ecotourists. This sort of commercial construction is manifest in the Montego Bay park 1998 management plan. Of the five action plans, the longest is the fifth, 'Financial sustainability', with the goal: 'To become financially sustainable through utilizing all possible sources of revenue, cost sharing and partnerships including fees, donations, grants, volunteerism and sales of goods and services, locally, nationally and internationally, from private, corporate, government and institutional organizations.' The associated sub-strategies are: a visitor centre at the park headquarters, an ecotourism programme, merchandising and franchising, generating park products and services, placing collection boxes in the area, corporate fund-raising, setting up a donor organisation, user permits, holding public events, participating in existing public events, establishing a park trust fund.

The neoliberal political-economic environment effectively put pressure on activists and managers to embrace ecotourism out of financial necessity, making market forces in the tourist industry the measure of value of the environment. And this in turn affected the ways that people like X, and the successors to Y in Montego Bay, understood their marine environment, thought about park waters and the actors who populated it. At the most obvious level, these people were constrained to see that environment and the things in it in terms of a commodity, access to which was to be traded for money, and they were constrained to see certain sorts of people as belonging there and others as illegitimate intruders.

For instance, X reported that hotel operators in Negril wanted her to ban all fishing in park waters. They said that their guests were complaining about the presence of Jamaicans in small fishing boats in park waters, apparently believing that any fishing was bad and that no fishing boat had a legitimate reason to be in park waters (for a similar situation elsewhere in the Caribbean, see Sandersen and Koester 2000: esp. 94–5). From what she said, hotel operators seemed to think the same. Two points are worth noting here. First, the park had not banned all fishing in all its waters. Second, access to the Negril town landing beach was through park waters, obliging fishermen to traverse those waters. X resented this pressure from hotel operators. Even so, she saw the views of these hotel operators and their tourist-guests as a real constraint, springing from commercial interests, and they affected the ways that she saw the marine environment.

Similarly, if more subtly, senior park management at Montego Bay regularly were interested in shaping park waters in ways that would attract ecotourists and satisfy hotel operators and others that it was worth paying access fees. Management wanted to know about consumer demand: what is it that divers, a particularly salient body of ecotourists, are looking for in a dive site? Here too, then, the neoliberal environment imposed a new layer of meaning on the waters, and in so doing identified certain sorts of people as properly in the seascape, indeed as necessary for its survival. Jamaicans in small boats belonged elsewhere.

While powerful institutions were imposing neoliberal constructions of the coastal waters upon these people, it appeared that the tourist sector was not playing the game. A recurrent concern late in the 1990s, when I was dealing with these activists and managers, was the reluctance of that sector to support the parks financially. In Negril, for instance, some hotel operators were prepared to offer a degree of support in kind for special projects, and similar support was offered occasionally in Montego Bay. However, activists and managers regularly complained that there was no chance of getting money on a regular basis. One activist, with substantial experience in conservation organisations in Jamaica, complained about what he saw as the unreasonable failure of the tourist industry to pay for environmental protection. He said that their situation is 'Just like in any business. It [the environment] is a maintenance cost.'

CONTESTING LANDSCAPES

In the preceding section I described the ways that the neoliberal orientation of the USAID and other bodies confronted activists and managers with novel meanings for the waters that they sought to protect, meanings which many of these people resented but saw no way to subvert. I said also that these meanings included understandings of how different sets of people ought to relate to and be in the landscape. One set of people were defined, in effect, as having no legitimate place there: Jamaican fishers. Neoliberalism itself did not define these people as unwelcome intruders. Rather, it made the opinion of tourists especially important to activists and park managers, and those tourists appeared to adhere to the Modern view that the truly natural ought to be devoid of human presence and impact (see, e.g., Cronon 1995). This put activists and managers in a difficult situation because fishers' cooperation was important for successful marine conservation: the truism is that fisheries management will be only as good as fishers allow it to be.

Like most of the English-speaking Caribbean, Jamaica has an open-access fishery, and fishers said that all people have a right to fish on the sea, as long as they do not trouble the next fisher. In fact, coastal waters in Jamaica appear to resemble what is called 'family land', held by all the children and grandchildren (and so on) of the person who originally acquired the land, though for coastal waters the 'family' is defined by national identity, part of the patrimony of being Jamaican. Family land is a safety net, a place where you can go when you are down and out, and find food and help until you are able to support yourself again with other resources or other work: 'For the greater part of family members, the land has been a place where they might go whenever they are in need, but not a place where they actually have chosen to live' (Olwig 1997: 151). If this assumption is correct, then fishers saw the coastal waters as something that is theirs by a combination of right and necessity.

I am proposing an analogy between coastal waters and family land, not an identity. Many of those who fished these waters were not temporarily distressed, in the manner of a stereotypical user of family land, but fished regularly as a main source of their livelihood and had done so for years. However, it is also true that a significant proportion of fishers were people who had come to these towns to seek work and who had failed to find a livelihood by other means. Typically these distressed immigrants took up spear fishing, which required little initial outlay and could be learnt relatively easily. Particularly in Montego Bay, spear fishing expanded markedly in the 1990s, and spear fishers there characteristically came from the city's most impoverished areas.[4]

In addition, it appears that fishing has another common significance in the English-speaking Caribbean. Price (1966) argues that it had a distinctive place in the slave and plantation economy that dominated the Caribbean through the early part of the nineteenth century. In particular, Price says that fishermen-slaves formed a relatively distinctive, privileged and independent group. As a consequence, communities of fishermen acquired a distinctive social identity as independent, self-reliant and skilled. Price argues that this identity remained important in the region and gave fishing communities a cultural and moral and even political force that is far beyond what their numbers and economic importance justified.

I have invoked Price's work and the idea of family land to suggest that the coastal waters carried a background set of meanings for the people who fished there, meanings that defined those waters as a part of people's national identity and independence, in a society where independence among males (the overwhelming majority of fishers) is highly valued. And these meanings populated the waters with hardworking Jamaicans who were fishing as part of their efforts to make ends meet.

But whatever the strength of these background meanings, the coastal waters were the place where these fishers did seek to make ends meet, either because necessity drove them to fishing or because they thought of themselves as fishers. Their fishing brought them into conflict with these marine parks. This is because the key way that the parks sought to protect the marine environment was by reducing the pressure on fish populations, which is to say, by restricting fishing. Neither park had banned fishing altogether, but both promulgated zone systems, which divide park waters into different areas, and prohibit different activities (including types of fishing) within those areas.

Fishers agreed with activists and managers that fish stocks had deteriorated markedly in the past decades, and they agreed that their fishing harmed these stocks. However, generally they dissented from the conservationist policy of these parks (the following paragraphs draw on Polunin et al. 2000: esp. 55–64). Their dissent was not expressed in terms of the background values that I have mentioned, though these doubtless underlay that dissent to some degree. Rather, the most articulate basis of their dissent sprang from the very environmental science outlook that activists had adopted to further their conservationist goals. However, fishers linked environment to politics, and so reversed the depoliticisation of the environment that is a common feature of that science.

Fishers argued that the harm caused by their fishing was minor compared to the environmental degradation brought about by urban growth and the tourist industry that fed that growth. (Recall that X and Y also thought that environmental degradation was important, as did other activists.) The case is clearest in Montego Bay. I have already noted that the city had a large and growing number of hotels, and the population of the city had grown sharply in the closing decades of the twentieth century as well (see also Bacon 1987: 105; for a smaller version of this elsewhere in the Caribbean see McMinn and Cater 1998: 689–91). This entailed the destruction of a substantial amount of the original coastline and the damage and dredging entailed in the construction of a new port facility to serve the growing city and to attract more and larger cruise ships. The situation in Negril was just as stark. The building of Norman Manley Boulevard separated the bulk of the Great Morass from the sea and the construction of hotels along that road involved the partial filling of the Morass. The coastline of Long Bay, the key part of the coastal waters of tourist Negril, was thus radically altered. The hotels and the tourists that they attracted sharply increased the pressure on the marine environment.

More narrowly, many fishers in Montego Bay argued that tourist activities harmed the marine environment. One common tourist attraction was boats that took tourists out snorkelling. There were a number of these, and fishers said that hotel guests who went snorkelling and diving often stood on the coral, killing it. Similarly, fishers who used one of the important landing beaches in Montego Bay pointed to the activities of a large tourist hotel nearby. This hotel operated a cruise catamaran in the mornings and evenings, and fishers said that this boat damaged a large amount of the reef in the area.

Thus, the dissent by these fishers expressed yet another set of meanings of the coastal waters, meanings that contained the historical growth of tourism but evaluated it in a different way. Tourism was not the economic motor of conservation, as in the neoliberal construction that park managers were obliged to accept, but instead drove environmental destruction. Tourists should not displace fishers, they should keep away, for it was Jamaican fishers who had the right and the need to be in these waters. These fishers, then, said that they should not be expected to give up their fishing while nothing was being done about the main causes of the deterioration of the marine environment, the tourist industry. This not only struck them as unjust, it also reaffirmed their belief that these two parks were not about improving the coastal waters for all those who used them, but were about benefiting the tourist industry.

CONCLUSIONS

I have focused on the coastal waters of Montego Bay and Negril to show how those waters carried different and even conflicting sets of meanings for different sets of people. I described the way that some of those meanings sprang from the biographies of individuals, notably the environmental activists X and Y. At the same time, I noted how those waters carried other sets of meanings, which contained moral visions waiting to be realised.

Some of these meanings were those of local fishers, and I looked at two different sorts of meanings that these waters had for them. One set I called background meanings, which sprang from the idea that coastal waters are part of the patrimony that comes with being Jamaican, analogous to family land, and which sprang from the historical nature of fishing in the English-speaking Caribbean. The other set sprang more directly from the activities of the marine parks, activities themselves shaped by the historical growth of tourism and the increasing influence of neoliberalism. These meanings reflected fishers' assessment of the overall orientation of these parks, one which supported the tourist industry at the expense of fishers. This orientation, these fishers argued, led the parks to ignore the growing tourism that caused environmental degradation, and instead unjustly to seek to restrict their fishing activities.

The confrontation between parks and fishers took place in the context of yet another set of important meanings that sprang from the neoliberal policies and requirements of the agencies that these parks dealt with. These meanings show that an awareness of the ways that biography and history shape the meanings of the landscape needs to be complemented by an awareness of the ways that larger forces, springing from outside the locality at issue, can have a crucial role in defining the landscape. And this imposed neoliberalism did not simply impose new meanings on these waters (as commodities), it also created a situation that made the meanings of yet other sets of people especially important (the meaning of nature that tourists seemed to hold).

This aspect of neoliberalism, the way that it made activists-managers attend to the views of nature held by hotel guests and divers, points to another aspect of the meanings of the landscape that I have described. These meanings do not simply give these waters personal and collective significance. They also populate those waters, for they identify the sorts of people and activities that are appropriate for those waters, and the sorts that are inappropriate. In making this point I have, in a way, come full circle analytically. While people's dealings with or in the context of the surroundings are important for giving meaning to the landscape, meanings also constrain those dealings.

And finally, in attending to the ways that these meanings populate these waters, I have pointed to the link between the realm of meanings on the one hand, and on the other socio-political conflict. The different meanings that these waters carried do not simply reflect the individual and collective histories of activists, managers, fishers and the like. In addition, they justify the exclusion of some people and activities from the landscape, as they justify the inclusion of others. These exclusions and inclusions do not occur automatically, by themselves. Rather, they occur because some of the actors and institutions that confront those waters are more powerful than others.

The result of these processes is that the waters of Negril and Montego Bay are a disputed landscape, burdened with history. Conservationists, who see that landscape in light of their personal histories and environmental science, increasingly have been obliged to see it in light of the dictates of the agencies with which they deal. Fishers, who see that landscape in light of their position as independent Jamaicans, increasingly have been obliged to see it in light of the dictates of the tourist industry. And these visions of the landscape conflict. Conservationists are under pressure to see fishers as a problem to be contained and ultimately eliminated. Fishers see conservationists as captives of the tourist industry, seeking to dispossess them.

ACKNOWLEDGEMENTS

Some of the field research referred to here was carried out as part of ODA (later DFID) project R6783, 'Ecological and social impacts in planning Caribbean marine-reserves'. Among those I spoke with in Jamaica, I thank particularly Jill Williams and Jeremy Woodley, as well as Janos Beyer, Gordon Glave, Malden Miller and Teo Schmidt, and of course the anonymous X and Y. In the midst of their own busy lives, all these people were forthcoming and hospitable in ways for which I am most grateful. Finally, as I have worked on the issues developed here, I received helpful comments from Kay Milton, Michael O'Hanlon and Dimitrios Theodossopoulos.

NOTES

1. Her approach is that put forward in Goreau et al. (1997), but it is worth noting that some marine biologists who have worked in Jamaican waters dissented from this approach.
2. Neoliberalism and virtualism have their own histories, of course, though I can not describe them here (see Carrier and Miller 1999; Cockett 1994; Miller 1998).

3. Ecotourism was attractive to more than just conservationists, for it was presented as an important way to increase commercial and state revenue from tourism, in a region of the world heavily dependent on increasingly uncertain mass tourism (see Pattulo 1996).

4. As this suggests, fishers were not a uniform group. In the following discussion I will be referring primarily to those who fished using traps or fishing lines, though impressionistic evidence indicates that spear fishers had similar views.

REFERENCES

Adams, J.S. and T. McShane (1996) *The Myth of Wild Africa*. Berkeley: University of California Press.

Adams, W.M. and D. Hulme (1998) *Conservation and Communities: Changing Narratives, Policies and Practices in African Conservation* (Working Paper No. 4). Manchester: University of Manchester Institute of Development Policy and Management.

Bacon, P.R. (1987) 'Use of Wetlands for Tourism in the Insular Caribbean', *Annals of Tourism Research* (14), pp. 104–117.

Bromley, D. (1994) 'Economic Dimensions of Community-based Conservation', in D. Western and M. Wright (eds) *Natural Connections*. Washington, DC: Island Press.

Bunce, L. and K. Gustavson (1998) *Coral Reef Valuation: A Rapid Socioeconomic Assessment of Fishing, Watersports, and Hotel Operations in the Montego Bay Marine Park, Jamaica and an Analysis of Reef Management Implications* (Report, Project RPO 681–05). Washington, DC: World Bank.

Carrier, J.G. (1997) 'Introduction', in J. Carrier (ed.) *Meanings of the Market: The Free Market in Western Culture*. Oxford: Berg.

—— (2001) 'Diplomacy and Indirection, Constraint and Authority', in J. Hendry and B. Watson (eds) *An Anthropology of Indirect Communication*. London: Routledge.

Carrier, J.G. and D. Miller (eds) (1998) *Virtualism: A New Political Economy*. Oxford: Berg.

—— (1999) 'From Public Virtue to Private Vice: Anthropology and Economy', in H. Moore (ed.) *Anthropological Theory Today*. Cambridge: Polity Press.

Ceballos-Lascurain, H. (1996) *Tourism, Ecotourism and Protected Areas: The State of Nature-based Tourism around the World and Guidelines for its Development* (based on papers presented at the Fourth World Congress on National Parks and Protected Areas, Caracas 1992). Gland, Switzerland, and Cambridge: IUCN.

Christie, P. and A.T. White (1997) 'Trends in Development of Coastal Area Management in Tropical Countries: From Central to Community Orientation', *Coastal Management* 25: 155–81.

Cockett, R. (1994) *Thinking the Unthinkable: Think-tanks and the Economic Counter-revolution, 1931–83*. London: HarperCollins.

Cronon, W. (ed.) (1995) *Uncommon Ground: Rethinking the Human Place in Nature*. New York: Norton.

Dixon, J.A., L.F. Scura and T. van't Hof (1993) 'Meeting Ecological and Economic Goals: Marine Parks in the Caribbean', *Ambio* 22(2–3): 117–25.

Edie, C.J. (1991) *Democracy by Default: Dependency and Clientelism in Jamaica*. Boulder, CO: Lynne Rienner/Kingston: Ian Randle.

Framhein, R. (1995) *The Value of Nature Protection: Economic Analysis of the Saba Marine Park*. Summary for the Government of Saba, September.

Goreau, T.J., L. Daley, S. Ciappara, J. Brown, S. Bourke and K. Thacker (1997) 'Community-based Whole-watershed and Coastal Zone Management in Jamaica', *Proceedings of the Eighth International Coral Reef Symposium* 2: 2093–6.

Hirsch, E. (1995) 'Introduction: Landscape – Between Place and Space', in E. Hirsch and M. O'Hanlon (eds) *The Anthropology of Landscape: Perspectives on Place and Space*. Oxford: Oxford University Press.

Leach, M. and R. Mearns (eds) (1996) *The Lie of the Land: Challenging Received Wisdom on the African Environment*. London: Heinemann.

McMichael, P. (1998) 'Development and Structural Adjustment', in J.G. Carrier and D. Miller (eds) *Virtualism: A New Political Economy*. Oxford: Berg.

McMinn, S. and E. Cater (1998) 'Tourist Typology: Observations from Belize', *Annals of Tourism Research* 25: 675–99.

Miller, D. (1998) 'Conclusion: A Theory of Virtualism', in J.G. Carrier and D. Miller (eds) *Virtualism: A New Political Economy*. Oxford: Berg.

O'Callaghan, P.A., J. Woodley and K. Aiken (1988) *Montego Bay Marine Park: Project Proposal for the Development of Montego Bay Marine Park, Jamaica*. TS.

Olwig, K.F. (1997) 'Caribbean Family Land: A Modern Commons', *Plantation Society in the Americas* 4: 135–58.

Pattulo, P. (1996) *Last Resorts: The Cost of Tourism in the Caribbean*. Kingston: Ian Randle.

Polunin, N., I. Williams, J. Carrier and L. Robertson (2000) *Final Technical Report: Ecological and Social Impacts in Planning Caribbean Marine-Reserves*. (DFID project number R6783.) TS.

Price, R. (1966) 'Caribbean Fishing and Fishermen: A Historical Sketch', *American Anthropologist* 68: 1364–83.

Sandersen, H. and S. Koester (2000) 'Co-management of Tropical Coastal Zones: The Case of Sourfriere Marine Management Area, St Lucia, WI', *Coastal Management* 28: 87–97.

Scura, L.F. and T. van't Hof (1993) *The Ecology and Economics of Bonaire Marine Park* (Environment Department, Divisional Paper 1993–44). Washington, DC: World Bank.

Watts, M.J. (2000) 'Contested Communities, Malignant Markets, and Gilded Governance: Justice, Resource Extraction, and Conservation in the Tropics', in C. Zerner (ed.) *People, Plants, and Justice*. New York: Columbia University Press.

EPILOGUE

Andrew Strathern and Pamela J. Stewart

If landscape is best seen as a process, what kind of process is involved? And why is controversy and conflict often involved in this process? In our comments in the Introduction we pointed out that landscape as a form of memory often comes to encode past conflicts that are revealed in its own form and which people think are relevant to the present and the future. We have characterised many of these conflicts in terms of a contest between heritage and development. The same contrast turns up in government regulations that require archaeological research to be done prior to the building of offices or factories on particular sites of potential historic interest. Here heritage and development are brought into partial alignment by an insistence that the needs of heritage be recognised prior to a particular development taking place. In this vision of the world, the landscape is often seen as endangered by industrial development. If the landscape itself cannot be preserved at least some of its record of the past can be retrieved.

As we have pointed out, what was at one time 'development' may later become 'heritage'. With the passing of previous technologies, old factories, whose impact on the environment may have been questionable and contested, may be turned into visitors' centres. People pay to see the quaint machines of the past. The underlying rhetoric here is still that which animated development in the first place: the narrative of historical 'progress'. The old technology may be criticised for its polluting effects. Alternatively, the tone may be nostalgic, lauding the kinds of social relations that were built around previous methods of production. Other types of visitors'/heritage centres may concentrate on aspects of the landscape or environment itself (geological, topographic, flora and fauna); or on the achievements of writers and artists who drew inspiration in part from a local area where they were born, or grew up, or with which they otherwise felt an identification.

In Scotland, for example, there is a visitors' centre in the area known as the Howe of the Mearns, a massive rolling stretch of mountainous countryside nowadays clad partly with the ubiquitous firs of the Forestry Commission. The centre is dedicated to an exposition of the life and work of Lewis Grassic Gibbon, a novelist whose writings often feature the area itself and the ways of speaking of the people within it. Here landscape is turned into the medium of memory and history through the narratives by the author and the centre's own narrative of the author.

This kind of secondary representation of landscape through another medium, usually the life of an individual, a set of people, or an institution is a phenomenon that we have found to be increasingly significant in the parts of Scotland and Ireland where we have travelled. One of the reasons for this lies in the emergence of the European Union as a major factor in people's consciousness and in their lives, not so much in an everyday or political way, but as a kind of background influence. The Union gives grants to support centres that are seen to be important in some way for a newly developing sense of European identity. Prehistoric sites often fall persuasively into this category, since early populations spread over what is now Europe long before the recent historical creation of large nation-states.

The site at Skara Brae in the Orkney Islands north of the mainland of Scotland, originally excavated by V. Gordon Childe, offers a prime instance of such a category. European Union support is always commemorated on blue plaques near the entrance to such sites. In Scotland, many historic sites are kept as preserved ruins (e.g. castles and forts), and Historic Scotland tends to look after these on its own; while from the level of the UK as a whole, support is often recorded as coming from the National Lottery Fund. In one place, situated in Kintyre, we found that a local centre, meticulously set up, complained of a lack of support from Historic Scotland. Yet, all around it, in the Kilmartin area, there were numerous collocations of large prehistoric cairns and standing stone assemblages, all of them in the care of Historic Scotland, for the benefit of visitors to the centre and anyone passing through. In this case there was a dispute between central government authorities and the museum about where a particular prehistoric stone, recently discovered, should be kept. The government wanted the stone to be kept in a museum in Edinburgh; the museum wanted it to stay in the local area. The example shows that the general argument, long mooted, over 'Who owns Scotland?' can extend from big, landed estates to organisations owned within the heritage business itself. The anecdote underlines the general point that visitors' centres are mechanisms whereby representations of landscape in a general sense are linked to varying scales of social identity.

Representations of identity are a means of defining and controlling people's senses of themselves, or of opposing other representations. Missionaries and other colonisers always make a significant impact on the environment by building large establishments that impose themselves on their viewers (Ballard 2002 on Irian Jaya, Indonesia). The roads built at the behest of government officers in Papua New Guinea fall into this rubric of control, as did the roads that Romans built when they colonised England. To this day, stretches of unusually straight roads can be recognised as old Roman roadways, built for efficient military movement to control the people. Remnants of Roman walls are preserved in historic towns, such as Colchester in Essex, wedged in between modern roads and walkways. The preservation of the marks of the colonisers in this way indicates the very general process by which development gradually turns into heritage. Sometimes the commemoration is carried out simply by preserving the records, taken from archives, of the controlling disciplines of colonial activity.

In the old city of Tainan in south-west Taiwan (Republic of China) in 2002 we were investigating temples dedicated to a regional goddess of great importance, Mazu, and one of the people who kindly helped us in our study gave us copies of maps that the Japanese colonisers had made of Tainan and its temples during the time when they controlled the island (1895–1945). The maps also pinpointed each temple exactly. These maps were made not as an aid to academic research but as a practical tool of control, since temples were and are a focus of mobilisation for local collectivities with strong senses of solidarity and shared interests in the temples themselves. The maps also charted the extensive canals made earlier by the Tainan people for the transport of trade goods obtained through mercantile activity into the city itself, and their dispersal into warehouses and stores. They therefore encoded two very different aspects of identity, but both were presented as a part of the city's history and therefore as markers of its people's identity. The Japanese themselves had used the temple areas as places to station some of their contingents of troops in the Pacific campaign of the Second World War, which had led to the bombing of some of the temples, as one of our temple manager guides told us.

Arguments over control often take place through the use of names or the use of particular language forms as against others in order to label the landscape. In the Ordnance Survey of Ireland, Gaelic names were anglicised by the surveyors with the aid of local collaborators. This was a part of the effort to stamp an English-speaking identity on a Gaelic landscape. It was by no means the first attempt. In the 'Plantations' of settlers from England and Scotland instigated in turn by Elizabeth I,

James VI and I, and Oliver Cromwell, a process of re-naming certainly took place; although the names chosen often reflected, at least in the case of County Donegal, Gaelic roots.

After the creation of the Republic of Ireland early in the twentieth century, there was a drive to re-establish Irish Gaelic as an official language of the new state along with English. Compulsory courses in Irish were imposed on all schoolchildren, and economic support was given to the western Gaeltacht areas. In these areas also road signs were made in Irish, forcing the traveller to take note of them. Much more recently, a counter-move has emerged from those parts of Ulster, including eastern County Donegal, that were extensively settled in the Plantation by Lowland Scots Presbyterians from counties such as Ayrshire. These people retain a strong sense of being 'Ulster Scots', in origin and in self-perception. Their colloquial speech is a version of Lowland Scots that has developed on its own since the seventeenth century. While Lowland Scots was known already as Lallans in the time of the poet Robert Burns, the Ulster Scots have come to call their own speech Ullans, a term derived from 'Ulster' and the second syllable of 'Lallans'. As a marker of identity, the proponents of Ullans claim, it too should be used as a way of labelling their Ulster environment. The issues are contentious, since they involve the whole history of Scots/Irish inter-actions and the troubled problems of Northern Ireland. It is in County Donegal, on the Republic side, that the clearest support for Ullans comes, and this is recognised by the establishment, on 1 July 2002, of an office to promote it in Raphoe, squarely within the ambit of Scots Presbyterian settlement. Interestingly, here too the European Union enters. Its officials have granted Ullans the status of a recognised minority language within the area coved by the Union, and have allocated a considerable sum of funds to support research on the language. A dictionary of Ullans is to be compiled to stand alongside a grammar that has already been completed and the extensive dictionary materials on Lowland Scots. In terms of the landscape, the debates over Ullans will certainly extend to road signs and names on maps if the movement gains impetus. Such labels will then become a part of cultural repertoires and arguments about them, within both the Republic of Ireland and Northern Ireland.

Three recent books on Scotland illuminate different aspects of the analysis of landscape. One, *The Landscape of Scotland: A Hidden History*, by C.R. Wickham-Jones (2001) explores, with extensive photographs and drawings, marks on the environment ranging from prehistoric times to industrial sites that are now largely abandoned. The 'hidden' part of the history lies in the fact that, over time, the signs of habitation and use tend to become obscured and have to be brought to light by excavation, field photography and special enquiries. The landscape brought to light is largely one of memory and history rather than contemporary conflict, but some of the book's entries intriguingly encode histories of conflict. The author remarks on Scot's Dike, in Dumfriesshire. This feature of landscape began its life in 1552 as an earthwork bank built during the reign of Mary Queen of Scots, the mother of King James VI and I. The bank still survives within a narrow band of woodland stretching across the countryside. The Dike was built just 'where the Border ran inland from the coast' (Wickham-Jones 2001: 158). The author writes that

In Britain today we are unused to political boundaries, though they have been treated with much more importance at different times in the past.... It is surprising to us, therefore, to realize that this thin stretch of woodland running across the gentle farm-lands of Dumfriesshire marks out an ancient boundary, and one the life of which has not yet, seemingly, come to an end. (2001: 158)

An anodyne acknowledgement of continuing contests over nationhood between the Scots and the English that, if anything, are sharpening rather than declining with the advent of devolution and the successes of the Scottish National Party. Perhaps the author was also forgetting in this passage the border between Northern Ireland and the Republic of Ireland, for example in Donegal and Derry (Londonderry). Here, although the material marks of the border are largely erased, a multitude of signs lie just below the surface in people's minds, and in their memories of killings during the Troubles since 1969. Remarkably, roads often just finish at the border and do not go across it. The boundary at one point follows the middle of Lough Foyle. From Donegal on the banks of the Foyle River, one looks across constantly at the farmlands on the other side, replicas of those on the Republic side, separated by a stretch of water and the memories of conflicts.

Another book on Scotland directly tackles issues of conflict and nationhood. This is *Scotland's Landscape: An Endangered Icon* by Anna Paterson (2002), which comes with an endorsement on its cover from the Historiographer-Royal of Scotland, T.C. Smout. The author begins her study by roundly declaring that 'Scotland's landscapes and cityscapes have become emblematic of the nation, parts of the citizens' sense of belonging – icons, to be venerated even if not understood' (2002: vii). This is an activist book, urging that more attention be paid to conservation – that is, heritage – and extensively discussing the 'stewardship' concept in relation to land. The book discusses governmental impacts (as well as bungles), criticises aspects of the European Union's policies, and argues that 'all tourism should be eco-tourism' (2002: 97). The author discusses the Land Reform Bill, which would give 'rights for tenant farmers to become free-holders and use the land in their own best interests, and limitations to power of the few who own so much of Scotland' (2002: 145). The author thus tackles issues of both heritage and development, and argues for a different vision of development itself, one that would give more control to local people. The book abundantly illustrates the class conflicts that surround landscape and are rooted in memory and history.

The conflicts took a particular shape in the Highlands Clearances and in the forms of farming adopted in what is called 'the Age of Improvement' in farming history. The third book we consider here is edited by David McClure and deals with the county of Ayrshire in the Age of Improvement (2002). It contains a set of contemporary accounts of the 'Improvements' themselves, which largely consisted in getting rid of the old community-based fermtouns and their riggs or strips of land, and enclosing the land with fences, bringing more of it into intensive use by draining, stone-removing and liming, thus enabling better crops to flourish and larger herds or flocks of cows and sheep to be maintained. These changes were instituted by 'improver' landlords, often ones who had made money in mercantile activities and used it to buy estates; but they were also made by many tenant farmers. To encourage these farmers, the owners gave them longer and more secure leases. Methods of rotation of crops were used to give land time to recover its fertility, and richer grasses were sown to feed stock. Landowners themselves planted many trees as windbreaks and places for game birds to exist. At this time also, and earlier too, large landowners laid out parks of trees, and extensive gardens, around their dwellings, giving them seclusion and dignity.

This, then, was a time of 'development' that made the landscape as it exists today in many ways, thus encoding a set of class values linked to a progressive ideology of the eighteenth century. Looking at the layout of the farms, visitors may see these as 'traditional'. Indeed they have become so. As 'traditional' phenomena, they have the potential to be parts of a general 'heritage'. The development of a previous age becomes heritage today. This may help to explain why no great resentment is overtly expressed against estate owners. To some extent these alterations of the landscape represent 'improvements' that are conceptually shared as 'heritage' today. The conflicts of the past become another 'hidden history' here; while pragmatic issues of conflict between tenant farmers and the estates to which their farms belong are very real and close to the surface. These Ayrshire farmers want to make and benefit from their own improvements to their farms, as Anna Paterson suggests. They want to have the satisfaction of creating their own landscapes and having full control over them. While the past, figuring today in the still existing big houses and gardens of the landowning gentry, is not a focus of overt resentment, the present, in the form of fixtures, fences and implements, is a source of anxieties and aspirations. The landscape overall is divided between these components, expressing respect for the past and frustration with the present.

Another set of conflicts surrounds the issue of the accessibility of land to ramblers (walkers) and campers. Farmers experience these categories of people in general as intruders who may cause difficulties or problems by leaving litter behind, leaving gates open, introducing diseases and the like. In the year 2000 an epidemic of foot and mouth disease swept British farms, leading to the wholesale closure to outsiders, by government notice, of all farm pathways. These restrictions were still in force in 2001 in both the UK and Ireland. In the summer of 2002, we found that some farmers had left the original notices up in order to discourage walkers, perhaps still in fear that disease could come in their wake. On one occasion at Malin Head in Inishowen, County Donegal, we came to a gate with a notice of this sort. We read it and turned back. At that moment the farmer came out of his house and called to us 'If ye're wantin to go through, ye can carry on.' Gratefully we did so and came to a delightful rocky area by the sea, with pockets of wild flowers and heather nearby. The farmer here expressed his own agency. He chose who should and who should not gain access to his property for their recreational purposes. He controlled the 'tourist gaze' rather than being the object of it. The issue of the wishes and demands of tourists *vis à vis* locals must be an important one in many parts of Europe today. Visitors to the countryside may look on farms and their animal stock as somehow existing passively in 'nature'. Farmers themselves know their landscape as products of generations of work, and therefore as artefacts of their labour and 'culture'. Indeed the farm as a whole is a cultural and historical artefact, whether visitors understand this or not.

Also in 2002 we stayed for one night at Tyndrum, a small village or town located south-west of the huge Grampian mountains near the Stirling region, Scotland. We were staying at a bed and breakfast accommodation and shared our morning table with a young Swedish couple who had come to hike in the area. Somewhat to our surprise they complained that in the 'villages' marked on their Ordnance Survey maps there was 'no culture, just farms'. By culture they seem to have meant shops, perhaps ones selling artefacts and other tourist items. We pointed out that the Ordnance maps list farms, with their associated buildings and sheds, as entities in their own right without linking them to villages. What was striking was this young couple's disinclination to recognise a farm itself as a complex form of culture in the landscape, with its own intricate history of continuity and change. If there is one thing the study of landscape can do, then, it is to make it clear that landscapes are culture, inscribed in fields, woods, crops, animal stock, buildings and roads, and in the sensory impressions and memories these evoke for those who live in them.

Returning here to the theoretical issues we raised in our Introduction (Chapter 1), we can ask again what the value is of studying landscape. Our answer has been that landscape as a concept brings together conventional themes in anthropology of place and community and sets these into a larger framework. People live in places and communities; they also find a wider field of life and imagination in the landscape that places and communities inhabit. The idea of landscape points to life-worlds, their potentialities, their conflicts and their deep associations with feelings of identity.

REFERENCES

Ballard, C. (ed.) (2002) 'The Signature of Terror: Violence, Memory and Landscape at Freeport', in Bruno David and Meredith Wilson (eds) *Inscribed Landscapes: Making and Marking Place*. Honolulu: University of Hawaii Press, pp. 13–26.

McClure, D. (ed.) (2002) *Ayrshire in the Age of Improvement: Contemporary Accounts of Agrarian and Social Improvement in Late Eighteenth-century Ayrshire*. Ayr, Scotland: Ayrshire Archaeological and Natural History Society.

Paterson, A. (2002) *Scotland's Landscape: Endangered Icon*. Edinburgh, Scotland: Polygon at Edinburgh.

Wickham-Jones, C.R. (2001) *The Landscape of Scotland: A Hidden History*. Stroud, Glos., UK: Tempus Publishing.

CONTRIBUTORS

James G. Carrier has taught in Papua New Guinea, the United States and the United Kingdom, and is currently associated with the University of Indiana in the USA and Oxford Brookes University in the UK. He has written extensively in economic anthropology and political economy, including *Gifts and Commodities: Exchange and Western Capitalism since 1700* (Routledge, 1995) and two edited collections, *Meanings of the Market* (Berg, 1997) and *Virtualism: A New Political Economy*, co-edited with Daniel Miller (Berg, 1998). His interest in conservation in the Caribbean springs from his interest in political economy.

John Gray is currently Reader in Anthropology at the University of Adelaide in Australia. He has conducted long-term fieldwork in two locations: a multi-caste village in the Kathmandu Valley of Nepal and a hill sheep farming community in the Borders of Scotland. His publications include *The Householder's World: Purity, Power and Dominance in a Nepali Village* (Oxford: Oxford University Press, 1995) and *At Home in the Hills: Sense of Place in the Scottish Borders* (London: Berghahn Books, 2000).

Pei-yi Guo obtained her PhD from the Department of Anthropology, University of Pittsburgh in 2001. She is currently an Assistant Research Fellow at the Institute of Ethnology, Academia Sinica in Taiwan. Her research involves historical anthropology, landscape, migration, trade and shell money among the Langalanga of the Solomon Islands, where she did her fieldwork.

Janice Harper is Assistant Professor of Anthropology at the University of Houston, and author of *Endangered Species: Health, Illness and Death among Madagascar's People of the Forest* (Durham, NC: Carolina Academic Press, 2002).

Ruth Lane is a human geographer employed at the National Museum of Australia, Canberra. She is currently researching community partici-pation in natural and cultural resource initiatives in the Murray-Darling

Basin, a major river catchment in south-eastern Australia. Recent publications include 'Authenticity in Tourism and Native Title: Place, Time and Spatial Politics in the East Kimberley', published in *Social and Cultural Geography* in 2001, and 'Environmental History in Museums: Objects, Subjects and Narratives', published by Oxford University Press in 2000 in *Environmental History and Policy: Still Settling Australia* (ed. S. Dover).

Stuart McLean received his PhD in Anthropology from Columbia University. He is currently a postdoctoral fellow at the Humanities Institute of Ireland, University College, Dublin. He is the author of *The Event and its Terrors: Ireland, Famine, Modernity* (forthcoming, Stanford University Press).

Michael O'Hanlon and Linda Frankland have done fieldwork with the Wahgi people in Papua New Guinea's Western Highlands Province at various times since 1979. Michael O'Hanlon is Director of the Pitt Rivers Museum at Oxford University, where Linda Frankland is Administrative Coordinator for the Oxford Internet Institute. Michael O'Hanlon's most recent book is *Hunting the Gatherers: Ethnographic Collectors, Agents and Agency in Melanesia, 1870–1930s*, co-edited with Robert L. Welsch (Berghahn Books, 2000).

Angèle Smith is an Assistant Professor in Anthropology at the University of Northern British Columbia, Canada. Her research concerns the intersection of space, place and landscape theory, and the politics of representation. Her publications include 'Landscapes of Power: The Archaeology of 19th-c. Irish Ordnance Survey Maps' (in *Archaeological Dialogues* 5(1), 1998) and 'Maps' in the *Encyclopedia of Historical Archaeology* (London: Routledge, 2002).

Pamela J. Stewart and Andrew Strathern are research collaborators and are both in the Anthropology Department, University of Pittsburgh. They have published many articles and books on their fieldwork in the Pacific and Europe (Scotland and Ireland). Their most recent co-authored books include: *Minorities and Memories: Survivals and Extinctions in Scotland and Western Europe* (Carolina Academic Press, 2001); *Remaking the World* (Smithsonian Institution Press, 2002); *Violence: Theory and Ethnography* (Continuum Publishing, 2002); and *Witchcraft, Sorcery, Rumors, and Gossip* (Cambridge University Press, forthcoming).

Veronica Strang is Professor of Anthropology at the School of Social Sciences, Auckland University of Technology, New Zealand. An environmental anthropologist, she works mainly in northern Australia and the UK, conducting research on human–environmental relations and issues relating to land and resources. Her recent publications include: 'Poisoning the Rainbow: Cosmology and Pollution in Cape York', in *Mining and Indigenous Lifeworlds in Australia and Papua New Guinea*, A. Rumsey and J. Weiner (eds) (Adelaide: Crawford House Publishing, 2001); and 'Life Down Under: Water and Identity in an Aboriginal Cultural Landscape' (London: Goldsmiths College Anthropology Research Papers, 2002).

INDEX

Aboriginal mobility 143
  and hunting areas 145
  in the 1990s 145–6
  and land rights 146
  and the Ord Irrigation Scheme 156
Abu-Lughod, Lila 37
Adorno, Theodor 59–60, 61, 63
agalo 196
Agamben, Giorgio 6
'Age of Improvement' 234, 235
alder tree 80
Alexander I (of Scotland) 22
Amazon 193, 199, 200
Ambodiaviavy 97
ancestors 197, 198, 202, 203, 204, 206
ancestral signs 195, 196
Andrianapoinimerina 98, 99
Anglican Mission 112, 113, 119
Anglo-Protestant gentry 76, 77, 83, 85
archaeology 9
  excavation of Céide Fields 49–50
  and Iron Age findings in bogs 53
Argyle Station 143, 144
artificial islets 189
  construction of 190, 206
  as cultural markers 192
  kinds of 195
  and supernatural power 196
  and identity 204
Australian Stockman's Hall of Fame 120, 121, 130
Austronesians 192, 199
Ayrshire 3
  in the Age of Improvement 234

Ballard, Chris 231
Ballymote 76
Barlow, K. and D. Lipset 183

Bashō, Matsuo, 9
Basso, Keith 194
Bayly, B.A. 192
Bender, Barbara 8, 9, 81, 194
Benjamin, Walter 60, 61
birds of paradise 5, 6
  as plumes for headdresses 169–71
Bloch, Maurice 193
bogs 11
  peat bogs 47–8
  as archives 50
  cleared by English settlers in Ireland 51
  drainage of 51–2
  as colonial topography 56
  peat-cutting in 58
  as definitional puzzles 64–5
bog-corpses 53–4, 66
bolyim house 170, 172, 173, 179
  and *mond* post 173, 179
Bord na Móna 58, 62, 65, 67
Bowman, Frank 108, 113
  killing of, accounts of 114, 117
  persons killed by 122, 123
  represents colonial oppression 123
  gravesite of 124, 129
Braudel, Fernand 50
Bruce, Robert 24
burial 13–14, 124–6, 174
Burns, Robert 232
Burt, Ben 199

cairns 230
Carlyle, Thomas 53
Carrick, Earl of 23
Carroll, Lewis 9
Carrowkeel-Lough Arrow 75, 76, 80, 82
Cars 183–5
  as skeletons 185

Catholicism, in Ireland 76, 77, 80
Céide Fields 49–50, 62, 63, 67–8
Celts 66, 80
ceremonial grounds 172, 173
Cheviot 26
Childe, V. Gordon 230
Christian symbols 7
   Catholic cross 181
clachans 76
Clifford, James 168
colonial representations 71–2, 120,
   163n.26, 200, 201, 204, 205
colonization processes
   in Ireland: *see under* maps
   in Aboriginal Australia 110–13
   'Golden Age' of 119
community 4, 5
compensation payments 169
   and *pati* among Wahgi 181
   for car accidents 185
conservation 11–12
   and issues regarding peat bogs 62,
     67
   and ethnicity 89
   ideologies of 91
   activists, in Jamaica 210, 211
   and biographies of activists 212,
     213, 216
   money for 218
   management plans for 218, 219
   and land, in Scotland, 233
cordyline 179
cosmology 126
County Donegal 52, 232, 235
County Mayo 48, 55
   north Mayo 62
crannogs 8–9, 11
Cromwell, Oliver 51, 232

Dacre, Lord 24
dancing
   in Waghi 173–4
Dante Alighieri 51
Deleuze, G. and F. Guattari 61
Derry 233
development schemes 136
   and environmental management
     139
   alternative views of 140
   historical picture of 142
   modernization vs. sustainability in
     160
   and roads 167
Devine, Tom 17, 31, 37, 45

diaspora
   Scottish 7–8
Dickinson, Emily 9
diviners 91
Douglas, Earl of 19–20
   and Battle of Otterbourne 34
Douglas, Tim 11, 20–2
Downs, Ian 166
'Dreaming' stories 143
Dryburgh Abbey 30
Dumfriesshire 233
Duna 3–4, 7, 196
   burials among 13–14
   'internal externality' among 176
Dunfanaghy 52

ecotourism 219, 220, 227n. 3, 233
Edinburgh 23
Ekit Kuk 6
Elizabeth I, of England 24, 231
emplacement 5–6
Enga 182
environmental activism 214, 215,
   225, 224
   see also conservation
English
   in wars with Scotland 22–5
   in Ireland 51
estates
   in Ireland 52–3
   mapping of 75–7
ethnicity 89
   conceptualization of 93, 94
   'Tanala' and 'Betsileo' 94, 96, 98,
     99, 104, 105
   and images of poverty 95, 97
   and health 95
Europe 50
European Union 62, 67, 230
European Union, policies of 233

fairies 51
farming 10–11
   in Scottish Borders 20
   and Irish tenants 85
   in Madagascar 92, 93
   by Australian settlers 139,
     149–51, 151–4
   and Australian pastoralism
     108–30, 143
   in Wahgi area 169
   in Ayrshire 234
   as culture 235, 236

Feil, Daryl 177
fenlanders 65
Finney, Ben 184
fishermen 221, 222, 223, 224
flying foxes 206
foot and mouth disease 235
forest regions
    in Madagascar 89, 90–4
Fox, James 192, 193, 198, 206

Gaelic society 81, 232
Gaeltacht 232
genocide 112, 116, 117, 123
ghosts 119, 122, 130
    calling out to 132
    among Wahgi 173, 181
    and car accidents 185
Gibbon, Lewis Grassic 230
Glamis 8
Glob, P.V. 53, 66
Gow, Peter 193, 201
Grampian Mountains 235
grief names (penthonyms) 197
Gupta, Akil and James Ferguson 168

Hawick 29
health conditions 97, 98
Heaney, Seamus 53
heritage 3, 8
    management of 9–10, 12
    sites of, in Australia 120
    and environment 139
    issues over 230–6
    and ecotourism 233
Herzfeld, Michael 38
Highlands Clearances 234
Highlands Highway 167
Hill, Lord George 52
hilltops
    and pastoralism 81
    and rituals 81, 82
Hindmarsh Bridge 130
Hirsch, Eric 2, 4, 201, 211
Historic Scotland 230
history
    rewriting of, in maps 78
    colonial, in Waghi 182
    see also landscape, memory, place
Hogg, James 33
'home' 5, 29
Howe of the Mearns 230
humour 21

identity
    in Wahgi, internal *vs* external 174
    see also landscape, memory, place,
        history
identity, senses of 4
    in Scotland 17
Inishowen 235
Inkerman, Jimmy 108, 113
    memorial to 109, 126, 127, 128
    killing of 115, 116, 117, 125
    memories of 122, 125, 126
'internal externality' 176
Ireland 47–70, 71–88, 231
Irish Farmers' Association 62
irony 17, 24, 25, 30, 34, 36
    as idea in M. Herzfeld's work 38
    in work of J. Fernandez and M.
        Huber 38

Jacob, Violet 8
Jamaica 210–28
James VI and I (of Scotland and
        England) 22, 24, 232, 233
Japanese 231
Jutland 54

Kahn, Miriam 204
kastom priest 190, 196
Kawelka 7
Keesing, Roger 191
Kilmartin 230
Kimberley, East 136, 148, 149
kin relations 143, 146, 147, 160
    and marriage in Wahgi, 174–8
    and concept of marriage road 174
    and maternal kin 174
    'road' idiom of 174–5, 177
    cursing of fertility among 176, 177
    and powers of women 177, 178
    and 'shadow communities' 178,
        179
    and warfare 179
    and ghosts 185
Knockcalltecrore 55
kol kep alamb ('road people') 175–6,
        177, 178
konggar 169–71
Kowanyama 122
Kristeva, Julia 61
Küchler, Suzanne 206
Kuk 14
Kununurra 144, 146, 149–51, 155

Labour Party (UK) 17, 31
Land Reform Bill (Scotland) 233,
    234
land tenure, in Ireland 75, 79
    and townlands 79
    in Madagascar 103
    in Australia 111, 122
    in Langalanga 195, 202, 203
    in Scotland, disputes over 233
landscape
    concept of, 2–3, 7–8, 236
    inner 7–8, 9
    ironic 25
    of Borders (Scotland) 26–7
    and colonial topography 56, 110,
        115, 118
    research on 71–2
    imagined 73
    adminsitrative 78, 79
    and hilltops in Ireland 81, 82
    and ritual 83, 126, 148
    and nature/culture idea 110, 118
    and land use 142
    and roads 167, 180
    and identity 180
    as process and inscription 190,
        200, 201, 202
    and boundary markers 194
    and the ancestral past 195, 196
    and migration stories 199
    text metaphor and 200
    among Australian Aboriginies
        201
    and bodily analogy 202
    and ideas of power 202, 203
    and meanings of water, in Jamaica
        211, 219, 223, 224
    and neoliberalism 217
    disputed meanings of 226
    and 'development' versus
        'heritage' 229–36
    as integrative concept 236
Langalanga 12–13, 189
    features of landscape in 194, 202
    snake narrative in 198, 199
    and shell money 199
Latour, Bruno 57
Laws of the Marches 23
Leyburn, James G. 66
Lough Foyle 233
Lowland Scots, in Ulster, 232
Lughnasa festival 81, 82

Mabo 122
MacKenzie, Maureen 183
Madagascar 89
    geography of 90, 91
    stereotyping of its people 92
    biodiversity of 93
    ideology of biodiversity 94
Makis 186
Malaita 189
    colonial history of 191
    cyclones in 191
Malin Head 235
malu 4, 7, 196
maps 11
    of Ireland 51, 71–2
    and the colonial process 71–2, 83,
        84, 85
    as artifacts 72–3
    as political instruments 73
    and state control 77, 79
    and historical structures 77
    and placenames 81, 82, 83
    and local identities 86
    of Tainan city 231
marriage,
    in Wahgi 175–9
    and links extended in colonial
        times 182
    and landscape 'tilted' by 183
    and comparative cases on 'roads'
        186
    see also kin relations
marshes 50–1
Mary Queen of Scots 233
Mazu 231
Meigs, Anna 176, 178
    on 'shadow communities' 178
memory
    contests over 10
    and history 10
    and contestation 72, 73, 106
    and placenames 78, 83
    held in the land 121, 122
    internal and external 128
    and commemorative stones 133
    and history of land use 142
    and artificial islands in Langalanga
        191
    as key to landscape 193
    and Israeli farmers 194
    and landscape 200, 203
    and names 203

Merina empire 99
Miller, Dan 226, n.2
Milne, A.A 9
mimetic faculty 60
Miriuwung and Gajerrong people
    137, 143, 144, 163
    bush meeting of women of, 157
modernity 58–9
Montego Bay 210
    Marine Park Trust 214
Morphy, Howard 110, 131, 193,
    200, 201, 206
Mount Hagen 6
mourning names (penthonyms)
    197
mourning songs
    among Duna 5–6
    among Australian Aboriginals 122
Munn, Nancy 110, 183
    and the 'Fame of Gawa' 183
museums 230
Myers, Fred 131

naming practices 6, 7
    and 'over-naming' 60
    colonial 78
    significance of, in Langalanga 196,
        197, 203
    see also grief names
nation
    Scottish 29–31, 36–7
National Farmers' Union 29, 30,
    32
Nationalism
    Scottish 16–46, 233
    Irish 85, 86
Native Title Acts 122, 130, 133,
    137, 139, 146
    and native title process 159
'natural history', as category term,
    59–65
Negril 210
neoliberal landscapes 217
Ngart-YapMalmanl 108, 116
Norsk Hydro 58
nostalgia 7–8, 229

O'Hanlon, Michael 2
Ohnuki-Tierney, Emiko 192, 204
oil 31
    as wealth of Scotland 33

Ongka 6, 7
Ord Irrigation Area 136, 139
    interviews with farmer settlers in
        149–51
    horticulturalists in 151–4, 158–9
Ordnance Survey 72, 74, 78, 79, 82,
    84, 231, 235
Orkneys 230

Pacific campaign (WWII) 231
Papua New Guinea 3–4, 5–6
    and 'first contact' in Highlands
        166
Payame Ima 13–14
peat-cutting 49, 53
    extraction works 58
    bans on 62
    techniques of 65, 67
Pig Festival 169–71
    significance of pig-fat in 171
    and grease-cycle idea 170
    and 'vertical' identity 179
    truncated 180, 181
Pitjantjatjara, cars among, 184
place, senses of 3
    concepts of 4
    and weather 27
    in colonial names 78, 79
    omitted in maps 82, 83
    clan-based, in Wahgi 171
    and festivals 173
    relating to cars 184
    and senses of self in Langalanga
        189
    in names 197
'Plantations' of Ireland 231
poetry
    Scottish 8 (Violet Jacob), 16–45
        (Tim Douglas)
    local themes in 17–18
    of Scottish Borders 18, 27
    Bedouin 37
    see also songs
political economy 217
politics 17, 31
porridge 29
Presbyterians 232

rain 27, 29, 32–4
Ranotsara 92, 93, 94, 95
    national park project in 94

description of 96, 97
health problems in 97
historical overview of 98–100
oral histories of 100–2
agriculture in 105
Raphoe 232
raskol 168
Read, Kenneth 186
reivers 18–19, 22–5, 26–7
    and landscape 26
    in Tim Douglas's poems 32–44
    as warriors against England 34–5
representations of identity 231
resistance 83, 84
    to Merina rule 99
    tavy as resistance 106
    to white Australians by
        Aboriginals 112, 117
    through oral history 121, 122
    see also reivers
revenge 115, 131
roads 12, 14
    roadscapes 14
    and environment 106
    and change 148
    in the Papua New Guinea
        Highlands 166
    and ideas of landscape 166–7
    Wahgi perceptions of 167–9
    dialectic between place and roads
        183
    and meanings of vehicles 183,
        185, 186
    Roman 231
Romans 26, 231
Rosaldo, Renato 192
Rose, Deborah Bird 110
rowan tree 80
Rumsey, Alan 161 n. 5
Rumsey, Alan and James F. Weiner
    199, 200
Rutland Plains 108, 112, 121

satire 21, 36
Schama, Simon 3
Scotland 16, 17, 30, 230
    and books on landscape 232, 233,
        234
Scot's Dike 233
Scots pine 62–3

Scott, Sir Walter 18–20, 22, 24–5,
    26
    burial place of 30
Scottish Borders 16, 18
Scottish National Party (SNP) 16–17,
    37, 283
Selwyn, Tom 201
September 11, 2001 10
shark, ritual significance of 190, 196,
    206
sickness 177, 178
Simbu 167, 184
Simpson, Colin 166
Skara Brae 230
slavery 98
Smout, T.C. 233
Solomon Islands 189
songs 5–6
    in Wahgi Pig Festivals 172, 173,
        174
Stoker, Bram 47, 54–7
    story of the Snake's Pass 55–6
    interpretation of the story 56–7
    life of 66
Strang, Veronica 3

tavy farming 93, 94, 95, 99, 100,
    101, 103
    meaning of, to locals, 105
tafurae 203
Tainan 231
Taiwan 231
taxes 75, 84
terror attacks 10
Teviothead 26, 45
Thatcher, Margaret 31
Thoreau, Henry 9
Tilley, Christopher 194
time, spatialization of 192, 198
Tinpis Run 167
Tone, Theobald Wolfe 66
Toren, Christina 193
tourists 2, 8, 12
    and tourist gaze 189
    in Langalanga 204, 205
    in Jamaica 210
    and ecotourism 219, 220, 227n.3,
        233
    criticism of, by fishers 224
    and land accessibility 235
townlands 79
Troubles (in N. Ireland) 233

Trubanamen 112, 113, 114, 119
turf-cutting
  see peat-cutting
Tyndrum 235

Ullans 232
Ulster 66
United Irishmen 55, 66
United Kingdom 17, 20, 30, 35–6
USAID 218, 219, 222

vehicles 183–5
virtualism 217
Visitors' Centres
  at Céide Fields 49–50, 63, 67–8
  and Heritage Service 65
  and nostalgia 229
  and the European Union 230
  examples of, in Scotland 230, 233

Wahgi 12
  mid-Wahgi people 167
  clanship relations in 168
Wamirans 204
warfare
  in Wahgi 177–8, 179
  see also reivers
Wars of Independence 22
Wassman, Jürg 206
weather 27–8, 33–4
Winer, M. 8, 9
witchcraft 7
World Bank 101, 103

Yir Yoront 110, 131
Young Irelanders 84

Zafimaniry 193
Zafindraraoto lineage 100–4